ORM IN THE ARAB WORLD

Stefano Bianca

URBAN FORM IN THE ARAB WORLD
PAST AND PRESENT

First published in the United Kingdom in 2000 by
Thames & Hudson Ltd, 181A High Holborn,
London WC1V 7QX

www.thamesandhudson.com

First published in the United States of America in 2000 by
Thames and Hudson Inc., 500 Fifth Avenue, New York, New York 10110

thamesandhudsonusa.com

Graphic design: Oswald Roth
Layout: Oswald Roth with Martin Josephy

British Library Cataloguing-in-Publication Data
A catalogue record for this book is available from the British Library

Library of Congress Catalog Card Number 99-67630

ISBN 0-500-28205-6

Printed and bound in Germany

Table of Contents

Preface

The main focus of the ORL Planning Institute (Institut für Orts-, Regional- und Landesplanung) at the Swiss Federal Institute of Technology (ETH) is on research and training related to national planning tasks. Yet, acknowledging the potential importance of other cultures with regard to the future activities of its graduates, the Institute is open to research topics transcending the narrow boundaries of Switzerland, and has encouraged the integration of planning tasks related to foreign countries into its curriculum.

When Dr. Stefano Bianca was appointed from 1978 to 1980 as a visiting professor at our Institute, a group of architectural students became involved in a number of research and planning projects in the Moroccan city of Fez, carried out under our joint supervision. The result of these studios, summarised in Chapter 12 of the present book, was first published by the ORL Institute in 1980 ("Städtebau in Islamischen Ländern", ORL Studienbericht Nr. 44). Subsequently, in 1990/91, our Institute hosted a research project on town planning in Islamic countries, co-sponsored by the Swiss National Research Fund, to enable Dr. Bianca to synthesize his more recent professional experiences in places such as Aleppo, Baghdad, Mecca and Medina, and to develop his analysis of the clash between traditional urban structures of the Islamic world and conventional modern planning methods.

We are happy to present this long-awaited new publication by Stefano Bianca, issued under the auspices of the ORL Institute, as a volume of our research series. The mandate of the ORL Institute is to nurture research related to the theory of town planning, as well as to engage in practical planning courses and exercises. The present book realizes both objectives in an exemplary way, as it combines a structural analysis of the historic urban form with a discussion of contemporary planning problems, illustrated by a number of actual case studies. Thus it has the potential of becoming a textbook for individuals and institutions interested in the urban dimension of the Arab-Islamic world, and particularly for those who care about the cultural implications of modern development.

Benedikt Huber
Professor Emeritus for Architecture and Town Planning
ORL Institute/ETH Zurich

Introduction:
The Subject and the Approach

When I first conceived this book in the late 1980's at the request of the Swiss Federal Institute of Technology (ETH), it was clear to me that I should not attempt to write another history of architecture of the Islamic world. A number of distinguished orientalists and art historians have already dealt with this daunting task with varying degrees of success. As a practicing architect and town planner, and occasional architectural historian, I am indebted to the existing stock of publications on this subject which, for lack of any better designation, continues to be labelled "Islamic Architecture". Having lived and worked in the Arab world for long periods since my first journey to Morocco in 1964 and having developed a strong interest in the traditional Muslim philosophy of life, however, my aim was to transcend the conventional categories of architectural history: rather than limiting the study to the stylistic aspects of architecture and urban form, I wanted to explore the inner motivations behind visual structures as the main sources of pre-formal shaping forces and morphological structuring principles.

I have applied this approach more extensively in some earlier studies, most of them written in German and all of them dealing with art, architecture and urban form in Muslim cultures. The present book draws on this material, although due to the necessary shortening and my limited command of English, it may be less eloquent and occasionally less subtle than its German predecessor ("Hofhaus und Paradiesgarten", C.H. Beck Verlag, München 1991). Yet what distinguishes this book from the latter publication is the attention given to the contemporary situation as well as the attempt to bridge the gap between past and present, which is also a divide between theory and practice. My contention is that, by looking into the deep-rooted human factors which gave birth to distinct formal and artistic expressions and to a specific type of built environment, it should be possible to reveal certain non-formal patterns which are, to some extent, time-resistant and which therefore contain the seeds from which cultural continuity can grow – even at times of disruption by strong outer forces. If this book can contribute to the discovery of such elements and to their future implementation in terms of adapted architectural and urban design, or if it can stimulate others to continue exploring these paths, then it will have achieved its purpose in spite of its imperfections.

The manifestations of Islamic architecture are not based on explicit formal prescriptions and have varied considerably from period to period and from region to region, which has given rise to the provocative thesis that there is no such thing as "Islamic Architecture". Yet from an early point in history (about the 9th/10th century AD onwards) there is a specific Islamic quality which becomes apparent in every appropriation and adaptation of pre-existing architectural and artistic heritage, be it of Roman, Hellenistic, Byzantine or Sassanian origin. The respective regional styles of Islamic architecture are not necessarily linked by formal resemblances, but they show inner affinities which are clearly based on related customs, patterns of use and corresponding structuring principles. This "common denominator" draws on various sources: there are, for instance, certain climatic conditions, socio-economic factors and vernacular building techniques shared by many regions of the Islamic world. There is, at least for some regions, the common basis of the Roman-Hellenistic building tradition, already "orientalized" in the context of Byzantine, Parthian and Sassanian cultures and brought to a new synthesis by Muslim craftsmen and architects. But above all, there is an unmistakably Islamic character that can only be attributed to a prevailing spiritual identity, as materialized through a consistent daily practice and the corresponding built environment.

Similarly to other ancient traditions, Islam has developed and maintained a set of ritualized patterns of human behaviour which embraced all aspects of daily life, on the individual as well as the collective level, permeating man's activities with constant references to an acknowledged religious truth. This may not be consonant with the secular beliefs of modern Western civilization which, for the sake of "individualism", tend to ignore spiritual hierarchies and thus to reject the idea of normative types of human conduct – without always recognizing that, by excluding service to higher realities, the human mind may become subservient to much more limited man-made ideologies and their constraints. In the traditional Islamic context, the divine order was a commonly accepted reality and accordingly, the given system of daily rituals was capable of infusing meaning and consistency to every single human activity. As vernacular architecture is a relatively direct spatial crystallization of man's thinking and behaviour, the built form could hardly remain unaffected by this cultural coherency. The real source of the inner unity of Islamic architecture, therefore, has to be sought in the realm of such pre-formal archetypes and not in ephemeral stylistic features.

What strikes most Western observers is the fact that the basic factors and patterns of Islamic life should have been subject to relatively little change throughout the various historical periods. Notwithstanding the development of a sophisticated civilization during the first two centuries after the

Prophet's death, Islam as a religious and social order has always maintained a certain archaic simplicity. Its way of life remained faithful to the original modes of human behaviour defined by the first nucleus of the Muslim community in Medina, which had absorbed the teachings of the Prophet Muhammad. Through later centuries, and until the 19th/20th century, this cultural mould was perpetuated generation by generation and continued to be followed by a growing number of societies in many different regions of the Islamic world.

To be sure, the outer conditions changed considerably during the history of Islam and, as Muslim philosophers of the past readily admitted and sometimes deplored, reality often fell short of the ideals. Yet most Muslim societies have never believed in "progress" in modern Western terms. They rather understood the course of history as a gradual decline and sometimes as a deviation from the original path. Possible aberrations were attributed to human weakness and did not affect the unquestioned validity of the divine order. Being supported by the enduring force of steadily reproduced archetypes, the ideal Muslim way of life thus remained the target, and although it could no longer be fully met, it still provided Islamic culture and its various expressions with a rare continuity throughout time.

As a result, divergent historic perspectives emerged in East and West: one could say that the evolution of Islamic culture proceeded along circular or spiral patterns, maintaining a permanent relation to its spiritual centre of gravity. In contrast, European civilization after the "Renaissance" (and especially since the 19th century) adopted a linear path of development, determined by the underlying utopia of man-made progress towards "the best of all possible worlds". Both perspectives obviously implied different basic assumptions, and thus they elicited contradictory philosophies of life as well as different modes of architectural expression. While it is impossible to weigh the achievements of a secular and rather single-minded technological progress against the benefits of a spiritually determined, more comprehensive (and arguably more realistic) tradition, it should be emphasized that both attitudes build on their own set of criteria, and that confusing the respective parameters will not result in adequate approaches, let alone judgements.

A case in point is the disillusionment of a number of modern Western art historians, who are unable to find real "progress" in Islamic art after a certain point in history, when most of the specific artistic tools of Islam had been articulated. This led them to the conclusion that Islamic art in its later periods had lost vigour and substance or had become a merely "mechanical" repetition of existing models. Nothing could be more misleading for the understanding of the real objectives of Islamic arts and crafts: in fact, for a craftsman in any traditional culture, the highest pride is to remain faithful to the models or archetypes he chooses to interpret, because they convey a distinct spiritual meaning. To him, the idea of "individual expression" for its own sake does not appear as a desirable value, for in fact it is already implied in the very process of the traditional artist's re-creation, which is nothing but a personal and temporal interpretation of an immaterial and timeless truth. Explicit emphasis on subjective expression would only distort the real message by subjecting it to the limitations of the transmitter.

Given the special nature of Islamic art and architecture, its essential qualities seem inaccessible to certain modes of interpretation used by conventional Western art history, which, being geared to other types of artistic expression, are often obsessed with analyzing external stylistic development. Such an approach is bound to reiterate the ideological prejudices of positivism, which has informed many aspects of Western science over the past 300–400 years but has little or no affinity with the essential shaping forces of traditional art and architecture. Understanding these forces requires a different approach, based on the identification and interpretation of cultural archetypes, their meaning and their formal variations through time and space. Admittedly, this method, which could be labelled "Platonic" rather than "Aristotelian", may be of little use for the study of post-medieval Western art and architecture, but it has its merits when dealing with Islamic architecture, which has fostered specific archetypes for architectural and urban form, as generated by prototypical patterns of behaviour.

Acknowledging that the traditional formal structures of Islam – be it in the arts, in architecture or in urban texture – represent significant crystallizations of non-material contents is the basis for the morphological analysis of the historic built environment intended by this book. Yet the same approach also proves useful when it comes to analyzing the contemporary problems resulting from the pre-industrial Islamic city being confronted with modern Western concepts of life. Indeed, it would be wrong to reduce this conflict to the aesthetic or functional dimensions of town planning, for the introduction of new architectural models into a different cultural context has a far-reaching impact. It cannot be limited to isolated "formal" or "technical" problems, but has to address aspects of local customs, human behaviour and, above all, the meaning of architectural forms as perceived by their users.

Urban structures are always three-dimensional projections of human beliefs. At best they can provide a mirror of a spiritual universe which integrates man in a meaningful order and provides him with essential inner fulfilment, by the very fact that his small personal world is in harmony with a much larger reality; at worst they are expressions of narrow ideologies which confine man to the cage of his own rationality, depriving him of the vital contact with his higher levels of existence. The clash between the traditional Islamic culture and modern Western systems of thought has to be seen in this wider philosophical context, for the controversial issue is the interpretation of "development" and what it should entail: should development enable the balanced realization of the totality of human faculties and capabilities, or should it reduce reality to limited aspects of material life at the expense of other qualities? Should it foster an increase in quantifiable production only, or should it support a different type of creativity, which includes more fundamental forces and experiences? As far-fetched as these questions may seem, they determine the cultural responses which eventually generate the built environment and its physical expressions.

Western models of urban life started exerting their influence on the Islamic world during the colonial period and mainly in the second half of the 19th century when Europe entered the age of applied sciences and modern technology, which in turn became the basis for its massive and extensive industrialization. The underlying aspiration was to establish a new man-made creation by mechanical means, anticipating a new golden age as a result of unlimited technical progress. Although (or perhaps because) this ideology was totally secular, it produced dogmatic beliefs and a somewhat perverted salvation myth of its own: implicitly or explicitly, the promise was to achieve "paradise on earth" by the joint forces of technological and economic development. A missionary zeal, combined with obvious commercial and political interests, pushed this new European civilization towards the exploration and conquest of the planet, up to the last physical boundaries it could reach.

Today, the failure of technology in fulfilling its promise is becoming increasingly evident, as is the destructive character of this civilization which drew, and still draws its main energies from the rapid consumption of finite natural resources and from the dissolution of self-contained social and cultural systems – paralleled by the destruction of the historic built environment. On balance, it seems that the environmental, social and economic implications of this development process are generating more new problems than they have solved. "Breakthroughs" often lead to subsequent collapses; these are then postponed or transferred by engaging a higher level of technological investment (and risk), which either constitutes liabilities for future generations or displaces the problems to other, still untouched areas of the world. Western civilization in its present form has proven to be unsustainable, and its export to the Third World, in spite of its proclaimed short-term success, exposes mankind to unpredictable long-term hazards on a global scale.

Seen in the context of the present ecological debate, the age-old wisdom of traditional cultures, hitherto considered as "backward", reveals itself to be much more realistic and indeed more timely than many obsolete modern utopias. It does not come as a surprise that the growing awareness of the limitations of technological progress and its architectural expressions allowed for a new appreciation of the cultural, aesthetic and social values of the pre-industrial built environment and the conditions that enabled its growth. Dismissing this interest in the past as mere nostalgia or branding it as an outdated revivalism would be too simplistic. The real issue is that human nature needs to respond to primordial emotional and spiritual impulses in order to achieve its full potential. Such responses are an integral part of the cultural framework of the traditional environment, while they tend to be suppressed by a dominant technology which can exert an almost hypnotic influence on man, since it substitutes natural processes with technical surrogates and makes him dependent on them.

Extreme situations tend to engender opposing trends and opportunities. At a time when the technological destruction of natural and cultural resources seems to be reaching its peak, new environmental sciences have sprung up, trying to re-establish the relation between man and the created world through a more holistic view of the universe. A similar phenomenon is to be observed in the spiritual realm: while modern Western civilization is threatening to eradicate the cultural identity of age-old cultures everywhere in the world, the West itself has produced thinkers who deeply absorbed the values and principles of traditional cultures and succeeded in transmitting their inner meaning. This knowledge has suddenly become more accessible and more explicit than it ever was before, even within the traditional cultures themselves. For as long as these cultures were not subject to external threats, there was no need to analyze their underlying raison d'être. Their self-evident spiritual principles were shared naturally by the society, and people practised them implicitly, without necessarily exteriorizing them. Today the situation has changed radically: a conscious awareness and support of basic values is needed to balance and master the impact of man-made development, as modern industrial civilization itself is unable to instil meaning to the products it generates.

Under such circumstances it seems a tragic irony that many Third World countries should have adopted obsolete Western ideologies, mistaking them for the miraculous instant solution to all their social, economic and political problems – at the very moment when the Western world is beginning to see the need to revise its previous concepts, re-consider its objectives and methods and take into account the negative effects of inappropriate technologies. Unfortunately, one should add, the intoxication by the Western "Myth of Development" was not overcome with the end of the colonial period, but has grown even stronger since the emerging Third World nations achieved political independence. One of the reasons may be that the local political "elites" were often trained in the West and still believe in development concepts which have little to do with the realities of the Third World and have now become obsolete in their own place of origin. The cloned Western type of development has produced the well-known architectural disruption in the physical environment of many Arab cities; but its effects were even more disastrous with regard to the social segregation it induced by introducing new categories of "rich" and "poor" according to a value system that was alien to traditional communities.

In addition, the pressures emanating from undigested "progress" tend to provoke a fatal split between "modernist" and "fundamentalist" movements, thus generating yet another rift in many contemporary Islamic societies. The resulting contradictions between "technocrats" and "traditionalists" are extremely hard to reconcile, as after the collapse of an integrated and overarching cultural framework there is no common ground on which they could meet. The battle between conflicting paradigms becomes more complex, and sometimes confusing, since both camps, consciously or unconsciously, distort their message by adopting and perverting the attitudes of the other side: "modernists" pursue their mission with a para-religious eschatological fervour, and "fundamentalists" often revert to the tools of a militant positivist ideology.

It would seem presumptuous to venture into the political and ideological consequences of this struggle, and the present book has no such intention. All it tries to do is to trace the cultural background against which the questions of conservation, adaptation and revitalization of traditional cities in the Islamic world are to be seen and discussed. It is my contention that this urban tradition is not to be considered as a museal heritage, but as a formidable cultural resource capable of regeneration and renewal. To quote an established principle of ecology, one should not, just for the sake of maximum short-term benefits, reduce the genetic variety of a rich flora built up over thousands of years, as this may cause a dangerous shortage of resources for coming generations. In a similar way, historic cities can be seen as containing the seeds of future cultural transformations. They may constitute an essential resource in case alien models of urban development should prove less viable than anticipated.

Therefore, the morphological study of traditional Islamic cities is not only of historical and academic interest, but bears practical consequences for architects and urban designers. It can indeed reveal many culturally determined patterns which carry with them timeless elements of cultural identity and can therefore be revived and re-integrated under new circumstances. Far from being a matter of replicating, cloning or freezing specific stylistic features, cultural continuity calls for sensitivity, imagination and high creative powers. Anyone who wants to pursue it must be able to recognize and to express the inner forces of architectural archetypes, distill the implicit meaning in its "liquid" spiritual state, as it were, and re-cast it into physical shapes which are adapted to new circumstances and yet constitute a natural link with the chain of a living tradition.

As far as this book is concerned, it is an attempt to make a contribution – modest as it may be – to the discovery of this potential continuity, both by analyzing and interpreting basic urban and architectural patterns and by exemplifying how some of them can be adopted or re-interpreted in a contemporary context. Taking into consideration the cultural disruption which occurred during and after the colonial period, the book is structured in three parts: the first section is devoted to the morphological and typological analysis of traditional architecture along the principles explained at the beginning of this introduction. The second section deals with the problems and incompatibilities caused by the impact of modern Western planning and design models, both in philosophical and in practical terms. The third section is an attempt to explore new alternative approaches which could reconcile traditional principles with contemporary needs, based on a number of case studies.

Given the intricate social, political and economical dimensions of the problem, nobody will expect the author, or anyone else for that matter, to provide readily and universally applicable solutions. It is my experience and firm belief that valid projects cannot be derived solely from theoretical principles, but must grow out of a careful and realistic study of the specific local conditions and existing resources. Hence the interest in presenting and discussing a variety of case studies in their context and with reference to the implementation problems encountered.

Whilst the case studies may illustrate desirable – as well as undesirable – approaches and principles, they are not intended to provide recipes. As architects, we should refrain from rash generalizations and schematic design transfers, which may be too rigid to match a complex reality. Individual solutions for each case and each site must spring from the careful interpretation of concrete circumstances and constraints if they are to meet users' needs and to support the growth of a lively human environment. Community resources, economic potentials and institutional mechanisms must be considered together with physical interventions and harnessed as driving forces of urban rehabilitation. Projects cannot be designed in an abstract manner, nor can they be imposed "by decree", which is perhaps the very reason for the ultimate failure of so many modern town-planning schemes.

After explaining at some length my approach to the subject, I would like to conclude this introduction with a few personal remarks. The first one concerns the fact that a Westerner has written a book which aims at promoting cultural continuity in the architectural and urban traditions of the Islamic world. The only argument I can invoke in my favour is that I have been a lover and admirer of traditional Islamic architecture for over thirty-five years now and that I owe many rewarding experiences to living and working in that environment, to studying Muslim poets, philosophers and historians and, not least, to the acquaintance of a number of Muslim friends and colleagues who contributed to the development of my thoughts and the case studies contained in this book.

I might add that with today's rapidly shrinking geographical barriers, the survival of the Islamic architectural heritage has become a universal concern which can and should be shared by Westerners. If there is such a thing as cultural solidarity and acknowledgement of timeless values, the relative distance of a foreign eye, combined with the necessary empathy for the subject, may be of help in unravelling complex problems which tend to appear even more confusing to those directly involved in the matter. An external observer certainly runs the risk of over-simplification (and I apologize in advance in this respect), yet given the present impact of an aggressive type of modernization, he has the advantage of having already experienced the results of a process which is now finding its way into the Islamic world.

There is room for hope that the young generation of Muslim intellectuals and decision-makers will be discerning and critical enough with respect to the crucial issues of cultural transformation and evolution. To be sure, the message of this book does not imply that Western tools and methods are to be rejected in toto, but that a selective process of adaptation and gradual integration should be followed, guided by a strong awareness of existing local values and by an informed evaluation of the successes and failures of modern development trends. This is a monumental task indeed, comparable perhaps to the earlier synthesis the Islamic world had to achieve with regard to the impact of Greek, Roman and Byzantine cultures. The future shape of cities in the Islamic world will tell to what extent such a synthesis is feasible and whether the impact of ubiquitous modernization trends still allows for local identities to be maintained, strengthened and developed.

Finally, I feel compelled to express my sincere thanks to all those who, in one way or another, have helped me develop the content of this book or assisted in its production. I am especially indebted to the late Titus Burckhardt, whose intimate knowledge of the traditional Islamic world is not only contained in his exemplary writings, but imbued his whole personality and his approach to the field work, which I was fortunate enough to take part in for a few years in Fez during the late seventies.

In Fez, Ahmed al-Iraqi and Abdullatif al-Hajjami (now the Director of the local conservation and redevelopment agency ADER) have closely cooperated with our Unesco team in establishing the conservation plan for the old city and later in developing the further proposals contained in this book.

In Jedda, I owe thanks to Dr. Sami Angawi, the founder and first Director of the "Hajj Research Centre", who initiated and participated in the project on the central area of Medina. He also commissioned the surveys on traditional housing in Fez, Aleppo and Medina, which allowed some of the new plans and maps published in this book to take shape. My former students Serge Schwarzenbach and Wolfgang Fülscher drew up most of them in many months of dedicated work.

In Aleppo, I must pay tribute to my friend Adli Qudsi, whose courageous initiatives were instrumental in stopping further wholesale demolition in the old quarters at a crucial moment in the city's long and distinguished history. He enabled me to engage in the revised Bab al-Faraj project and became the driving force behind more recent rehabilitation efforts in the old city.

In Baghdad, I am grateful to Rifat Chadirji, the distinguished architect then in charge of all building activities in the capital, and to Dr. Sabbah al-Azzawi, the chief of the town planning department, for giving me and my colleague Giorgio Lombardi the chance to develop the conservation and redevelopment project for the inner city contained in this book. We were able to draw on the valuable assistance of Dr. Ihsan Fethi, whose knowledge of Old Baghdad was always inspiring. It was a major setback to all of us when this important project was aborted in 1984 due to a tragic and unnecessary war at the very moment its implementation seemed to be within reach.

At Unesco, I wish to acknowledge the support of Dr. Said Zulficar and Dr. Mounir Bouchenaki, now Director of the Cultural Heritage Division, who deeply care for the cause of conservation in Muslim countries and who commissioned several consultancies which allowed me to deepen my field knowledge in Fez, Aleppo, Damascus, Cairo and Sana'a.

My colleague Werner Muller, now in Baltimore, was a dedicated companion who assisted me in the Medina and Baghdad projects and produced the perspective sketches featured in the respective case studies.

The production of this book would not have been possible without the joint support of the Swiss National Research Fund in Berne and the Planning Institute (ORL-Institut) of the Swiss Federal Institute of Technology (ETH) in Zurich. My special thanks go to Professor Benedikt Huber, Director Emeritus of the ORL-Institut, whose support and patience during the various phases of the project were of great help to me.

Oswald Roth, illustrator at the ORL-Institute, and Chester Romanutti from the ETH press (vdf Hochschulverlag AG an der ETH Zürich) saw the book through during the production phase and coped gracefully with the author's demands and delays. Martin Josephy took care of formatting text and illustrations in sensitive and efficient manner. Together with them, I would also like to thank Jacques Feiner, a young ETH graduate who prepared, redrew or processed many of the plans and maps in this book. His enthusiasm for the subject eventually led him to participate in new projects in Sana'a and Shibam.

Urban conservation and planning in general cannot materialize without a collective effort which brings together institutional decision-makers, international organizations, financing agencies, architects, historians and professionals of various other disciplines, researchers, committed citizens and opinion-makers, and, last but not least, the community concerned and their representatives. In this sense, I would like to acknowledge the help and support of many other individuals who have not been named in this introduction, but whose efforts have contributed to the cause of renewing the traditional urban heritage of the Islamic world and continue to do so.

Postscript

The raw version of this book was almost completed in late 1992 when I joined the Aga Khan Trust for Culture in Geneva to build up the newly established "Historic Cities Support Programme" (HCSP). This challenging task did not allow me, until the summer months of 1996, to finalize the work on the book. Looking again into the manuscript at a distance of several years was somewhat frustrating, and anyone having gone through a similar experience will probably sympathize. While one's basic views may remain the same, the desire to re-structure the material according to more recent thinking and experiences emerges – but cannot be satisfied, as it would mean recommencing from scratch... Eventually, I acquiesced and retained the "historic" shape of the book. Only in the conclusions did I take the liberty of inserting more recent pieces of writing. I am consoled by the fact that no book on this subject will ever be exhaustive, final or perfect, and I trust that interested readers will still find enough food for thought to pursue on their own.

Trélex, December 1998   Stefano Bianca

PART I
The Historic Arab-Islamic City

Basic Principles of Islam and their Social, Spatial and Artistic Implications

"As far as architecture is concerned, it is the haven where man's spirit, soul and body find refuge and shelter ..." (From an urban management manual by Ibn Abdûn, an Andalusian judge from the 12th century)

In every genuine cultural tradition, architecture and urban form can be seen as a natural expression of prevailing spiritual values and beliefs which are intimately related to the acknowledged cosmic order of the world. Whether such a three-dimensional representation is intended explicitly, by "mirroring" the universe in the microcosmos of man-made material structures, or whether it is simply an outcome of traditions and daily practices which correspond to certain spiritual principles, is of secondary importance; it merely reflects the difference between consciously planned, often "monumental" works of art and the more modest vernacular architecture built by the inhabitants themselves or by anonymous craftsmen.

As a rule, there is a close interaction between what people build and what they believe, and this equation works in both senses: man structures his environment, while he is also influenced and confirmed by it in his attitudes as a result of interacting with it over time. This certainly holds true for traditional societies, where human activities were guided by distinct spiritual values which thus succeeded in permeating the whole built environment. "Tradition" means the chain of revealed truth, wisdom and knowledge, which is transmitted and renewed generation by generation, thus linking various successive layers of temporal existence to the primordial reality which originated them. All spiritually founded traditions – and Islam is one of them – aimed at materializing and manifesting their individual perception of universal truth, filtered through the "medium" of their own cultural conditions. Therefore, the various religious doctrines, in spite of relative differences originating from their embodiment in specific communities, times and places, do not necessarily exclude, but complement each other; they all represent particular aspects of a sacred universe or, in other words, different approximations to the supreme reality which can never be fully captured by man.

Compared with other religious traditions, the distinctive feature of Islam is that it has given birth to a comprehensive and integrated cultural system

1 Within the traditional Muslim city: the transition from the market street to the ritual space of the mosque courtyard (see also plates 6 and 7).

by totally embedding the religious practice in the daily life of the individual and the society. While Islam did not prescribe formal architectural concepts, it moulded the whole way of life by providing a matrix of behavioural archetypes which, by necessity, generated correlated physical patterns. Therefore, the religious and social universe of Islam must be addressed before engaging in the analysis of architectural structures. In doing so, we will limit ourselves to some of the essential issues, which – directly or indirectly – have conditioned the structure of the built environment.

Islam is the youngest of the three monotheistic religions which trace their tradition back to a common ancestor, the prophet Abraham, and all sprang up in the Middle Eastern area. It accepts its forerunners Judaism and Christianity as "religions of the book", but sees itself as the ultimate confirmation of the primordial faith, restored by the revelation of the Prophet Muhammad, the last in the chain of prophets. Unlike Judaism, Islam does not believe in a chosen people as exclusive carrier of spiritual truth; and unlike Christianity it does not claim divine status for its founder. While Christ is worshiped as the son of God, Muhammad saw himself as the human transmitter of the divine message – the Qur'an – dictated to him by the Archangel Gabriel.

The existence of the Prophet Muhammad is a historic fact, and in this respect Islam benefits from an unbroken and genuine tradition. The Prophet was buried at his house in Medina, today the second holy place of Islam after the Ka'aba in Mecca. His own and his companions' deeds and sayings were recorded by contemporary followers, as was the case with the Qur'anic revelations, which were memorized and recited during the Prophet's lifetime, then fixed in written form immediately after his death. They have since continued to be recited by Muslims all over the world in their daily prayer.

Islam means the peaceful submission to Allah, the one and only Lord of the Universe, who has made man his vice-regent on earth, but who continues to control both worlds. Man was entrusted with the custody of God's rule, but the Qur'an makes it clear that he should never assume the role of the Lord, for he is only the instrument of His supreme and unscrutable will. Ontologically speaking, *all* human beings, regardless of their relative status in worldly terms, are therefore considered servants of the sole God. This reduced to a considerable extent the relevance of earthly hierarchies by marking them as accidental and revocable distinctions, and at the same time it stressed the equality and solidarity between human beings.

On the one hand, the Qur'an emphasizes that Allah is beyond the limited human capacities of imagination and that nothing should be directly associated with the idea of God, in order to preserve the purity of the Divine. "La ilaha ill'Allah" (no Divinity but God) is therefore the prime credo of

Islam, coupled with the recognition of the Prophet Muhammad as messenger of the revelation. On the other hand, the Qur'an again and again stresses the omnipresence of God within his creation: His forces permeate the creation and manifest themselves in the countless "signs" (ayât) of nature, which should induce man to reflect on the omnipotence of Allah. God is therefore seen as both *transcendent*, i. e. above all rational or material explanations, and *immanent*, i. e. inherent to his creation and therefore perceivable by virtue of symbolism and analogy. As his presence can be felt everywhere on earth, the world as a whole participates in the sacred character of the creation. Yet man must beware of identifying God with his limited perception of Him and should avoid any attempt to seize and fixate the divine in human artefacts. Accordingly, it is a major concern of Islam to maintain a clear distinction between the two levels of existence, one being the human or temporal realm, the other being the Divine or timeless realm. Blurring the division line between them is considered a blasphemy.

Nevertheless, both spheres are always seen in close interaction: while Islam emphasizes the uniqueness of God, it also affirms the fundamental oneness of His creation, which ultimately implies the unity of both worlds. Similarly, the Prophet insisted on the transcendent nature of the Divine, but this did not prevent him from acknowledging and accepting human factors. Wordly concerns, motives and desires were in no way ignored, belittled or condemned, but rather transcended by their integration into a comprehensive religious system, the prime objective of which was to interconnect the temporal and the timeless, the earthly existence being seen as a transient emanation of eternal life.

One could say that the strength of Islam lies precisely in this interconnection of both worlds, which operates and is expressed in very practical terms. The Qur'an – in the eye of the Muslims the word of God – contains prescriptions and recommendations which are directly related to the daily life of the first community around the Prophet and are still followed by millions of Muslims. Similarly, the Prophet Muhammad, by virtue of being a *human* receptacle for the Divine message, became the supreme model of the "universal man" for all later Muslims, especially as, besides being a man of God, he also led his earthly life as head of his family, as political and military leader and as ruler of the first Muslim community in al-Medina. Therefore, not only his ethics and his teachings but all aspects of his actual behaviour in life became significant. Accounts of his character, his sayings, his deeds, his reactions in specific situations were collected and constituted a complete philosophy of life which covered all aspects of human experience, from the sublime to the mundane and from the intimate to the public sphere. These accounts of the "sunna" (habits) of the Prophet became exemplary for all later Muslims, thus leading to a veritable "imitatio pro-phetis" which was instrumental in shaping the character of a Muslim society. Together with the Qur'an, they served as sources for the constitution of more formalized compendia of orthodox Islamic law.

The new Islamic law was established during the 8th/9th century AD, about 200 years after the death of the Prophet, at a time when Islam had expanded well beyond the Arabian Peninsula, absorbing the heritage of the late Roman, the Byzantine and the Sassanian empires. Obviously, major cultural and political changes took place, as the small original community of al-Medina, ruled by the Prophet and the first four rightful "Khalifas", i. e. his appointed vice-regents (Abu Bakr, Umar, Uthman and the Prophet's son-in-law Ali) turned into a major empire, with Damascus and Baghdad as its new capitals. According to Ibn Khaldun, the famous Maghrebi historian of the 14th century, the "period of miracles" and the original unity forged by the Prophet had given way to the normal course of life, marked by inevi-table political and religious struggles, such as the division between Sunnite and Shi'ite Muslims. The later caliphs were shrewd political leaders but unable to fully match the model of the Prophet and his first successors. Powerful tribal and military leaders (sultans) had emerged, who were to secure the Islamic dominion, but did not always act according to religious rules. Finally, large masses of non-Arab populations had converted to Islam, asking to have their share in cultural, religious and political matters.

In this situation, the formation of Islamic law (Shari'a) became the tool for safeguarding the Islamic identity of the empire and ensuring the religious "unité de doctrine", which was needed to establish the cultural coherence of Islam in a rapidly changing world. Interestingly enough, existing Roman models which had contributed a lot to the new material civilization of Islam were completely discarded when it came to the question of law and justice. Instead, a deliberate return to the origins took place, by going back to the first community of Medina for guidance and reference. The prescripts from the Qur'an, complemented by an interpretation of the deeds and sayings (Hadith) of the Prophet and his first companions, thus became the prime sources of the new Islamic law. For cases where no direct reference was found, conclusions by analogy were permitted and, failing that, the indi-vidual search (ijtihad) and the consensus of religious leaders could be cal-led upon. The creative period of Islamic jurisprudence ended when the "door of individual search" was closed and the four established orthodox schools of law became canonic. Later generations confined themselves to an interpretation of the then existing stock of secondary sources.

Due to the character of its sources and its objectives, Islamic law differs considerably from Roman law, which continued to serve as a basis for most

European legal systems. Firstly, Islamic law constituted a religiously based, not a secular compendium of prescriptions. Secondly, it did not originate from abstract principles but from the live experience of an exemplary society. And finally, its main concern was not to settle economic and social disputes, nor to define a rigid penal code, but to promote an exemplary pattern of individual and collective human conduct. It was therefore not limited to "negative", i. e. restrictive regulations, but implied a complete "positive" system of human behaviour (including a codex of good manners), which was highly ritualized. The resulting body of religious and social customs became instrumental in shaping and preserving the social identity within the whole Muslim "umma", or mother-community (a virtual extension of the first nucleus around the Prophet in al-Medina) and conditioned what could be called an Islamic "liturgy of daily life". In a certain way, the comprehensive social rules of Islam may even be compared to those of the monastic orders in medieval Europe, except for the fact that orthodox Islam never accepted the dualism between the "spiritual" and the "material" realm and never introduced a distinct class of clergy or any special preconditions for a contemplative life, such as celibacy. Therefore, it can be said that the "monastic" aspect of Islam was diffused and integrated into society as a whole.

The constitution of Islamic law, and later its development and daily application, was the responsibility of the "ulema", the religious leaders of the community. Thanks to their knowledge of the sources and their special education, they acted as trustees of Qur'anic law and custodians of the social life of the community. While, over the centuries, Islamic law may have become somewhat sophistic and dogmatic, its great merit was that it represented a direct deduction from divine rules and prophetic models. It set an exemplary yardstick of ethics and justice which could not be corrupted by arbitrary human interventions and preserved the ontological primacy of the Lord as the real ruler and the only legislator of the community. From the beginning, Islam had excluded the concept of sacred kingship, as it was common in Asia, and even during the European Middle Ages. No caliph or sultan was ever bestowed with legislative authority, and the role of the Islamic ruler was only to "promote the right and to prevent the evil" in accordance with the given Islamic law which he had to implement.

During the later period of Islam, when it was no longer possible to combine spiritual and political authority in one person, this religious limitation of regal power became extremely important. The sultans usually established their political supremacy through a ferocious natural selection process which was hardly in line with religious ethics. Therefore, the pre-established Islamic law, the so-called "street of the believers" (shari'a), was a useful corrective against potential excesses of princely power and ruthless worldly leadership, and became the main tool that was used to warrant the intended unity between religious and worldly matters after the integral leadership practised by the Prophet and his first successors had been broken.

Obviously, this system also enhanced the role of the ulema and of religious sheikhs, who came to rule the daily life of the urban community. The leading "civil servants" of the traditional Muslim government, such as the kadi (judge), the mufti (expert in religious matters) or the muhtasib (market inspector) were taken from the ranks of the ulema, as were the teachers in the mosque and the secretaries of the ruler. Being rooted in the local urban society, the ulemas could legitimately represent the population. This fact, combined with their spiritual authority and their wide network of social connections, enabled them to counterbalance the rulers' interests wherever they went against those of the community. Occasionally, they could also mobilize public resistance in the mosque and the market against unpopular decisions by misguided rulers, which enhanced their negotiating powers.

The special character and the practice of the Islamic religious order could not but influence the corresponding social structures and living habits. These were in turn clearly reflected in certain spatial preferences, basic urban layouts and artistic concepts, which shaped the physical appearance of the Islamic built environment. The following paragraphs will address these influences in greater detail, acknowledging that they occur on a pre-formal level, so to speak, which does not fully define all formal aspects of Islamic culture but strongly conditions the inner structure of its urban and architectural expressions.

The social implications of the religious practice of Islam are perhaps most evident in the so-called "five pillars of faith", which include the basic affirmation of faith (shahada), prayer (salat), almsgiving (zakat), fasting during the month of Ramadan, and the pilgrimage to the Ka'aba (hajj). *Prayer* is recommended to be done collectively wherever possible, five times a day. On Friday noon it brings the whole local community together in an event which has strong social and even political connotations. The sequence of the five daily prayers structures the life of the community and consequently the course of commercial activities in the city. The physical act of prayer itself, with its prescribed bodily movements and its orientation to Mecca, has distinct spatial implications, which will be addressed when describing the structure of the mosque. *Almsgiving* is a duty with obvious social benefits and traditionally involved at least four percent of each individual's yearly income, as a kind of religious tax. The daily *fasting* from dawn to sunset during the month of Ramadan is a major collective effort and thus a social event which reverses people's daily life and calls for a set of related reli-

2

gious and social festivities, culminating in the "Eid-al-Seghir", the smaller
one of the two major Islamic holidays. The *pilgrimage* to Mecca unites
believers from all over the Muslim world in the heart of their religious cosmos after a long and tiresome journey from the "periphery" to the "centre".
It thus provides them with a unique geographical, social and human experience of the Islamic community (umma). The pilgrimage ceremonies in
Mecca last for several days. They include first the gathering of the pilgrims
in the plain of Arafat, then the mass procession towards the inner city of
Mecca, with intermediate stations where ritual duties have to be fulfilled,
and finally the circumbulation of the holy Ka'aba. The concluding ritual
sacrifice on the last day marks the end of the pilgrimage and is celebrated
by Muslims all over the world as the "Eid al-Kabir". It is the major religious
festival of Islam which unites and centres the whole community by allowing
it to participate in the ceremonies performed by the pilgrims at the heart of
the Muslim universe.

Its emphasis on community matters, combined with its concern for social
harmony and formalized human interaction, gave Islam a distinct civic character and made it, at least potentially, an urban religion. No doubt, its
original background was the tribal society of the Hejjaz with its Bedouin

2   The tent city of pilgrims gathering in
the plain of Arafat during the Hajj period
(from Snouck Hurgronje, around 1890).

roots, yet urban culture was not unknown in Arabia (especially in the southern part of the peninsula), and intensive trading had kept the Arabian tribes in contact with some of the major urban centres of the Near East long before the times of the Prophet. Eventually, Islam sustained the early revival of urban civilization all around the Mediterranean in the conquered former Roman provinces, including Syria, Egypt, Spain and North Africa. In this respect, the Islamic conquest compares quite favourably with the intrusion of Eurasian tribes into the northern provinces of the later Roman empire which in effect led to a century-long cultural collapse in central and northern Europe.

Perhaps the most significant social implication of Islam was the fact that the strength of its ritualized living patterns dispensed with the need for many formal institutions. A large number of administrative structures which are normally identified with cities – at least in Europe – did not develop, simply because the society had internalized its structuring constraints, which minimized the need for external controls. Its coercing mechanisms worked from within, so to speak, and needed little or no institutional support. Traditional Islamic cities had no municipalities comparable to those of the Western world, and the Crown and the Church in the institutional sense of Medieval Europe did not exist. Hence, the Muslim "res publica" was not the result of civil rights wrested from oppressive authorities but the outcome of the shared desire to follow certain religiously prescribed patterns of life which would hopefully provide man with peace and welfare in this world and salvation in the next world.

The only Muslim institution which combined certain aspects of royal patronage, religious domain and civic functions was the establishment of religious endowment (waqf, plural: awqaf). It was based on pious donations by the powerful and the wealthy, which were given for a social purpose and became forever the inalienable property of the community, administered by the kadi. These donations could consist of funds to build and/or maintain social welfare buildings such as mosques, schools, baths and fountains (which were sometimes combined with the tomb of the sponsor). Or they could consist of land, commercial facilities or houses, the returns from which were allocated to social welfare purposes. Since they were inalienable and could accumulate over centuries, waqf properties eventually covered large parts of urban real estate. In practice, the institution of the waqf thus provided the public funds which were needed to finance and to run the public domain of Islamic cities. It also strengthened the role of the kadi as the responsible representative of the community, especially vis-à-vis the ruler, who was not entitled to use the accumulated funds for his own purposes.

The absence of dominant civic institutions in the Islamic city increased the need for social consensus and the importance of certain mechanisms of human interaction. A set of implicit rules and conventions known and accepted by everyone helped society to maintain a self-regulating inner balance. The kadi and the muhtasib, the ulema, the sheikhs of the various professional guilds and the heads of the major family clans and ethnic groups were instrumental in achieving and maintaining this balance. Their relations with the ruler were based on a kind of implicit social contract, which had to be confirmed every Friday by quoting the name of the ruler in the official prayers. In cases of conflict, the urban community could manifest its discontent by abstention from the official prayers or by collectively shutting the markets, both of which were clear warnings to the ruler.

Physically, the lack of formal institutions resulted in the absence of outstanding government buildings such as city halls, courts or audience halls and related formal open spaces. Most of the institutional functions were fulfilled by the Friday Mosque, the prime public building, which, in line with the Islamic philosophy of life, had not only religious but all sorts of political and social functions. Embedded as it was in the framework of the central markets, the mosque seldom took monumental forms (as European cathedrals did), except in cases where the prestige of royal sponsors was involved. While being the major religious building, it usually remained a polyvalent structure integrated into the urban fabric, with no intention of expressing the power of religious or secular authorities.

Another consequence of Islamic society's inbuilt control mechanisms and the corresponding absence of institutions was the redundance of planning in the modern sense of the word. Most traditional Islamic cities, with the exception of royal palace cities, followed an "organic" pattern of growth, marked by the presence of certain archetypes of built form which acted as architectural "seeds". Such archetypes could develop a wide range of related physical shapes according to site constraints, community size, economic resources, building materials etc., as will be described in the following chapters on the components of urban form. Due to this common origin and mutual affinities, the resulting buildings, i.e. houses, mosques, public facilities, caravanserais and markets, could combine into larger structures in an unforced and quite natural manner. The commonly accepted rules of building, as determined by the codex of social behaviour, did away with the need for central planning; combined with the casual freedom of individual variations, they resulted in the striking balance and homogeneity of the Islamic townscape which is so different from planned uniformity.

Paradoxically, it can be said that it was the highly formalized way of life which allowed for relatively informal urban layouts and a corresponding freedom of individual architectural expression in the Islamic city. The re-laxed attitude (or even hesitance) with regard to formal modes of planning is based on the consciousness of well-defined individual and social duties, as fixed by religious conventions. In addition, it also reflects the conviction that the plans of the Lord can only be executed by inspired and co-ordinated actions of living human beings. Islam never believed in the intrinsic value of "dead" institutions founded and controlled by man for his own purpose. In harmony with its basic tenet ("La ilaha ill'Allah"), it was inclined to let God be God and man be man, i. e. to respect God's prime control over human matters without attempting to interfere with heavy artificial structures, as these may end up restricting human freedom rather than enhancing it. The fact that Muslims were aware of the provisional and transient character of human establishments made them accept more easily certain shortcomings and imperfections inherent to man's worldly existence. The effects of this attitude can easily be observed in the physical structure of the urban environment.

3

The visible physical expressions of any given traditional culture are essentially defined by the way it chooses to deal with the sacred in spatial, architectural and artistic terms – the sacred being the supreme reality which generates, conditions and permeates the various layers of the material world. In the case of Islam, one can observe an obvious reluctance against any attempt to capture and contain the divine qualities in any material spaces, structures or images. While the dangers of idolatry certainly are of concern, the overriding idea is to maintain the direct and effective link-age between God and his creation As the Qur'an emphasizes again and again, God is transcendent, but also immanent in every single feature of the created world. Nature and man are signs and reflections of His power, and therefore the beauty of creation is to praise and to mirror His excel-lence. However, any human endeavour to constrict and isolate the sole creator's attributes into places or objects shaped by man would necessarily curtail their real power and disturb the divine order. In addition, it would represent an arrogant and fallacious attempt to compete with the only bestower of life (Qur'an XVI/17).

The most conspicuous confirmation of this attitude is the character of the prime sacred place of Islam: the Ka'aba with its inlaid "black stone" is not a monument in the conventional sense of religious architecture, but literally a cube marking the focal point of a cosmic system both in the geographical and in the spiritual sense. Its simple geometric volume is a condensation, as it were, of the physical world, with its faces relating to the six primary direc-tions of the earth – the zenith, the nadir and the four cardinal points. Sym-

3 Tunisian miniature from the 11th century showing the Ka'aba as the focal point of the Muslim cosmos.

4 The Haram of Mecca in the late 19th century (from Snouck Hurgronje).

bolically, it represents the intersection of the human world with the celestial spheres, both being connected by the vertical "axis mundi" around which the rotation of the universe takes place.

Thus the Ka'aba is the transmission point between the eternal and the temporal world. By the ritual act of circumambulation (tawaf), one experiences bodily the essence of the centre and participates in the harmonious movement of the universe. This experience is of an existential nature. Accordingly, the Ka'aba is not venerated as an idol or as a significant work of art but as a source of strong spiritual energies which emanate from the cosmic centre and manifest the divine presence on earth. For this reason, it is also called the "House of God". Following an old Semitic tradition, it is wrapped with a black cloth which protects its holiness and prevents human beings from being exposed to the unfiltered impact of the sacred.

Being the radiating spiritual centre of Islam, the Ka'aba creates a magnetic field, so to speak, which extends through the whole of the terrestrial sphere. This allows Muslims anywhere in the world to evoke the divine and to communicate with it, simply by facing to the cosmic centre of the Islamic universe. The orientation towards the Ka'aba, as achieved by the

4

"qibla" direction, confers to each respective place of prayer a potentially sacred character, which is maintained during the ritual act. The holiness of a space is therefore not bound to the spell of a specific building but can be produced anywhere by symbolic representation – a philosophy which matches the Islamic idea of the omnipresence of God: "God has blessed my community by giving it the face of the whole world as a sanctuary", as the Prophet said.

The spiritual charge bestowed by the qibla on any given place is complemented by the ritual consecration of man before performing the religious act. Islam has formalized this consecration by the state of "ihram", which is imposed on pilgrims visiting Mecca. It requires that pilgrims exchange their normal dress for just two pieces of simple seamless cloth (to be worn around the hips and over one shoulder), in order to underline the passage from the temporal into the timeless order during the days of the Hajj. Thus, all worldly differences between the believers are extinguished to remind all men of their primordial status as "servants of God". Another type of consecration, pertaining to the daily religious duties, is the prescribed sequence of ablutions which precedes every act of prayer. It consists of a cleansing of the head and limbs or of the whole body (according to circumstances) with clean running water – the Qur'anic sign of eternal life. Symbolically speaking, the ablution releases the believer several times a day from his temporal condition and concerns, allowing him to enter a state of purity from which he can communicate with the spiritual world.

Necessarily, this particular concept of experiencing the sacred and dealing with it in spatial and physical terms had important repercussions on the architecture of Islam. Unlike a Christian cathedral or a Hindu temple, the mosque is not seen as a sacred place per se but simply as a polyvalent assembly space which can be enhanced for religious purposes by virtue of the qibla orientation and the ritual act of prayer. It is thus invested with sacredness by delegation, as it were, which also means that the presence of the sacred is not limited to religious structures but is potentially available in every place or building. This fact, which is consonant with the absence of a formal priesthood in Islam, has greatly influenced the spatial articulation of Islamic cities. Consecrated spaces are by no means exclusive and are not subject to social and spatial hierarchies in the urban system, nor are they limited to specific types of architecture. Accordingly, the notion of sacredness could be extended to social and architectural domains other than the mosque, and particularly to the family and its home.

Although marriage, being considered as a social matter, is not given sacramental character, Islam qualifies the private sphere of the family as "hurm", which means sacred and, in this case, both inviolable and ritually

5 The city centre of Mecca today, after the modern extension of the Haram, around 1970 (from National Geographic Magazine).

5

6

forbidden to strangers. The related word "haram", which is often identified
with the secluded female section of a house or palace, therefore has a much
wider religious connotation, which is also expressed in the previously
described state of "ihram". The special status of the family unit (bait), seen in
both social and architectural terms, is underlined by the fact that the family
head acts as the "imam" (i. e. the responsible religious leader) of his domestic community, which makes the cell of the house virtually independent from
any intermediate civic or religious institution.

The Islamic approach to religious and social institutions, combined with
its high appreciation of tribal structures and the family clan, therefore gave
rise to a particular concept of sacred space. On the one hand, the religious
building of the mosque is fully integrated into the social life and the architectural fabric of the town and fulfills comprehensive civic functions. On the
other hand, the private home has acquired a degree of sacredness which is
probably unique in comparison with other civilizations. Accordingly, it can
be said that the sacred within the Islamic city does not stand out in concentrated and isolated form but spreads over the urban fabric as a whole – not
unlike the multitude of fountains which give life to the many houses and
mosques of the city. Totally immersed in the cellular structure of the town, it
imbues man's built environment with a continuous remembrance of the
divine, without ever confusing the timeless and the mundane.

The physical effects of this attitude are visible in the homogeneous and
yet highly differentiated structure of traditional Muslim cities. While the architectural fabric tends to be continuous, i. e. undisrupted by massive free-

6   The ablution fountain in the courtyard
of the Qairawiyin Mosque in Fez.

7   Aerial view showing the Qairawiyin
Mosque in Fez embedded in the urban
fabric.

8   The continuous roofscape of the old
city of Isfahan, from the prayer hall of the
Friday mosque to the covered market and
an adjacent caravanserai.

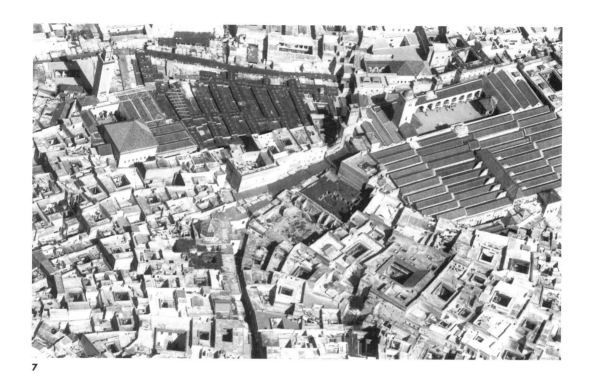

7

8

9

10

standing religious or public buildings or by major open spaces highlighting individual monuments, it also shows a clear internal differentiation into a series of self-contained cellular compartments, which allow the private or sacred character of individual spaces to be protected where and when needed. As a rule, the public spaces lack the rigid layout which is imposed by highly formalized institutions, allowing for a high degree of interaction between various social activities, including religious functions. The mosque, as the main public core, is usually embraced by markets, and together they form a coherent architectural complex. As the prayer space has to meet special requirements of cleanliness, it is always neatly defined, and marked by gates and thresholds where visitors take off their shoes. The transition from the secular to the sacred spheres, both contained within the same public section of the urban fabric, is accomplished by a few steps, which allows for easy interaction between the mosque and the market.

Meanwhile, the residential districts are shielded off from the main streams of public life. The houses, often closely knit together, or built wall to wall in the case of courtyard structures, form inward-oriented autonomous units which are protected against visual intrusion from the street or from neighbouring buildings. The access from the public areas to residential quarters is usually tortuous and broken into successive hierarchical sections which herald increasing degrees of privacy. Dense residential quarters tend to swallow the street space and to convert it into private access corridors. Thus, the sanctuary of the house is not directly exposed to alien influences: it can assimilate the external world after the circulation has been gradually filtered by various intermediate sections of the street network. Dead-end alleyways and a progressive sequence of gates and thresholds are the pre- ferred tools for achieving this protection, which preserves the "aura" of the family sphere and prevents frictions with the public realm.

9 A main alleyway in a residential district in Fez, with a gateway leading into a semi-private dead-end alley on the left side.

10 Inside a dead-end alleyway, looking towards the entry gate.

11 Typical structure of a cluster of courtyard houses around a ramified dead-end alleyway.

12 Typical structure of a residential district in North African cities, composed of individually accessible cluster-units.

In accordance with this spatial logic, the public street network of traditional Islamic cities was reduced to the sheer minimum required to provide connections between the main city gates and the central markets and to ensure the selective accessibility to private quarters. The major circulation streams were deliberately channelled around the "islands" of ritually pure space and protected private domains, so as to avoid an inappropriate mix of activities. Public open space was detached from the main arteries in order to differentiate it according to specific uses and to integrate it into corresponding public buildings, such as mosques, madrasas and caravanserais. Available open spaces in the residential areas were absorbed by the housing clusters, where they emerged in the form of enclosed courtyards which often became the core of individual dwelling units, allocated to well-defined social purposes.

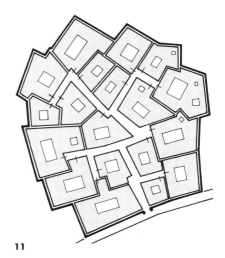

11

The clear attribution of open space to specific social and architectural entities meant that there was no "anonymous" ground to be managed by public institutions. Since Islam conceded a large amount of autonomy and responsibility to various social groups within the society, city planning in the modern institutional sense was practically absent. The groups, whether family clans, foreign ethnic communities or professional corporations, were always allowed to take charge of the respective sections of public open space running through their "territory", in both residential districts and market areas. Former thoroughfares were often deliberately interrupted to cut direct access and privatize the street space. Since the definition of private territorial identities was so dominant, this led to the absence of representative civic space in the Western sense, and also to the lack of undefined public open space which, if it ever existed, tended to be neglected or rapidly appropriated for other uses.

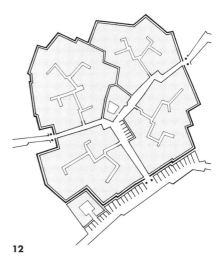

12

These religiously sanctioned ways of dealing with public and private space resulted in townscape principles very different from those of the classical European tradition. Except in palatial cities, there was little or no intent to impose formal planning principles through the street layout by creating large avenues, representative public spaces and rational land subdivisions. The prevailing attitude was to transform anonymous (quantitative) space into personalized (qualitative) space by defining and enclosing a multitude of self-contained individual volumes and developing them from within, in ways which made them virtually autonomous. The coordination between single units occurred implicitly through the inner affinity of their structuring principles, and not through outer geometric arrangements. Buildings thus tended to become architecturally self-sufficient, imposing their law on the street system rather than depending on a predetermined circulation layout. With the composite growth of such individual nuclei, public space was often constricted or reduced to a kind of interior corridor system, framed by adjacent buildings and leaving no loose residual spaces. The internal structuring system of residential units followed similar principles: rooms were not created by mechanical subdivision of the available space but by a cellular aggregation process, which allowed the main reception rooms to become almost autonomous, self-centred shells and create "houses" within the house, so to speak. The internal circulation system of the whole housing unit was subservient to this principle and had to adjust to the access requirements or restrictions imposed by the shapes and functions of the main rooms.

The structuring laws of both the house and the city were thus based on progressive differentiation of "interior" niches from "exterior" spaces, the notion of "interior" and "exterior" being relative values within a large spatial spectrum which ranged from the small private room to the complete urban structure. The resulting cellular structure of the house and the city was predicated on the "wholeness" of each self-contained unit, regardless of its relative position in the urban system. The outcome was the typical multi-focal pattern defined by the countless "centres" of individual buildings rather than by a rational grid of streets and squares. Yet the morphological homogeneity of that pattern allowed the multiple individual forms to merge into a lively and highly differentiated architectural unity.

While the analysis of urban structures may reveal a number of basic cultural shaping factors, as filtered through social models and corresponding architectural patterns, the visual arts are perhaps the most transparent manifestation of the guiding spiritual principles. To be sure, the genesis of Islamic art could not draw on explicit religious prescriptions or recommended artistic practices. Moreover, in the early centuries it was heavily influenced by the cultural heritage of Byzantium and Iran, as well as various tribal traditions from Inner Asia to North Africa. Yet it was Islam which established the spiritual parameters within which the assimilation of the various inherited elements could take place. This assimilation process occurred in full strength during the 8th/9th centuries AD, quite in parallel with the formation of Islamic law. Both processes reflected the desire of the Muslim community to articulate a framework of life consistent with its essential beliefs.

The intent and the character of Islamic art can best be appreciated by referring again to the central guidelines of Islam. In accordance with every traditional (i.e. religiously inspired) art, its main concern is to express and translate its own vision of spiritual reality. As stated earlier, this supreme reality, in the Islamic view, is nothing which could be captured in material works of art or images. God being the sole creator of life, man should not attempt to create artificial surrogates of reality. The only appropriate way to

13 The interior of the dome of the "Pavilion of the Two Sisters" in the Alhambra of Granada (13th/14th century).

13

deal with the divine forces was therefore symbolic representation. While the artist could never grasp the essence of creation, he could allude to it through his works, so as to raise the mind of the viewer to the state of contemplation which is required to approach the mysteries of creation and to perceive its hidden unity, unfolded in the wide spectrum of its manifestations.

For Islamic artists and craftsmen this task meant exploring the intermediate realm between spiritual ideas and material representation: on the one hand they had to appeal to the visual sense, as the eye is the organ through which the inner meaning of art is carried to the human intellect; on the other hand they had to stay away from naturalism, which would have betrayed the transcendent character of the message. This attitude corresponded to the paradoxical goal of Islamic art, which was to pursue the dematerialization of physical reality, while at the same time seeking the embodiment of the invisible reality. The best method of resolving this ambivalence was to remain on the narrow ridge between physical and metaphysical forms, that is, to capture reality in its vibratory state, as it were, before it solidifies into concrete manifestations.

Given the dominant symbolic and "non-iconic" orientation of Islamic art, it is clear that it never really cared about imitation of physical reality in the sense of post-Renaissance European art which, for centuries, was preoccupied with the development of illusionary representation techniques, such as perspective. From an Islamic point of view, such an approach was inadequate as it was bound to miss the real target of artistic creation and lead the artist astray. Even the Byzantine and Medieval concepts of the holy icon, although closer to contemplation, did not satisfy the requirements of Islam, as the essential character of both revelations was different: Christendom relies on the incarnation of God in Jesus Christ, and the narrative character of the Bible called for pictorial illustration. For Islam, however, the Prophet is a human being, and the only incarnation of God is the Qur'an as the holy book containing His message. Accordingly, the analogy to the holy icon in Islam is the acoustic or visual recitation of the Qur'anic verses or "ayat". Calligraphy was thus elevated to the status of a sacred art and came to play an essential role – not only in the arts of the book but also in architectural decoration and even in the adornment of crafted objects of daily use. It enabled Islamic artists to pervade the whole human environment with a permanent rhythmical reverberation of divine presence.

Besides calligraphy, the two other main tools of artistic expression cultivated in Islam were geometrical patterns and the so-called arabesque, which developed on the basis of the vine leaf scroll ornament inherited from late antiquity. Both arabesque and geometrical patterns were often interwoven, overlaid or juxtaposed with calligrapy to form frames and panels of

14

15

14 Calligraphy combined with arabesque and geometric patterns on a decorated wall surface (Fez, 14th century).

15 Interlaced stone layers in two masonry spandrels (Syria, 12th century), showing the influence of nomadic patterns (after Herzfeld).

continuous decoration. If the geometrical patterns of Islamic art represent the "static" face of creation, the arabesque incorporates its "dynamic" aspect, i.e. the natural growth and decay of all expressions of life or, to use Qur'anic images, the continuous unfolding and annihilation of the creation by the Lord. The evolution of arabesque was sustained by the impact of cultural traditions from nomad tribes, which repeatedly injected their vigorous sense of rhythm into the sedentary Islamic art. They also contributed their stylized or abstract way of rendering figural motives which, once freed of naturalistic forms of representation, could be easily integrated into the arabesque pattern.

The webs of geometrical patterns provided the most appropriate "illustration" of the supreme credo of Islam, which confirmed the intrinsic unity underlying the multiplicity and variety of manifested forms. In Islamic art, geometric figures are crystallized manifestations of the wide range of potential forms contained in the circle – the symbol of the origin and perfection of the universe. As they can be derived by geometric procedures from the basic elements of the circle, they are all interrelated and refer to an overarching common framework. Combination of individual geometrical elements can result in intricate ornamental networks which become complex and playful expressions of corresponding principles.

Through their complexity, such patterns assume a multi-dimensional character open to different interpretations: while each figure is balanced and contained in itself, it can also be read as a component of an endless continuing pattern, or as a composition of several overlapping or juxtaposed "centres" producing geometrical networks at various hierarchical levels.

16

17

16/17 Ornamental geometric patterns derived from subdivisions of the circle (after Issam el-Said).

18

19

18 Calligraphy and geometric patterns on the interior of the dome of the Barquq mausoleum (Cairo, 14th century).

19 The courtyard of the Madrasa al-Sahrij in Fez (14th century), an example of a perfectly balanced architectural composition, kept in suspension by the mirroring in the central pool and the transfiguration of ornamented wall surfaces.

20

21

The multifocal structuring principle, which also emerges as an implicit "leit-motiv" in composite urban patterns, found its purest expression in the lucid geometrical composition of ornamental networks. It not only overplays the divisions between self-contained geometrical elements but also transcends the scale attached to individual manifestations, making one realize that the small unit can stand for the larger one and that all are part of the same underlying order. By demonstrating how the macrocosm can be reflected in the microcosm, the ornamental art of Islam became a tool for the philosophical – or rather meditative – comprehension of the inner laws of creation.

While Islamic art favoured plane surfaces (such as walls, panels, arcades, lintels, etc.) for its use of geometrical patterns and arabesques, it also developed a three-dimensional geometric pattern which, through its intermediate character between architecture and ornament, became an important vehicle of artistic expression. The basic component of this three-dimensional adornment is the "muqarna" – a small niche used in a variety of different sizes and composite aggregations. It probably originated from the subdivision of the Sassanian corner squinch, which was used to achieve a better transition from a rectangular base to the overarching cupola or, in other words, to smoothen the passage between plane and spheric surfaces. The precise history of the muqarnas has not been fully elucidated, but

20 The progressive development and refinement of Islamic arabesque, starting from the late Roman scroll ornament (after Kühnel).

21 A carved wood panel (Egypt, 10th century), showing stylized figural motives integrated into the flow of arabesques.

its rapid propagation and sweeping success throughout the Islamic world during the 12th century AD can only mean that it perfectly met the intents and desires of Muslim craftsmen of all provenances. Ever since, the muqarnas have become a hallmark of Islamic architecture. Their use was by no means restricted to the supporting corners of vaulted structures but became a ubiquitous decorative element, filling the interior of domes, the cavities of niches and the projecting edges of balconies and cornices with their so-called "stalactites" or hanging niches.

The deeper rationale for the indulgence in this decorative pattern was the ability of the muqarnas to overcome and transcend the sharp division between two geometric orders, that is the order of square (or the cube), and the order of the circle (or the sphere), the first one representing the static material world and the second one symbolizing the rotation of the universe around its immaterial point of origin. At the same time, the composite structure of imbricated muqarnas of different sizes created an interplay between ascending and descending hierarchies of forms, which blurred the perception of scale and dimension and therefore helped dissolve the impression of a heavy material reality. Similarly to the geometric patterns derived from the circle, the articulation and progressive subdivision of endless series of interrelated niches provided a non-figurative metaphor for the unfolding of creation and for the inherent unity underlying the multiplicity of generated forms.

Through its abstract and geometric character, the ornamental language of Islamic art became an integral part of built form, but while adorning and enhancing the architectural shell, it also invalidated the structural laws of the building, injecting a different dimension of reality into architecture. Far from being "decorative" in a superficial sense, the ornament could actually transform and transfigure a building, lifting it, as it were, into a realm where physical laws are virtually suspended and the structure becomes transparent for a more ethereal reality behind the material appearance. The veiling of architectural structures by the ornament – a recurrent device in Islamic architecture – was therefore meant to dematerialize the building masses and to reveal a hidden spiritual reality. This process is particularly conspicous in the way the filigrane carved ornaments and particularly the honeycombs of muqarnas capture, absorb and reflect light, transforming flat surfaces into vibrant and luminous screens which seem to glow from within (see picture on page 41).

These few examples demonstrate that Islamic art was not just an ornamental by-product of a sophisticated material civilization but an essential and integral component of Islamic culture. Its malleable design language relied on being transmitted by the crafts, which made it applicable to and

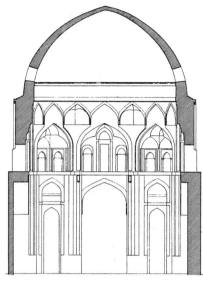

22

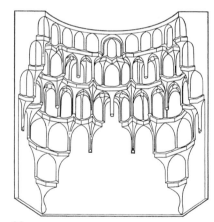

23

22 Dome structure on rectangular base, with tiers of intermediate squinches (Isfahan, Friday Mosque, 12th century).

23 Typical detail of hanging niches or "muqarnas".

compatible with all formal expressions of human life – from monumental public buildings to domestic architecture and to the humblest objects of daily use. As the inspiring, transforming and unifying factor of the built environment, Islamic art fulfilled a primordial role in the life of Muslim cities. Its ubiquitous presence served as a permanent reminder of spiritual reality and offered man a direct visual access to truth – an access which did not rely on abstract scientific theories, but on a refined sensorial experience appealing to the heart and to man's sense of intellectual vision.

Environmental, Cultural and Historic Shaping Factors of Islamic Architecture

Islam emerged in a desert region and later occupied the large belt of hot and arid zones reaching from North Africa to India. These areas were always marked by a strong nomadic hinterland and prevailing tribal structures. The given natural living conditions prompted specific environmental and architectural responses which had their impact on Muslim architecture, as did the nomadic background. While the growth of cities, spurred by the cultural heritage of Rome, Byzantium and Iran, brought to bear a set of new parameters, the urban civilization of Islam remained strongly influenced by the nomadic roots of a tribal society.

The major achievement of the Prophet as a statesman was that he succeeded in uniting the dispersed energies of the Arabian tribes (which were often spent on inter-tribal fights) and harnessing them under the auspices of an overriding religious idea. In this process, archaic nomadic and tribal concepts were not abolished but integrated into a more complex cultural system, which eventually was strong enough to absorb and assimilate foreign cultural influences without losing its identity. Islam took over many forms of ancestral nomadic thinking and behaviour, charged their archetypical character with a new symbolic dimension and perpetuated them by religious rituals. This applies to many Islamic customs, such as the rites of pilgrimage, the prayer movements or the way the floor surface is used for sitting, praying and socializing. The veneration of water as source of life and element of ritual purification may relate to the same origins. In general terms, the whole spiritual "climate" of Islam, with its deep-rooted belief in the transient character of this world, can be seen as influenced by nomadic concepts. Even in the urban context, and up to the present time, the social structures of Muslim communities have remained deeply imprinted by tribal models.

Looking at the cultural history of Islam, nomad and urban ways of life can be understood as different modes of the same existential status, one more "liquid" and the other more "crystallized" in its consistency, but both intimately correlated. Nobody has seen and expressed this complementarity more lucidly than Ibn Khaldun, the Maghrebi philosopher of the 14th century AD and author of the "Muqqadima" (Introduction to History). In his fundamental book, he states that urban civilization, with its flourishing com-

24 A cultural archetype: an oasis within the city and a paradise within the house (garden courtyard in Marrakesh).

merce and the corollary achievements in the arts and in science, is the climax of every cultural development, but that it is liable to rapid degeneration unless it is periodically rejuvenated by the influx of fresh energies. He sees the nomad tribes as the carriers of the required unspoiled potential of strength, vigour and pride, which is continuously reproduced under the hard environmental conditions of the desert. This potential can only be released and fully materialized once the nomad tribes emerge from the shapeless sea of the desert to inject their vital forces into the islands of urban civilisation – which they will first attack and partly destroy, then rebuild and renew. The key agent of this process is the strong social cohesion ("asabiyya") of nomad societies, as developed under desert conditions. It fosters strong leadership and group solidarity, qualities which are essential for building empires and cities (and for sustaining them over time), but which urban civilization is unable to produce by itself. To be able to flourish, cities therefore depended on the nomadic resources which, however, were subject to decay after several generations of sedentary life and therefore exposed to the thrust of subsequent Bedouin waves waiting for their historic moment to rise.

Ibn Khaldun thus understands nomad and urban societies to be closely interrelated and even interdependent, inasmuch as they are two components of a natural growth and decay process which nourishes and regenerates urban civilization. The potentially violent character of the cyclical encounters between nomads and sedentaries does not escape him, but he accepts it as part of the natural law of the survival of the fittest, especially with regard to the ruling dynasties. He also acknowledges the fact that the qualities most successful in dynastic struggles do not always conform with religious ethics. Yet a strong ruling class was needed to protect and support Muslims of urban societies and therefore political compromises had to be found in the interest of Islam.

This rhythmical interaction between nomad and sedentary forces has determined the course of history of the Muslim communities again and again. The migration and sedentarization of Arab tribes in the Fertile Crescent had already happened well before the advent of Islam, as witnessed by the earlier presence of Arab dynasties in Mesopotamia, such as the Lakhmids. With Islam, however, this movement gained a new momentum and led to the establishment of the first Arab-Islamic empire reaching from North Africa and Spain to Iran and Transoxania. During the Abbasid Caliphate (750–1258 AD), the security of the Islamic empire became dependent on the services of Turkoman slave-soldiers, who were brought in large numbers from the Transoxanian steppes. Their importance increased with the growing influence of Persian culture at the Abbasid court. With the est-

25

ablishment of the Seljuk dynasty (1040–1243 AD) the Turkoman tribes became a dominant power in the eastern part of the Islamic world. The Mamluk rulers of Egypt (1250–1515 AD) grew out of a selected and specially
educated caste of warrior slaves, again brought in from Transoxania. Later,
the tribal influx from inner Asia was continued by the Mongols and by the
Ottomans, the former occupying Iran and India during the 13th and the 16th
centuries, the latter succeeding the Seljuks in Turkey, and occupying parts of
southeastern Europe, North Africa, the Fertile Crescent and the Arabian
Peninsula. The Ottomans were the last Islamic dynasty of tribal origin and
kept the nominal tradition of the Caliphate until the collapse of their empire
in World War I.

In the western realm of Islam, similar waves of nomadic intrusion originated from the Saharan Berber tribes, resulting in the rapid succession of
the Almoravid, Almohad, and Merinid dynasties between the 11th and the
14th centuries. In most cases, the cyclical invasion by Bedouin tribes caused
considerable turmoil and even destruction, yet it was often also followed by
political, artistic and even religious rejuvenation, since the invading tribes
were usually freshly converted by a spiritual leader and their religious fervour gave new impulses to the "decadent" urban environment. It is conspicuous that the geometrical sense of Islamic art was repeatedly renewed
and enhanced by this process in the Maghreb and elsewhere.

25 Tribal settlement on the edge of the
desert, between nomad and sedentary
zones of civilization (Southern Morocco).

Besides violent invasions there was, however, also a continuous peaceful infiltration of the urban "milieu" by Bedouin and rural immigrants. The social structure of Muslim cities was dominated by family clans and tribal units which had their genealogic roots in rural or desert areas and often drew other clan members into the city. In addition, rural people from the surrounding hinterland tended to settle near the gates of the cities or form new rural suburbs, which gradually became more developed quarters "extra muros" as the population underwent the corresponding social urbanization process. This phenomenon, which was always present in latent form, has exploded in modern times, with waves of immigrants flocking to the cities in search of better opportunities.

The relative autonomy of clans and tribal units within the city found its most significant expression in the collective urbanization pattern of the "khittat", as applied in the early Muslim settlements and especially in the garrison towns of newly conquered areas in Mesopotamia and Egypt. These first Arab city foundations in Basra, Kufa and Fustat, occurring within one decade after the death of the Prophet, were carried out with the objective of sedentarizing the immigrant troops and their families. While in the beginning architecture was very primitive, probably consisting of tents and simple reed and mud structures, the organizational pattern of these settlements (related by the early historians al-Baladhuri and al-Ya'qubi) was to become significant, if not typical, for later Muslim cities: the foremost act of city planning was the marking and enclosing of the common meeting and prayer place, which was to serve as the integrating factor for the various tribes, fulfilling both religious and political purposes. Sometimes this enclosure, which anticipated the later formal mosque, was equipped with a palmtree structure and simple shades on part of the surface to provide better climatic protection. In all likelihood, the side facing Mecca was marked with a more or less solid qibla wall. Close to this meeting place or "masdjid" was the "dar al-imara", i.e. the seat of government, which was mostly attached to the qibla wall. In the open space around the masdjid there were markets which developed spontaneously around the most densely used public spaces. It can be assumed that they initially consisted of informal tent structures, probably comparable to the rural markets which have survived in many Arab countries up to the present day.

It is interesting to note that these first settlements did not follow explicit geometric planning concepts and that, at least in the early times, they were not even walled. Beside the demarcation of the central core and the reservation of a number of major access lanes (reportedly fourty spans wide), the remaining land was allotted to the various clans, tribes and ethnic groups for their own development. Planning authority was thus delegated to

26 Enclosed rural market area (Southern Morocco).

27 Typical semi-sedentary settlement in the Atlas mountains, composed of hedges enclosing individual spaces, which are filled with simple huts.

26

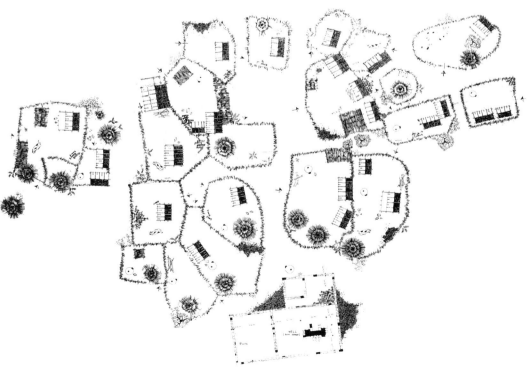

27

individual social groups which were responsible for the autonomous management of their allocated space. Within the given territorial boundaries, the definition of land usage was left to internal agreements, i. e. to the individual clans and families and their respective sheikhs. Each of these ethnic or tribal quarters had its own masdjid to settle community affairs and to resolve internally whatever conflicts might arise from diverging development interests.

The khittat system can be understood as the prototype of later and much more refined urban development concepts. It demonstrates many typical features which continued to be applied in most Muslim cities, such as the relative lack of institutional control, the absence of predetermined formal layouts, the autonomy of the residential units and sub-units, the supremacy of private arrangements over public regulations, the indulgence with regard to private space encroaching onto public space and the reduction of the circulation network to a bare minimum.

Similar trends can be observed in the adaptive re-use of existing Roman-Hellenistic town structures by the new Muslim population. The prime examples of this transformation process are the Syrian cities of Aleppo and Damascus, where the two major public spaces, the old agora and forum in Aleppo and the former temple square in Damascus, were occupied by new mosques. Interestingly, these buildings – important forerunners of many later mosques – in certain ways merged the functions of the forum and the temple into one single facility. The viability of this combination was due to the changed concepts of religious practice and governmental authority pursued by Islam. The task was to bring together in one place related social, religious, administrative and representational functions by introducing a flexible and polyvalent use of space. This could be achieved by maintaining a large central courtyard, surrounded by shaded arcades on three sides and faced by a pillared hall in the tradition of Roman market basilicas. The building was to provide both covered prayer space and the audience hall of the ruler. It is not without deeper significance that the old idea of placing a religious monument in the centre of the space, as found in the layout of the Roman temple square in Damascus and later in the construction of the church of St. John that replaced the temple, was deliberately rejected.

An equally significant urban metamorphosis took place with the large central avenues of the Roman cities in Syria – the Via Recta in Damascus and the main spine of Aleppo, leading from the western gate to the Citadel. These avenues, representative of the civic pride of Roman civilization and symbols of the central authority in the provincial towns, had lost their ancient meaning and were no longer used by horse-drawn carriages, since the Muslim city had returned to a predominantly pedestrian circulation. Thus the available space in the shaded lateral arcades and in the central traffic

28

28 The southern wall of the Umayyad Mosque in Damascus, featuring some of the original Roman stonework.

29 Plan of Damascus showing the original Roman-Hellenistic street grid superimposed on the later Muslim circulation network. (The black rectangular square corresponds to the temple square, which was later occupied by the Umayyad Mosque.)

30 Plan of the Umayyad Mosque in Damascus, built into the precinct of the temple square (see also page 106).

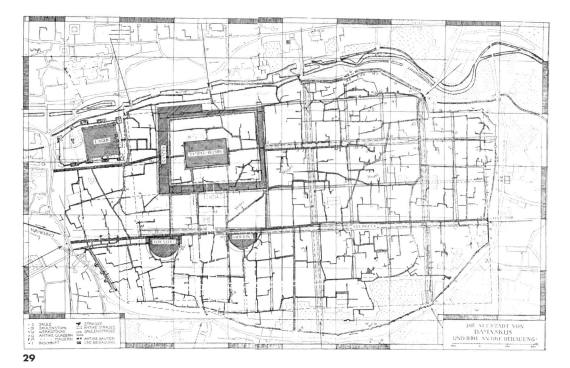

29

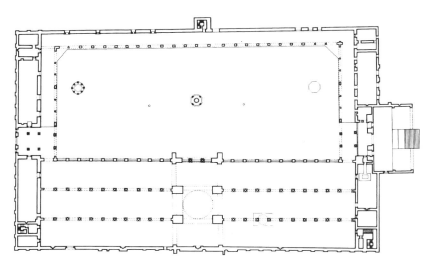

30

lanes was gradually occupied by merchants who started erecting booths along the main pedestrian flows – first as temporary, then as permanent structures. This process, which is consonant with traditional appropriation patterns in rural open-air markets, led to a number of narrow parallel pedestrian lanes framed by shops and eventually fostered the typology of the classical urban suqs.

In the residential districts, the orthogonal grid layout of Roman streets was to be gradually transformed into a much more irregular pattern. This change relied on the fact that the street layout in the private quarters was no longer controlled by a central civic authority and that individual houses, for reasons of family links, social convenience or simply lack of space, tended to grow together into larger clusters which interrupted, privatized or simply swallowed the existing street network. The result was an internalized access system with private corridors, dead-end lanes and cul-de-sacs, branched on semi-private residential alleyways which in turn provided connections with the main public thoroughfares and the markets.

The cases described are typical examples showing how continuous daily practice, rooted in ancestral customs, shared religious values and corresponding social rituals, can shape and transform a built environment. They also demonstrate how vernacular building patterns can interact with, supersede or integrate more formal architectural styles – a process which had a great impact on the evolution of Islamic architecture and its various regional expressions. Before addressing the influence of more monumental architectural typologies, which had their origin at the imperial courts rather than in rural areas, it is important to dwell on some of the basic concepts of vernacular architecture, which formed the solid trunk on which more hybrid branches of "historic" architecture were grafted.

Vernacular architecture in the Islamic world came forth as a perfect response to the living conditions of both the natural and the social environment, based on age-old regional experiences with local building material and appropriate techniques of climate control. Perhaps the best example to demonstrate this is the case of the courtyard building: the extreme climatic conditions prevailing in many regions of the Muslim world, ranging between cold winter nights and burning summer days, called for a tight architectural envelope with protected interior spaces, as independent as possible from the outside world. Incidentally, this requirement also matched the strong social and religious urge for a secluded private family space. The courtyard house, an age-old oriental invention already fully developed in the plan of the Sumerian city of Ur (around 2000 BC), responded ideally to these concerns. It was to become a timeless prototype of vernacular archi-

tribal roots

courtyard building

31 View of a model representing the historic city structure of Aleppo, with the Roman avenue transformed into covered suqs and the agora into a mosque (see also page 127).

32 Interior of the courtyard of the Umayyad Mosque of Aleppo.

31

32

33

34

tecture in most geographic regions of the Muslim world. In terms of historic connections, it had already passed from the East into Roman architecture and was brought back again to the oriental provinces of the Empire, where more vernacular versions had of course survived throughout the centuries.

The basic architectural gesture of the courtyard house is the enclosure, which defines and qualifies a specific space, marks it with an individual identity and singles it out from the surrounding environment. In the context of Islamic architecture, the enclosure has become a ubiquitous feature which pervades the whole building repertory from the private house to the caravanserai and the mosque. Applied in both rural and urban areas, it emerges as the result of certain basic forms of behaviour in space, translated into corresponding architectural prototypes such as the tent, the village house or the

33 Berber tents in southern Morocco, during a local festival.

34 Domed dwelling units constructed within enclosed family courtyards in a rural area of northern Syria.

35 Imaginative reconstruction of the Prophet's courtyard in Medina (after J. L. Leacroft).

urban residence. Even the tent can be seen as an encapsulated personal space extracted from the infinity of the desert, as it were. Aggregated in larger compounds, tents often form circular enclosures protected by a thorny fence, such as the North African duars. There the tents become individual sub-units oriented towards a central courtyard. The same principle is to be observed in hard versions of rural architecture such as the so-called "beehive structures" in northern Syria or the farmhouses of the Maghreb, which were often built as mud-brick structures. The North African examples show the transition from circular to rectangular shapes, which allow for better integration of the single units into compact houses and thus pave the way for densified urban structures.

A specially significant prototype of the rural enclosure was the house of the Prophet in Medina, which he is reported to have built with his companions on an empty piece of land at the place where his camel stopped and sat down when he entered the oasis. The structure of this house could be reconstructed from narrations of contemporary eyewitnesses: it consisted of a simple walled enclosure and the large courtyard, surrounded by a number of dwelling units, walls and a simple shaded portico on one side, and was to become the centre of the first Muslim community and the functional prototype of all later mosques.

In many places on the edge of the desert, fortified enclosures were developed to protect people, livestock and commercial goods. This was the case of the caravanserais (khans), fortresses (ribat) and enclosed market places, which were built as strongholds and seminal points of sedentary life in barren areas. It equally applied to fortified forms of dwellings, such as the "kasbas" in southern Morocco or the tower houses of southern Arabia,

35

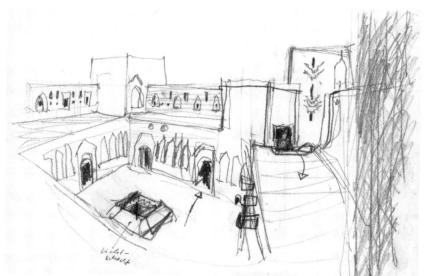

36

37

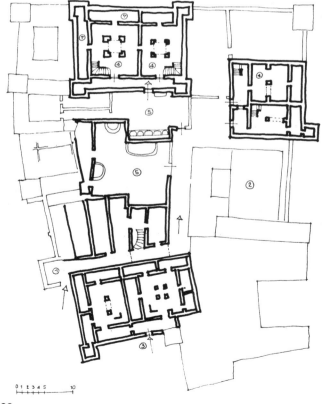

0 1 2 3 4 5   10

38

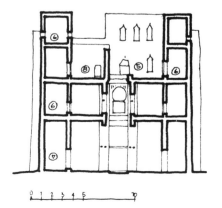

0 1 2 3 4 5   10

which reduced the courtyard to an air shaft or replaced it by a covered central room. Both included stables and storage room for grain and other food reserves on the lower floors.

Much of the later Islamic architecture can be seen as a refinement and further development of such rural prototypes, transposed to urban conditions. The enclosure is a recurrent theme which underlies most urban buildings, whether private or public, and shapes the layout of the city at various hierarchic levels of its internal structure. The connections to the rural origins were also stressed by the fact that many Islamic cities kept certain agricultural activities within their walls, including orchards and paddocks, and that the houses included corresponding storage and processing facilities. Often the urban population retained close bonds with related ethnic groups in rural areas, from where they attracted not only immigrants but also specialized skills and trades needed for construction and maintenance of the city.

Another "leitmotiv" of Islamic architecture intimately connected with the enclosure was the idea of the walled garden, which was congenial to people living on the edge of the desert and which, in hidden or overt form, interprets the Qur'anic image of the oasis turned into paradise. It is significant that Islam should have developed the concept of the celestial garden in contrast to the Christian idea of the celestial city or the heavenly Jerusalem (which was to inspire the Gothic cathedral). The Qur'anic images of paradise depict abundant water, fragrance and fruit trees and feature lofty

the walled garden as paradise

Quaran depicts paradise w/ water, fruit trees, Fragrance, and shade.

39

36 Upper terrace level of a fortified family stronghold (kasba) in southern Morocco.

37 Detail of the staircase.

38 Plan and section of a kasba compound.

39 Aerial view of a fortified caravanserai and adjacent village between irrigated land and the desert in central Iran (G. Gerster).

40

shaded places, where the believers can sit in perfect peace and enjoy exquisite pleasures. (See, for instance, Qur'an 56/11-33 and 88/8-20). Such vivid descriptions in the holy book could not but appeal to the senses and the mind, and were certainly a source of inspiration for the wide range of formal and informal gardens in the Islamic world.

Historically speaking, the cultural and religious predisposition to the garden theme was met by the Iranian concept of the "firdaws" (paradise garden), which was introduced into the Middle East in the early centuries of Islam but can be traced back to the Achaemenid period. The traditional Persian garden is based on the "chahar bagh" concept, i.e. four garden sections enclosed by a wall and divided by two crossing water channels symbolizing the four rivers of paradise. It has greatly influenced most Islamic palace gardens, starting with the Abbasid palaces of Samarra, built in the 9th century AD. From there, the paradise garden concept migrated westwards, to Egypt, Andalusia and the Maghreb. In the East it was revived in Iran itself, especially under the Safawid dynasty, and taken over by the Timurids in Samarkand, from where it reached the Indian subcontinent under the Moghuls.

Such royal gardens could stand on their own, sometimes outside the city walls, and in this case they served as "reception camps", featuring light pavilion structures only – as can still be seen in the Shalimar Gardens in La-

40 Mughal miniature from the 17th century showing the emperor Babur supervising the construction of his walled garden.

41 Scheme of the palace district of Isfahan in the 17th century, with the main spine of the Chahar Bagh (A) leading to the bridge across the river (B) and holding together a series of walled gardens. The palace area, slightly tilted with respect to the gardens, is bordered by the "Meidan" of Shah Abbas (F), a large open space which also served for polo games. The Meidan articulated the interface between the gate of the Palace (G), the Shah Abbas Mosque (J) and the central market complex (K), linked with the Friday Mosque (M) by a bazaar spine (L).

42 Plan of the Shalimar Gardens in Lahore (17th century), showing the typical cruciform subdivision of "paradise gardens" by water channels. The lower square on the north, with the entry gate (A), was the public zone, the upper square in the south (B) served as the private garden of the emperor, and the intermediate level with the big pool provided the official reception area.

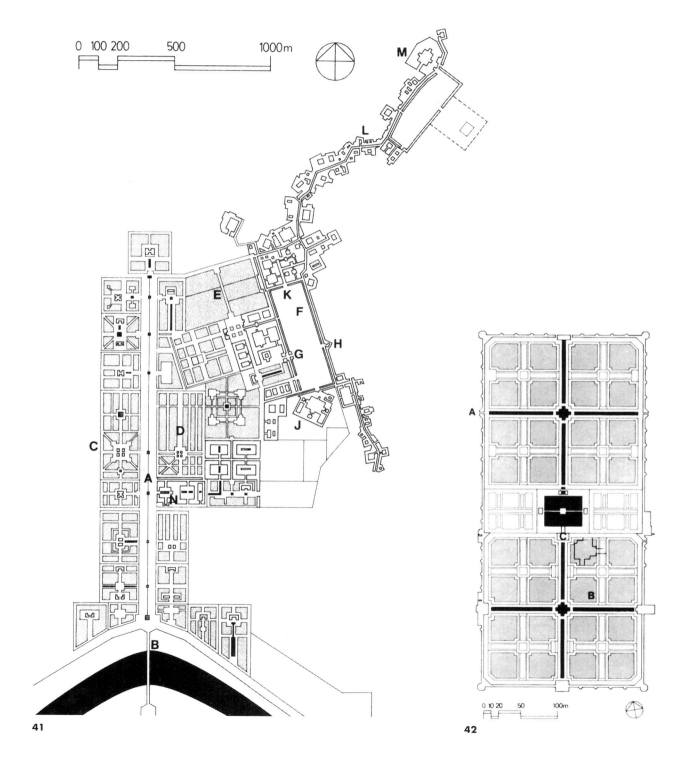

41

42

43

44

43 Pavilion over a fountain at the centre of a cruciform interior garden (riyadh) in an 18th century private mansion in Marrakesh.

44 Courtyard with central pool and musicians' estrade in an 18th century private house in Aleppo.

45 Sketch of a Moroccan interior garden (riyadh) by A. Laprade.

hore. Or they could be integrated into a more substantial palace structure, as was the case in the "Court of the Lions" of the Alhambra in Granada. In Isfahan, they extended into urban dimensions, forming the backbone, as it were, of the whole royal city of Shah Abbas. In Moghul India, pleasure gardens were often combined with the construction of a tomb complex which turned into a memorial place after the burial of its deceased patron or his beloved ones – the most famous example of this type being the Taj Mahal.

However, it would be erroneous to think that the paradise garden was confined to the realm of kings and princes. Descending from the courtly sphere to that of the urban bourgeoisie, it eventually became an immensely popular concept and was reproduced in smaller size in countless courtyard houses in many regions of the Islamic world. Even in its most modest form it made an essential contribution to the quality of life in Muslim cities.

It has been noted by cultural geographers that large-scale agriculture, as introduced by the Romans in their North African and Near Eastern provinces, was somewhat neglected under Islamic rule. In fact, peasants did not enjoy the same social status as merchants in the Islamic world, and regular farming was often compromised by Bedouin raids. Nevertheless, there was a definite impetus given to gardening, and in fact the wide geographical range of Islam and the regular trade connections to the Far East resulted in many exotic fruit and flower species being introduced into the western regions, including Europe. The traditional palm groves were often combined with orchards, using various layers of vegetation: the high date palms provided shade to the lower citrus trees, which in turn protected the ground cover consisting of spicy shrubs or flowerbeds.

Larger plantations, orchards and pleasure gardens were usually located at the same distance from the city, but could also be included within the city walls, adjacent to the urbanized areas. Smaller gardens could easily be integrated into the courtyards of individual houses. Their practical function, i. e. the yield of fruits, shade and climatic improvement, was combined with aesthetic pleasure and with Qu'ranic connotations of symbolic nature. This multiple benefit harmonizes with the fact that there was a joint religious and economic incentive for cultivating land: Islamic law considers the vivifying of "dead" land as a good deed to be rewarded, and the corresponding action, implemented on clearly abandoned ground, entitles the individual to ownership of the respective piece of land.

Water, too, had to fulfill a multiple function within the built environment of Islam: besides being an essential resource for survival in the most practical sense, there was also a religious and an aesthetic dimension attached to it, for it was the element of ritual purification and the symbol of eternal life. Within the palace, the domestic courtyard, the mosque or the walled

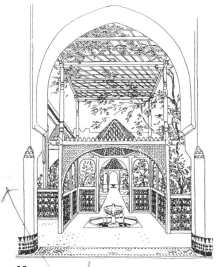

45

became common

*– yield fruit
's shade, aesthetics
– symbolic nature,
cooling effect*

*water: ritual
purification and
eternal life.*

46

47

water

garden, it helped cool enclosed outer spaces and even the interiors. Together with the garden, it improved the micro-climate of the house, allowing the inhabitants to endure the hot summer months. But combined with an appropriate architectural and landscape setting, it also served as a source of sensual pleasure and aesthetic delight. To understand these special qualities one only needs to look at the sophisticated way in which the flow of water is celebrated in the many types of fountains, channels, ramps (salsabil) and pools all over the Islamic world. Compared with the fountains of Renaissance and Baroque gardens in Europe, water is displayed in a far more subtle and intimate manner. The soft bubbling of a spring in a pool, the rhythmical trickling of an overflowing basin, or the silver-like veil of water coating the stone surface are more evocative to the Muslim mind than the dramatic outbursts of large arrays of fountains. Hand in hand with the ornamental tapestries adorning architectural enclosure walls, gardens and water became key factors in producing that contemplative state of mind which, according to the Islamic philosophy of life, enables man to open a window into the realm of timeless existence.

gardens + water produced contemplative state of mind ... timelessness

Obviously, the garden culture in most Muslim countries would not have been possible without elaborate irrigation methods. These were also needed to cultivate fields, orchards and gardens and to supply water to the cities, including their mosques, public baths, private houses and industrial facilities, such as mills, dye-works and tanneries. In the geographical context of Islamic civilization, cities appear like islands in a vast sea of uncultivated

46 Irrigated fields in the Algerian Saoura valley.

47 Irrigation channels passing under and between the houses of the city of Fez.

48 Distributor for irrigation of private fields in the Algerian oasis of Timimoun (after H. Imesch).

or barren land, connected by the caravan routes which replaced the paved roads of the Roman Empire. These routes were in need of well-distributed rest stations, combined with springs, wells or oases, to enable travellers to survive the journey. Here, caravanserais acted as outposts of urban civilization between the cities. Together with well structures and other facilities, they were usually built as pious foundations, especially along the trade and pilgrim routes leading to Mecca.

Irrigation techniques for urban settlements varied from place to place: wherever the geographical conditions allowed to do so, water was diverted from existing rivers and fed into a separate irrigation and discharge system. Equitable distribution mechanisms had to be devised to subdivide the flow of water according to socially agreed rules. In many cases land ownership was combined with precise water rights and specific water allocations. Cities located at the feet of mountains which were rich in springs and perennial waters often developed such supply systems to great perfection. The city of Damascus, for instance, lived in close symbiosis with its oasis (the Ghouta), which was fed by the springs of Mount Kassioun. Fez, against all strategic rules, was laid out at the bottom of a natural conch, which allowed for easy irrigation, using the incoming stream of the upper plateau and discharging it onto another riverbed at the bottom of the valley. In Cairo, water from the Nile was driven up by animal force to the top of a tower located on the riverbank, from where it was carried into the city by a large aqueduct. This was a monumentalized form of an age-old irrigation technique which is still used in the present day in rural areas of the Nile valley.

In other, less fortunate places, water had to be obtained by wells from the subsoil and distributed into the fields, as it was the case in Sana'a, where most wells were connected with mosques. In the Hadramut area, the orchards were located outside the city and not watered by wells, as in Sana'a, but by an irrigation system which regularized, distributed and exploited the floods of the wadi by a sophisticated system of dams, drains and decanting basins. A much more labour-intensive method was the construction of underground channels to tap the subsoil between different geological layers of mountainous areas and drain their water reserve into the city. This method, which required constant maintenance of the underground channels by a long series of vertical shafts drilled into the ground, was widely used on the Iranian plateau and also in the Saharan plains. The irrigation channels were called "qanat" in Iran and "ghettara" in Morocco, and it is believed that at least the Iranian ones are of pre-Islamic origin. Once the water was close to the city, sophisticated distribution systems allocated the right amount of water to individual landowners.

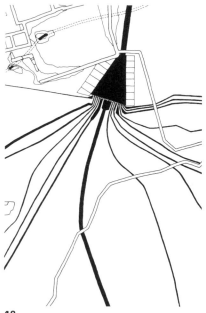

distribution
water system

48

The timeless vernacular architecture of the Islamic world provided the mainstream of built form, out of which the peaks of monumental architecture could emerge, bearing the imprint of certain historic periods, individual patrons or exceptional master builders. The representative buildings commonly associated with the term "Islamic architecture" are mostly cross-breedings between local vernacular traditions and the products of a more refined court civilization which absorbed, assimilated and propagated inherited building models, often of Roman, Byzantine or Sassanian origin. From the court cities such new typologies could in turn filter down in many variations into the repository of vernacular traditions.

The monumental, or "imperial" architecture of Islam to be addressed in this context, is basically the product of royal and princely patronage. Ibn Khaldun noted that the tribal energies, once emerged from the desert and having attained their urban accomplishment, necessarily led to the establishment of royal authority and dynastic rule, with the corollary needs for corresponding cultural and architectural statements. Very early in the history of Islam, the traditional caliphate, which combined spiritual and political authority, was de facto substituted with the more secular rule of sultans and emirs, who tended to usurp the positions and titles of the early caliphs without really disposing of their religious legitimation. The ensuing divorce of spiritual leadership from political power was a recurrent subject of grief in Muslim history, but was unavoidable. Spiritual matters now tended to fall into the realm of the ulema and the Sufi brotherhoods, which both dealt with the religious concerns of the Muslim community – the former in a more dogmatic, "exterior" manner, the latter in a more contemplative, "interior" sense. Meanwhile, the newly established royal dynasties, such as the Umayyads and the Abbasids, were keen to patronize the arts as a physical expression of their newly established political power. The idea of confirming their status and gaining in legitimation by sponsoring great works of architecture was certainly not alien to them.

The rising Islamic empire, which grew in the vacuum left by the declining rival dominions of the Byzantines and Sassanians, was to become a logical heir to the sunken Roman Empire, at least in the Middle Eastern and North African provinces. The first Muslim patrons could hardly avoid continuing this imperial tradition if they wanted to enhance their royal image. It was therefore natural that they harnessed the economic and artistic potential of the area to produce great works of architecture; it was equally inevitable that late Roman, Byzantine and Iranian building traditions were to become the point of departure for the evolving monumental architecture of Islam for the simple reason that the existing resources of local artists and craftsmen had a major role to play in the process.

49

The earliest buildings of the new Islamic empire therefore indicate a somewhat eclectic approach, adopting available typologies, construction techniques and modes of ornamentation to meet the emerging new architectural needs. The models which were to exert a direct or indirect influence on the development of Islamic architecture were mainly the "apadana" (the monumental pillared reception hall used by the Persian kings), the Roman basilica, the Sassanian iwan scheme, prominently represented by the palace of Ctesiphon, and the Byzantine dome structures, such as the church of the cloister at St. Simeon in northern Syria. The impact of these models was not always immediate and not necessarily comprehensive, as the borrowing of specific prototypes could result in important transformations and variations of the original scheme according to the changed context and patterns of use.

Although it is not the purpose of this book to discuss the history of monumental Islamic architecture in its formative period, it may be apposite to quote a few significant examples illustrating the adaptation process which took place during the first centuries of Islam. A widespread and rather simple case of absorbing the monumental heritage was the re-use of Roman columns for enhancing the primitive pillared halls of the early mosques in Mesopotamia, originally built with palm trunks. This method was often continued for the construction of new mosques, using the columns as convenient supports for formally designed arcades. An interesting evidence of the early use of the "apadana" scheme is provided by the surviving mosque in Shibam (northern Yemen) from the 8th century AD, which features slender timber columns and an elaborate timber ceiling. The adoption of the Basilica scheme in the Umayyad mosque in Damascus has already been mentioned and will be discussed in greater detail in Chapter 5. It is interesting to note that the Byzantine-style mosaics in the arcade of the mosque show only ideal landscapes, dispensing with the representation of human beings – a first

Borrowing architecture of previous cultures

Roman columns

49 Courtyard elevation of the Sassanian palace at Ctesiphon. One of the four monumental iwans was preserved until the end of the 19th century.

indication of the emerging Islamic preference for non-figurative artistic expression. The Sassanian iwan scheme had a strong and direct impact on palace architecture as soon as the centre of the Islamic empire moved to Baghdad during the Abbasid period, and later it was to influence the mosque typology in certain regions, as well as domestic architecture. The Byzantine cupola appeared in the first monumental building of Islam, the Dome of the Rock in Jerusalem, built in 692 AD by the Umayyad caliph Abdel-Malik with clear political intentions. However, its influence was hardly felt in early mosque architecture, but rather in the later typologies of funerary monuments and mausolea. The dome of the Hagia Sophia was "discovered" by the Ottomans in the 15th century AD after their conquest of Constantinople, but had no major influence on Turkish mosque architecture until the arrival of the architect Sinan in the 16th century.

In terms of construction techniques, there were two important sources on which the Islamic empire could draw: the age-old Mesopotamian tradition of building with sun-dried or burned clay bricks and the stonemasonry of northern Syria and Armenia. Both were further developed under Islam and coexisted or alternated according to regional preferences. In Egypt, during the 11th/12th century AD, a decisive shift from brickwork to stone took place under Syrian influence, while Mesopotamia and Iran continued to adhere to brick architecture. The choice of building materials was closely related to corresponding ornamentation techniques, since the Middle East had become the repository of a number of decorative wall cladding or facing methods: glazed tiles had been known for ages in Mesopotamia; the Roman and Byzantine mosaic was still widely used in the 7th/8th century; elaborate carved plaster facings had been developed in the Syrian provinces after the late Roman period, and Coptic Egypt excelled in highly decorative limestone carvings, which gave an almost textile character to the ornamented walls, combining stylized figural motives with geometric patterns and the late-Roman wine leaf scroll. Thus local artists in the Islamic provinces were provided with a wealth of resources, of which the emerging Islamic art took full advantage, moulding them together and adapting them to create a new language of their own.

The main internal shaping factor in this gradual assimilation process, which led to the development of an unmistakably Islamic architecture, was the attitudes and the distinct socio-religious practices of the Muslim society, as they placed the adopted formal elements in a new functional and semiotic context, and thus gave them a new meaning. The previously described ritual and spatial patterns of Islam had a great importance in this metamorphosis, especially as they were instrumental in redefining architectural typologies and in establishing a new urban framework, into which individual buildings were integrated. Last but not least, it was the concept of Islamic ornamental art, as developed and promoted from the 9th/10th century AD onwards, which helped integrate and unify the adopted architectural elements by infusing it with a specific Islamic character.

In the following chapters, we shall discuss the specific building typologies encountered in the urban architecture of Arab-Islamic cultures, as well as the way in which the various components of urban form merged into larger integrated units. The analysis of the various building types will put emphasis on the traditional patterns of use and the corresponding architectural implications in order to throw light on the cultural meaning of the architectural forms described. Readers interested in additional historical and architectural details will welcome the bibliography at the end of this book for further study.

Islamic ornamentation infused what is known as specific Islamic character.

Components of Urban Form I:
The Residential Unit

Private houses and clusters of houses are the determining component of the urban fabric in Muslim cities, not only because of their sheer quantitative dominance but also because of the particular attitude of Islam towards formal civic institutions and its relatively low emphasis on monumental public buildings. It therefore seems appropriate to start the discussion of the traditional Islamic city structure with an analysis of the residential unit, in spite of the fact that it is probably the most complex of all elements of urban form. Being strongly rooted in an age-old vernacular tradition, the domestic architecture of Islam shows a great range of local and regional varieties which, from a stylistic point of view, may appear to be quite different from each other. Before discussing specific regional styles, we shall therefore first address the common conceptual and functional issues, which will make it easier to grasp the shared values transpiring through the variety of architectural forms.

The philosophy of housing in the Islamic world may be illustrated by analyzing the content of the three Arab terms "iskan", "harim" and "dar". The word iskan, derived from the root s-k-n, means dwelling and housing. Its etymological connotations evoke the ideal of a peaceful environment protected from inappropriate intrusions. The general meaning of the word harim has already been dealt with in Chapter 2. In the context of housing it emphasizes the inviolability of the private domain: the interior of the house is identified with the sacred family sphere, the hearth and the clan's faculty of progeniture; the term harim thus also came to signify the female group of the family living in the house, as well as the corresponding physical and spatial realm within the house. As the woman represents this sacred aspect of the house, she was traditionally encouraged to veil herself when leaving the protective shell of the house and entering the public realm of the city – a basically male domain. The strong identity perceived between the architectural receptacle and its social content is clearly expressed by the words "dar" and "bait", which mean "house" both in the sense of the physical premises and of the social unit or family clan. Interestingly, the word dar is applied in various dimensions which can transcend the scale of the house. Its etymological root has to do with the idea of encircling, and dar therefore means the encompassed area or community – any space or social unit

50 The inner world of the house: view into the courtyard of a traditional 17th/18th century house in Cairo.

which is centred in itself. Dar al-Islam, for instance, refers to the Muslim family at large, in the sense of the whole religious community of the "umma" and the geographic sphere it occupies. Speaking of "both houses" implies an allusion to both worlds, i. e. the terrestrial and the eternal realm. In the urban context, dar means the well defined private territory of the family or the clan and the corresponding architectural shell which is identified with the inviolable "body" of the family group.

Age-old magic practices, some probably of pre-Islamic origin, testify that this identification is understood in actual physical, and not just symbolic terms: the protected territory will be defended, if needed by force, against illicit intrusion by strangers; possible areas of interface, such as all transition points between the "inside" and the "outside" world, are treated with special care, in order to protect the "aura" of the house, as it were, and to avoid mixing with alien influences. Many hidden or overt rites regarding the protection of the entry gate and its threshold confirm this concern with potentially dangerous interferences. Architecturally, this concern is reflected in the special care with which necessary openings in the architectural skin of the house are treated. Windows are often "veiled" by lacelike wooden latticework ("mushrabiya"), or dissimulated by the ornamental patterns of the wall surface. Doors often have smaller door leaves incorporated into the big gate, so as to minimize the aperture wherever possible. Entry vestibules are positioned in such a way as to obstruct the view of the inner realm of the home.

Islamic legal practice was particularly strict concerning the risk of strangers looking from the street or from adjacent buildings into the interior of

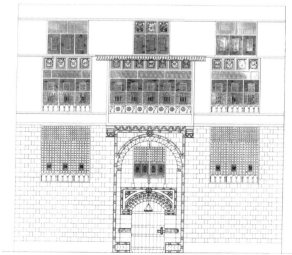

51

52

private houses. Any visual intrusion into the family sphere had to be excluded, much in the same way as acoustic and environmental nuisances from
nearby commercial and industrial premises. It was the task of the
muhtasib and the kadi to handle problems of such nature, preventing them
if possible or settling them in a rather pragmatic manner. The surviving man-
uals of "hisba" from the 11th and 13th centuries AD give us a vivid insight
into the practice and methods of urban arbitration. In general, however, the
Islamic code of good behaviour, as shaped by the Qur'an and the "sunna"
of the Prophet, did everything to avoid infringement on privacy. Any type of
spying was banned as strictly illicit, and specific rituals were devised to
ease the problem of entering private homes. Thus, the Qur'an explicitly
exhorts the believer to observe certain precautions when asking to be admitted into and entering a private home (Qur'an 24/27-28). In practice, this
meant that the male non-family members had to wait outside the gate until
they were conducted inside by male family members, while women and
children had almost unrestricted access to the female territory of private residences. Women had a quite different perception of the residential areas of
the city, as the secluded individual houses were totally permeable to them.
They were also the priviliged users of the often contiguous roof terraces,
which offered a wide platform of female space on top of the city.

The social unit of the traditional Muslim house was usually an extended
family covering several generations, which itself was part of a larger clan
or tribal unit. The agnate family clan was marked by a dominant male ancestry and by the patriarchal character of its social structure, at least as far as
the representation towards the outside was concerned. Seen from within,
the house was dominated by the female society, with the mother or grand-
mother as the leading personality. When the grown-up sons married, the
dar often had to undergo a cellular division in order to accommodate a new
individual unit within its enclosure. One room or a group of rooms was then
arranged as a "house within the house", an additional storey was added,
new units were attached to the main house, or existing neighbouring houses were connected to the main house. Such architectural transformation
processes linked to the social evolution of the family group are characteristic
of most Muslim cities. They often involved changes in the access system by
turning semi-public street sections into private corridors or by building on the
airspace above the street – a practice which was tolerated by Islamic law if
agreed to by the neighbours.

The alliance between two dars posed subtle ritual problems with respect
to the adoption or neutralization of an alien "family spirit" introduced
together with the bride. For in accordance with the agnatic system, it was
always the bride who had to move into the house of the groom. If there was

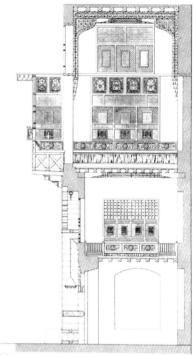

53

51 Visual protection of interior rooms
and bay windows through the filigree
lattices of the "mushrabiya" in an 18th
century mansion in Cairo (after G. Ebers).

52 Street elevation of an early
19th century house in Cairo showing the
screening effect of the "mushrabiyas"
(after P. Coste).

53 Section through gateway and first
floor bay window of the house featured on
the foregoing page (after P. Coste).

no consanguinity between bride and groom, special precautions had to be taken for the transfer of the bride from one home to the other, which explains the importance of elaborate marriage rites and ceremonies in Muslim countries. The problem could be minimized in cases where the young man and the girl were cousins, a solution which was widely favoured in Muslim societies.

The concern of Islam with preserving the integrity of each dwelling unit could have led to an excessive isolation of individual buildings, had it not been balanced by other social factors. But it was complemented by the equally important emphasis on being a good neighbour, as expressed by the Qur'an and in the sayings of the Prophet. Neighbours, whether related or not, were exhorted to avoid mutual harm and to actively support each other in case of need (Qur'an 4/40). There is also a hadith by the Prophet saying that nobody who has lived in affluence while his neighbour remained hungry will enter paradise. Other hadiths request all neighbours to grant each other mutual right of pre-emption on their estates, to observe equitable distribution of water resources and to allow each other to fix a beam in the outer wall of the neighbour's house. This latter recommendation was indeed instrumental in building houses wall to wall on one or several sides – a fundamental prerequisite for establishing the characteristic urban fabric of Muslim cities, and quite in tune with the saying of the Propheet that believers "should stick together like the bricks of a wall". Good neighbourly relations thus became a specific form of solidarity, shaping the social and physical fabric of residential districts in Muslim cities. The social cohesion was

54 Roof terrace of a house in Fez, showing the integrity of the protected domestic space, the shared walls and the opening of the central courtyard.

55 Courtyard corner in a house in Fez, turned into an improvised dining-room with the help of a transportable copper tray and mobile mattresses.

56 Simple kitchen in a house in Soakin (after J. P. Greenlaw).

favoured by a natural symbiosis between richer and poorer families which was of advantage to both sides. Important families often had a circle of "clients" who benefited from their influence and could in turn provide important services. This informal adoption could almost equal conventional ethnic bonds and was an efficient means of social integration.

The closely interlocked pattern of Muslim neighbourhoods also relates to the fact that ostentatious display of wealth and power was branded as arrogance by the social code of Islam. Wealth was certainly regarded as a distinction bestowed on an individual, but also as something lent to him by the Lord; it was therefore not automatically identified with personal merit and had to be used in a socially acceptable form. Spending funds on artistic decoration of the house was definitely not illicit, and the search for beauty was inherent to Islam, as evidenced by the Prophet's saying: "God is beauty and loves beauty". Yet the architectural richness was mostly displayed *within* the walls as an element enhancing the idea of the sacred interior space of the home. Exteriorizing it was considered inappropriate or simply bad taste. Accordingly, the urge to expose and enhance the streetfront of the house and to link it with considerations of social status and prestige was almost absent in the townscape of Muslim cities, quite in contrast with most European towns. This in turn facilitated the agglutination of individual houses to integrated urban entities.

55

The interior disposition of the Muslim house was usually based on a number of major cellular units which were grouped around a central distribution space or a courtyard. Each one of these sub-units tended to have an individual access and to be complete in itself, since it was complemented by ancillary rooms for storage and services adjacent to it. The cellular system inside the house was a reflection of the need to subdivide larger family groups into several smaller and virtually independent units. In fact the word "bait", which is often used for such autonomous rooms, can also designate a house, and therefore confirms the concept of "houses within the house" from a linguistic point of view. This type of subdivision was facilitated by the fact that single rooms could be used for many different purposes, as Muslim domestic life did not distinguish between living rooms, bedrooms and dining rooms.

56

The polyvalent use of space in the Muslim house recalls the underlying nomadic simplicity and implies a minimum of permanent furniture. Closets and cupboards were mostly integrated into wall niches. Mattresses could either be folded and stored away or remained on low benches along the walls, serving both sitting and sleeping purposes. Tables were usually designed as shallow copper trays which could easily be removed or replaced by a simple cloth spread out on the floor. Cushions made up for

Exterior kept plain. Interior decorated, elaborate display

57

58

chairs, which were virtually unknown in the Muslim household. The dominant posture, at home as in the mosque, consisted in sitting or kneeling on
the floor, which of course explains the ubiquitous use of carpets and the consistent concern with ritual purity. The living room, devoid of heavy furniture,
could in fact always serve as an improvised prayer area for the family and
for guests, and therefore the custom was to take off one's shoes outside the
room, similar to the practice in the mosque.

The relative independence of the individual sub-units of the house, as
well as their multi-functional use, was a prerequisite for shifting domestic
functions from one place to another – a need which could occur in various
ways and for various reasons. A major, and to some extent permanent shift
in the use of rooms could be caused by changes within the family structure,
due to the marriage of one or several sons, to the death of the father, or to
the takeover of the house by one of the sons. But there were also possible
short-term shifts of a seasonal nature, depending on climatic conditions: in
many Islamic countries, the use of the house was different during summer
and winter, with a predominant occupation of the lower floor (or even the
basement) during the hot summer period and preference given to the sun-
nier upper rooms during the winter months. In other instances, the roof terraces were used for open-air sleeping during hot summer nights. Another,
almost daily shift of functions occurred as soon as the family group was confronted with non-related male visitors. In this case the normal use of the
house had to be suspended and the rooms were polarized into "male
spaces", which would allow for temporary access and reception of outside

57 View of a male reception room of a
rich 18th-century mansion in Cairo, seen
from the upper floor balcony, which was
reserved for ladies.

58 Narrow section of the ladies' gallery,
with mushrabiya shutters looking down
into the male reception room.

visitors, and "female spaces", where family life could retreat and continue in parallel without being seen or disturbed by external visitors.

In more modest houses this internal divison into "public" and "private" spheres, or "selamlik" and "haramlik", was usually done ad hoc by assigning one of the main rooms, preferably one near the main entry or close to an independent staircase, for temporary reception purposes whenever the occasion arose. In important mansions, reception took on a more formal character and therefore required the establishment of an exclusive and permanent place for this purpose. The result was the creation of special reception rooms occupying a considerable part of the house. In some cases, they extended through several floors, surrounded by family rooms on the upper levels, which allowed the women of the house to glimpse through special windows into the "public" enclave of their home without being seen. In a way, such reception rooms resembled covered public squares transposed into the house and reserved for friends, guests and clients of the influential house owner. Depending on the social status of the family, these rooms could take palatial proportions and become a place for displaying rich ornamental features, commensurate with the wealth of the owner. Their architectural vocabulary often reproduced prestigious elements taken from the typology of royal palaces, such as domes, iwans and loggias.

In spite of its semi-public character, the domestic reception room was always perfectly integrated into the envelope of the house, for the functional differentiation did not take place by segregating the respective architectural volumes, but by accommodating the internal circulation network in such ways as to achieve the desired levels of accessibility. Each major component of the house had its own centrality and needed to be linked with, as well as separated from the remaining parts of the building and the main entrance. This implied a rather complex system of interior corridors, thresholds, doors and buffer spaces within the house. In the case of normal family use, the internal circulation network was totally permeable, whereas with the arrival of external male visitors the various sluices, barriers and sub-divisions were put into use. As a result, there are clear similarities between the internal circulation structure of the house and that of the residential cluster: the position of a reception room with regard to the surrounding house corresponds to the relation between the house as a whole and the encompassing residential structures. The internal corridor of the house replicates, as it were, the function of the alleyways within the residential district. Similar structural principles were thus reflected at different hierarchic levels, which set the ground for the extraordinary structural unity of the overall built form.

Within the urban system, the physical coherence between the various components was based on the graded articulation of a chain of polarities between included and excluded spaces, that is, between "inside" and "outside", or "private" and "public". The courtyard of a house, for instance, was outside with regard to the rooms around it, but inside with regard to the house. The residential alley was outside with respect to the house, but inside with respect to the residential quarter, which was also enclosed by walls and gates. The subtlety lies in the fact that each polarity was overcome by the integration into a larger unit on the next hierarchic plane. Eventually this resulted in the successful merging of individual parts into a larger whole, without any component losing its individual identity.

This particular spatial thinking can be observed in most traditional Muslim cities. But it becomes most evident in those areas and places where the courtyard house was used as the basic unit of the urban fabric. The courtyard house was indeed the favoured typology of most Arab-Islamic cities, whether in North Africa, Syria, Iraq, Iran or in the central part of the Arabian Peninsula. Its enclosed and introverted private space responded ideally to the requirements of the Islamic social order. In addition it offered valuable environmental and climatic advantages: the walled precinct provided protection against desert storms and allowed special climatic conditions to develop at the centre of the house. The hollow container of the courtyard, sunken into the building volumes, produced shade and could act as a temperature regulator by storing the cool air collected during the night. In

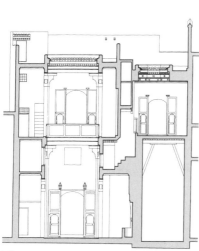

59 Extremely narrow house in Fez, with the courtyard transformed into a light well and upper floor rooms bridging the public alleyway.

60 View of a partly covered alleyway in Fez providing shade and a cool microclimate.

59

60

some cases, windcatchers were added on the roof to collect cool breezes and drain them into the lower rooms.

While being an age-old architectural prototype of the Middle East, the courtyard house was developed and articulated in different ways in various Muslim regions according to existing local traditions, available construction materials and the given environmental constraints. In the following, we shall attempt to present an overview of the main typologies, limiting ourselves to a number of distinct geographical regions. Due to the limited lifespan of domestic architecture, it is difficult to find houses older than 200–300 years, and therefore most examples used in this documentation stem from the 18th/19th century. Yet it can be safely assumed that the tradition embodied in these houses dates back much further, a fact which can sometimes be proved by archeological evidence, or by cross-reference to conserved palaces of earlier periods which show similar typologies.

The region which features the most consistent and the most formalized courtyard typology of domestic Islamic architecture is certainly North Africa, from Morocco to Tunisia. Historically speaking, the *Maghrebi courtyard house,* as seen in Fez, Rabat, Marrakesh or Tunis, is an offshoot of the Moorish architecture of Andalusia, and it is no wonder that there should be a close affinity between the palace of the Alhambra (13th/14th century AD) and the surviving North African town houses of the 18th/19th century. The residential quarters of this Andalusian palace have been destroyed, but the "Court of the Myrtles", the king's reception hall, clearly incorporates the model of an urban mansion, whereas the "Court of the Lions", the pleasure garden of the ruler, engulfs two small but exquisite buildings on either side of the central garden, which are miniatures of courtyard houses. While the elaborate muqarnas dome covering the interior courtyard is an exceptional architectural feature, representing the vault of heaven (see page 41), the plan of these two buildings corresponds exactly to the "bait" of much later Maghrebi houses and exemplifies the close interrelation between palatial and domestic architecture which existed in many parts of the Islamic world.

The dominant formal characteristics of the Maghrebi house are the absolute centrality of the courtyard, called "wust ad-dar" (centre of the house), and an ideally symmetrical layout of the main rooms around it. The hollow volume of the courtyard shapes the building, as if it were the imprint of a powerful invisible matrix into a soft mass of clay. The main rooms form a strongly articulated inner belt around the courtyard while ancillary facilities are relegated to the periphery of the building, where they can be aerated by a separate air shaft if needed. The plan of the house therefore shows an interesting architectural dialectic between the mostly irregular contours of the plot and the perfectly geometric incision of the courtyard, which is the deter-

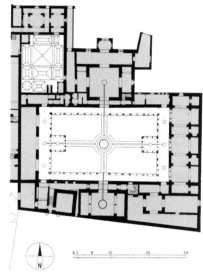

61

61 Plan of the "Court of the Lions" in the Alhambra of Granada featuring two pavilion-like dwelling units with covered courtyards north and south of the garden courtyard.

mining factor for the development of the built form. The main rooms follow the geometric pattern of the courtyard, while the minor rooms are used as "filling material" to absorb the change of directions and mediate between the chosen geometric framework and the given irregular plot shape.

The strong formal statement of this architecture is not a matter of aesthetics only but reflects (or induces) an existential experience of being centred in space. The shape of the courtyard establishes a strong vertical aspiration by the simple fact that its upper rim constitutes the primary window of the house, orienting the eye and the mind towards the skies. The secondary windows from the rooms to the courtyard are intermediate openings which receive air and light from above. All doors and windows of the main rooms are focused on the hub of the courtyard, which is often marked by a fountain, emphasizing the vertical axis of the building. Symbolically speaking, the symmetrical and totally balanced order of the courtyard can be interpreted as the timeless centre of gravity of the house, while the periphery responds to the given circumstances and pressures of the earthly environment. The timeless quality of the courtyard space is also enhanced by the symbolic dimension of the ornamented walls with their geometrical patterns and occasional Qur'anic calligraphies, which support the concept of the home as the sanctuary of the family.

The size and character of the Maghrebi house obviously vary with the dimension and the proportions of the courtyard. The majority of houses show courtyard walls of six to ten metres length, which allows for the presence of a central fountain and a few fruit trees. However, there are also smaller courtyards which resemble an air shaft and larger ones which convert their central space into large interior gardens (riyadh). In the vertical direction the building usually extends over two or three floors, although exclusive ground floor structures are also found. Each main floor is usually four to five meters high, and occasionally two-metre-high storage rooms are interjected between two main floors. The courtyard elevations of the oldest type of house, going back to Marinid models of the 14th/15th century, follow the traditional peristyle order, either with continuous columns soaring up to the projecting roof or with two layers of columns interrupted by a first floor gallery running around the courtyard. A more recent typology, going back to the 18th/19th century, shows plain elevations without columns or galleries, but retaining the projecting roof. In the case of narrow courtyards, the colonnaded galleries could be replaced by simple balconies connecting opposite rooms. The staircases, mostly more than one, are placed in strategic corners of the building without being exposed to the courtyard.

The main rooms, or "baits", usually face each other and are accessible from the courtyard or the gallery. As a rule, their main dimension is defined

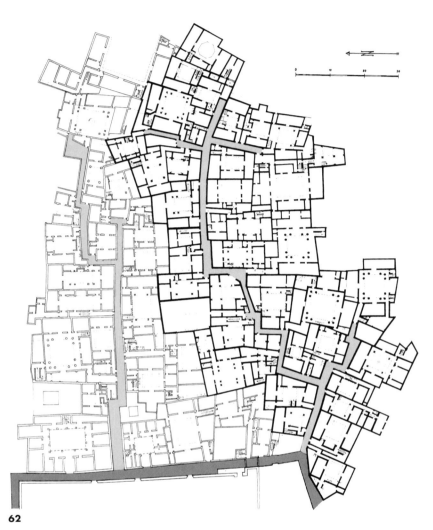

62

by the length of the courtyard while the depth, irrespective of the length, rarely exceeds about three metres. This measure may be due to the practical limitation of beam lengths (building materials had to be transported through the narrow lanes of the city), but it may also have to do with the traditional way of using the interior space. In order to receive a large number of persons during festivities, continuous benches were placed along the whole circumference of the room, allowing people to lean on the wall and to face each other, thus producing a sense of centrality within the room. A depth of around three metres provided the right distance to feel comfortable, and the very long space allowed for a convenient subdivision into a central access zone and two lateral sitting bays. The large double-winged portals

62 Plan of two residential clusters in Fez, immediately east of the al-Qairawiyin Mosque, with a variety of self-contained courtyard houses (see also page 144/155).

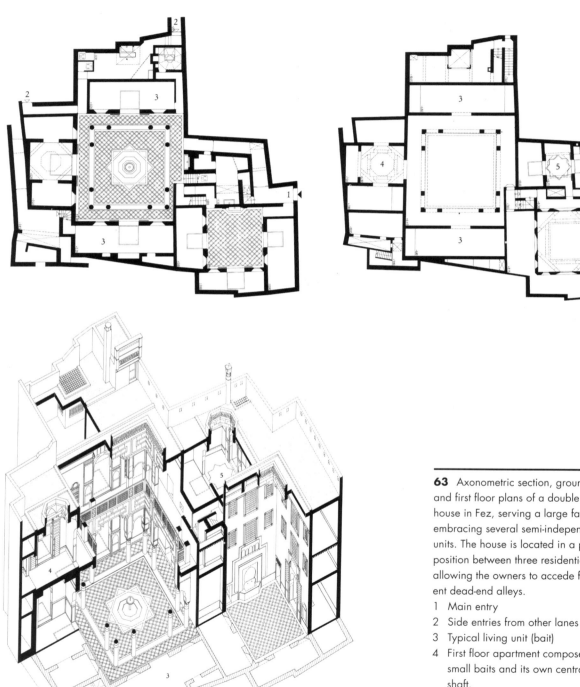

63 Axonometric section, ground floor and first floor plans of a double courtyard house in Fez, serving a large family and embracing several semi-independent sub-units. The house is located in a privileged position between three residential clusters, allowing the owners to accede from different dead-end alleys.

1 Main entry
2 Side entries from other lanes
3 Typical living unit (bait)
4 First floor apartment composed of two small baits and its own central light shaft.
5 Separate upper-floor apartment (masriya)

64

65

of the "bait" opened towards the centre of the courtyard and had "doors within the doors" in order to allow the inhabitants of the house to adapt the opening to different occasions and climatic conditions.

The building materials used for Maghrebi houses were sun-dried or baked bricks and cedar wood. The floors and the lower part of the walls were covered with tiles, often producing highly decorative patterns, while the upper parts of the walls could be enhanced by ornamental panels of

64 Central courtyard of a Marinid type of house in Fez, with the double doors of four "baits" facing each other across the courtyard. The location of the house is shown in the comprehensive plan on page 150.

65 The interior of a "bait", with a view through the small door openings into the courtyard of the same house.

carved plaster featuring geometric patterns, arabesques and calligraphy. The elaborate decoration of the interior elevations around the courtyard helped constitute the inner realm of the house as a qualitative space of its own, totally detached from the external world.

The *Syrian type of courtyard house,* as it can still be seen in the old cities of Aleppo and Damascus, represents another regional tradition, showing architectural features quite different from those of the Maghreb. The oldest surviving houses stem from the 17th, possibly 16th century AD and benefited, at least in Aleppo, from the solid stone construction which increased their resistance to the effects of aging. In fact Northern Syria, including Armenia, is the place from where stone architecture was brought into other Islamic countries such as Egypt as early as the 10th/11th century. During the Ayyubid and Zengid rule (in the late 12th and early 13th centuries AD), Syria was exposed to Seljuk influences and experienced a new cultural impetus, which resulted in the flourishing of the local stone architecture combined with the introduction of Iranian elements, such as the "iwan". The residential buildings of Aleppo have maintained and per-petuated essential elements of this architectural vocabulary well into the 18th/19th century, in spite of the later Ottoman occupation.

67

68

In comparison with the Maghrebi house, the Syrian courtyard house has a more complex and less regular structure, especially with regard to the courtyard shape and the interior elevations of the house. Both building types share the tight outer enclosure wall, which creates a total introversion while allowing for lateral attachment of neighbouring houses. Yet the courtyard of Syrian houses is less formal in shape and there is much less concern for symmetry in the frontages facing the open space. In fact, the courtyard here takes the character of a shared family square, providing the intermediate connection between the various components and sub-units of the house which have a higher degree of independence and self-sufficiency. Symmet-ric layouts are often applied within these components but are not extended to the central courtyard.

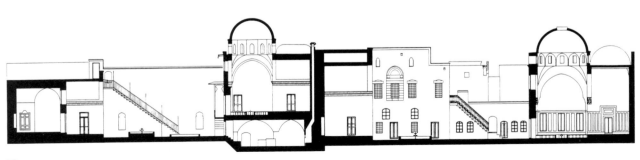

69

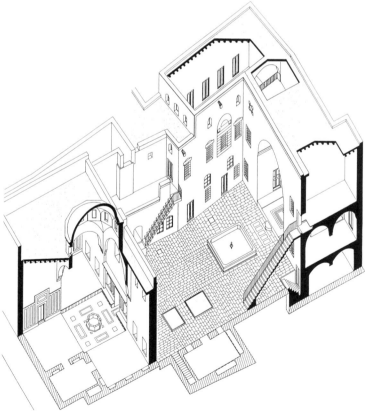

70

66 Longitudinal section through two adjacent houses in Aleppo, cutting through the "iwan" and the "qa'a" of both houses.

67 Exterior view of a "qa'a" with its projecting dome across the courtyard of a 17th-century house in Aleppo.

68 Interior view of a "qa'a" dome.

69 View of the courtyard and the "iwan" of the house below.

70 Axonometric section of a 17th/18th-century house in Aleppo, featuring a typical "qa'a" with three raised interior iwans around the domed central space. The iwan is located opposite the "qa'a", and two staircases lead up to independent small apartments. The location of the house is shown in the comprehensive plan on page 151.

This holds especially true for the "qa'a", the fully developed reception room of richer houses, which constitutes a house within the house by virtue of its autonomous architectural system. The qa'a consists of a high-domed central space of square shape which can be entered from one side, normally through a door from the courtyard. This central piece is usually surrounded by three iwans, two facing each other and one facing the entry door. The front of each iwan is marked by a wide arch, and the roof can either be vaulted (if built in masonry) or flat (if made of wooden support structures). The floor level of the iwans is always raised by one or two steps. The three walls forming the niche of each iwan are mostly solid, which stresses the centripetal orientation of the niches towards the sunken square. This central space, acting as the "courtyard" of the qa'a, is often equipped with an interior fountain and enhanced by a high dome which lets in light and air through the openings of its polygonal or circular drum. The frontage of the qa'a facing the main courtyard contains only minor window openings, emphasizing the dominant vertical orientation and the self-contained character of the central space.

The reception rooms of more modest houses could not reproduce in full the scheme of such palatial structures but often adapted the qa'a in fragmentary form, with only one bay and a small anteroom, directly accessible from the main courtyard. The single iwan of these simplified qa'as was also raised by one or two steps with respect to the entry zone close to the door. This subtle vertical differentiation between lower circulation space (where one would take off one's shoes) and higher living and sitting areas became so ubiquitous that it was adopted for almost every room, even if the sunken entry space behind the door was sometimes reduced to less than a square metre. The resulting steps formed a threshold which was called "atabe", meaning retardation, at the entrance of the main room.

In addition to the qa'a, there was often an open iwan directly attached to the courtyard, which could serve as a family sitting area or potential open-air reception space. It was usually oriented northwards to avoid direct sun radiation and to catch the cool breeze during hot summer days. It could also be flanked by two small lateral rooms which were accessible via the iwan and formed another sub-unit of the house. Separate individual living rooms could be accommodated on any side of the courtyard, including intermediate sections between the six- to eight-metre-high structures of the qa'a and the open iwan. Some of these independent dwelling units were called "murabba", or "square", and could provide separate quarters for family members or guests. They could be located either at ground level, directly accessible from the courtyard, or at first-floor level, and were often serviced by individual open stairs.

The *Egyptian courtyard house* has a complex history, since Egypt has been a melting pot of various cultural influences during the Islamic period. Through the centuries, it was subject to frequent dynastic and cultural changes which were also reflected in its domestic architecture. The excavations of Fustat (covering the period of the 8th and 9th centuries AD) inform us of the existence of courtyard houses with regular central squares, relatively symmetric introverted rooms and T-shaped reception rooms with central iwans – a typology which was possibly introduced by the Tulunid dynasty and would therefore reflect Persian influences, as filtered through Abbasid court architecture. Accounts written by travellers in the 11th century tell us about the high tower houses in the popular districts of Misr (an extension of Fatimid Cairo), of which no physical or archeological evidence has remained. The typology of surviving Cairene houses from the 16th to the 19th century is, however, linked to the model of 14th and 15th century Mamluk palaces which eventually influenced the structure of later private residences, as well as Qur'anic schools and mosques.

71

Many features of the Mamluk palaces were strongly influenced by Syrian models, but eventually the Cairene qa'a, as developed during the late Mamluk and early Ottoman period, became a distinct typology in its own right. It was characterized by two deep iwans facing each other across a sunken central space ("durqa'a") which shows the typical features of a covered courtyard. The durqa'a functioned as an entry space which gave access to the raised iwans. It was usually enhanced by highly ornamented floor patterns and a central fountain integrated into the floor. The space above the durqa'a extended vertically across the surrounding volumes of the house, creating a central void which was usually covered by a pyramidal roof on a pierced polygonal drum, allowing light and air to penetrate. The private living rooms in the upper floor, located above the iwans or around the vertical shaft of the durqa'a, often had screened windows overlooking the central space of the qa'a, which permitted the female group of the family to watch activities in the male reception room.

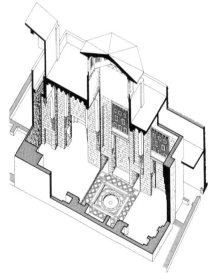

72

A characteristic feature of the Cairene house, also to be found in the architecture of the Red Sea (in cities such as Jedda and Soakin), is the "porosity" of large portions of the external walls and internal partition walls. In these places the hot and humid climate called for a maximum of cross-ventilation, which in principle conflicted with the need for privacy. The solution was to provide densely screened openings allowing for glimpses into the outside world and, above all, for effective air circulation throughout the house. The timber lattice screens, which eventually came to dominate the outer and inner elevation of domestic buildings, were called "mushrabiyas" or "rowshans". The term mushrabiya is derived from the verb "ishrab" (to

71 Covered central space between two opposite iwans in the 15th-century Qait Bey Madrasa in Cairo.

72 Axonometric section through the qa'a of a late Mamluk house from the 15th/16th century (after B. Maury).

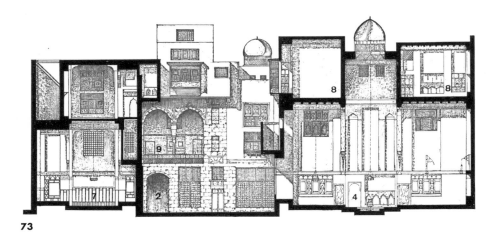

73

73/74 Cross-section of ground floor and first floor of Bait as-Suheimi, a complex private mansion from the 17th/18th century in Cairo, formerly belonging to a sheikh of al-Azhar University.

1 Alleyway
2 Bent entrance with mastaba for doorkeeper
3 Informal covered reception space
4 Formal male reception room (mandara)
5 Private teaching room
6 Kitchen
7 Prayer room
8 Upper floor family rooms
9 Family loggia (maqad)

drink), and in fact the custom was to keep water jars of unburned clay close to the screens, to benefit from the natural cooling effect of the draft. Often, the mushrabiyas were shaped in such a way as to project into the street or to form protected bay windows with integrated benches. Thus they added attractive niches to the rooms while creating elaborate and intriguing street frontages. In addition to the mushrabiyas, many Cairene houses were also equipped with wind catchers ("malqaf"), which directed cool breezes from the roof into the lower rooms.

75

76

75 View from the first floor loggia (maqad) of Bait as-Suheimi across the courtyard, towards the screens of the main female reception room, which sits above the informal covered reception space.

76 Interior of the main female reception room facing the courtyard.

With the exception of the "rab", a multi-storey apartment whose typology is linked to the housing units of the caravanserai, the traditional layout of Cairene houses was organized around a central courtyard. Similarly to the Syrian houses, there was no emphasis on the symmetrical interior elevation of the courtyard, since the use of more formalized layouts was confined to the interior of the reception rooms. Within the qa'a, there was a greater degree of transparency, since the rooms could have mushrabiya openings to both sides, i. e. to the courtyard and to the street, whenever a street front was available. The qa'a was the basic architectural scheme used for the large male reception rooms ("mandara") on the ground floor and could take monumental proportions, with the central part extending through three floors and being separated by mushrabiyas from the surrounding family rooms. However, the qa'a could also be repeated on a smaller scale on the upper floors as the nucleus of the family rooms and the female apartments, to the point where many rich houses in fact became aggregations of a number of qa'as, interconnected by corridors, staircases, service rooms and open terraces. Within this sequence of upper-floor rooms there was often a "maqad", a covered loggia that overlooked the courtyard and was predominantly used by women. As in most Arabic-Islamic houses, access from the street into the courtyard consisted of a bent corridor connected with a small anteroom and a bench ("mastaba") for the doorkeeper.

The *Iraqi type of courtyard houses* shows a greater concern for a regular layout of the courtyard, without necessarily insisting on bi-axial symmetries. None of the existing historic houses in Baghdad is older then 100–150 years, due to the termite plague which, together with periodic inundations by the Tigris, affected traditional building structures with their predominant building materials of brick and timber. However, the surviving samples of residential architecture clearly show very old Iranian influences, especially with regard to the elevated colonnade ("tarma") and the recessed bay with two front columns, called "talar". Both elements are well known from Iranian palaces and pavilions of the Safawid period and can be traced back to Achaemenid times. In the domestic architecture of Iraq, the tarma is used predominantly on the first floor of the house, providing a colonnade running around one or several sides of the courtyard, often combined with the iwan-like recesses of the talar, and giving access to lateral bays and closed reception rooms ("ursi").

In many houses the first upper floor performed the function of a "piano nobile" with the tarma linking the main rooms of the house, while the ground floor contained only service rooms, and occasionally a shaded recess which was used for open-air sitting and informal reception at the courtyard level. Large parts of the ground floor were sometimes occupied

77 Typical view of Iraqi courtyard house with first floor "tarma" (after O. Reuther).

78 Section of medium-size Baghdadi house from the 19th century, showing typical elements:
1 Tarma
2 Ursi (elevation)
3 Kabishkan
4 Nim
5 Courtyard

79 Diagram showing basic "tarma" dispositions within the Iraqi house (after J. Warren, I. Fethi).

77

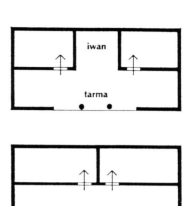

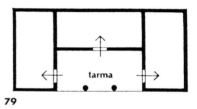

79

78

by the void of high living rooms located at basement level ("nim"), which were mainly used during the hot summer period. As the representative upper floor was easily five metres high, it allowed the inclusion of split levels in the corners, for instance on both sides of an ursi or a talar. This produced low mezzanine rooms ("kabishkan") to which the women could retire if the main floor was used for a male reception. The kabishkans had strategically located windows through which the women could look into the ursi or the tarma just beneath them and also watch the lower courtyard level across the open colonnade. Whenever first floor rooms had a front to the street, they tended to project into the air space of the street. In such cases, the cantilever was often irregular with respect to the ground floor walls, as the regular courtyard shape reflected by the projecting rooms was not always parallel with the irregular contour of the plot. The resulting triangular corbels produced the typical dented street elevations.

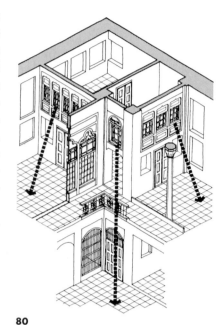

80

While the examples of urban courtyard houses described above are not exhaustive, it must be acknowledged that there are regions which have adopted different typologies. Most notable among these are Anatolia and parts of the Arabian peninsula, including cities such as Jedda, Mecca and Sana'a. Although the courtyard element may be absent in these buildings, the spirit in which the main components of the house were laid out and used remains closely related to the basic ideas put forward in the introductory paragraphs. Covered halls often made up for the missing courtyard, and centrality played a major role in the layout and interior decoration of the main reception rooms.

The structure of the *Anatolian house* is again based on the relative autonomy and the polyvalent use of the house's major components. The layout of the main rooms is handled in such a way as to ensure their mutual independence, while they can be easily aggregated into complex larger houses. In more rural conditions, where enough land was available, the house formed a pavilion-like structure within an enclosed plot. Often the back of the building was connected to the enclosure, while the front side faced an enclosed garden space. The front rooms, orientated towards the garden, were preceded and connected by a covered hall ("hayat") which was often raised above the ground floor, not unsimilar to the colonnaded tarma of the Iraqi houses. Since the outer enclosure with its main gate protected its intimacy, the hayat was accessible by an open staircase from the garden. In larger and more complex houses, this entrance hall was pulled into the centre of the building and symmetrically surrounded by a series of living rooms ("oda"). This central hall ("sofa") then performed the function of the courtyard but, being covered, it had obvious advantages in the

80 Axonometric section showing strategic position and views from the ladies' "kabishkan" on the mezzanine of the upper floor.

81

82

climatic context of Anatolia. In some cases, the sofa was enlarged into a cross-shaped core structure, with four lateral bays reaching out to the periphery of the building, while the four main rooms were geometrically located at the corners of the building, which produced an extremely formal layout. In some respects, the bays could be compared with iwans, although the lighting through the extroverted windows gave them a different character. Usually they performed the traditional function of informal sitting niches

81 Engraving from the 19th century showing the special typology of houses on the riverfront, with a "tarma" overlooking the Tigris.

82 Residential alleyway in the old city of Baghdad, with the typical projections of upper-floor rooms into the street.

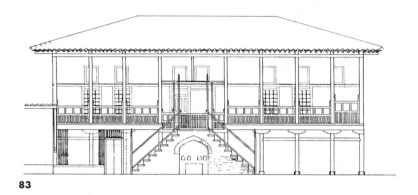

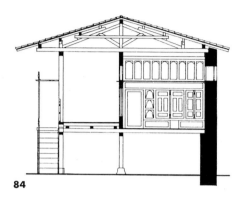

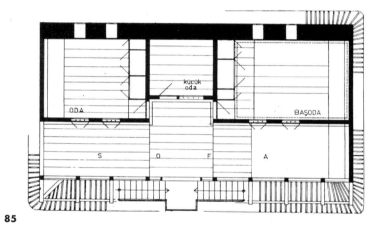

inter-connected by a common central space. The inclined roof of Anatolian houses contrasts with the roof terraces of North African and most other Middle Eastern houses. The need for protection against the cold and heavy rainfalls precluded the possibility of vertical openings.

The *South Arabian tower house* has a long historical tradition going back to pre-Islamic times. It was conceived as a stronghold to protect a family, its livestock and its agricultural products. The house could be built from clay or sun-dried clay bricks, but also partly or fully from stone, depending on the local materials available. Obviously, the prototypes of this typology were of rural character and conceived as free-standing towers. In Yemen, one still comes across such examples with massive round tower shafts supporting rectangular dwelling units. In the context of villages and cities, however, the towers needed to be attached on one or two sides, forming contiguous rows or clusters of buildings.

83–85 Elevation, section and plan of an 18th-century house in Bursa (after S. H. Eldem).

86 Top-floor male reception room (mafraj) in a tower house in Sana'a.

87 Highly decorated elevation of an 18th-century tower house in Sana'a, showing the old type of fenestration, with small circular alabaster discs.

The example of Yemen shows how the rural economy could be perpetuated under urban conditions, even in large cities such as Sana'a, and how
this conditioned both the environment and the construction techniques: in
the city of Sana'a, for instance, the sunken orchards interspersed among the
urban fabric were in fact the quarries from which the clay needed for the
construction of the surrounding houses was extracted. In exchange, their soil
was fertilized with the carefully collected human and organic waste from the

86

87

surrounding households. Both the rural and the urban tower house were characterized by a functional vertical division. The lower floors were used for animals and for the storage of merchandise or agricultural products, while the upper floors were reserved for residential purposes. On the residential floors, the individual rooms were usually held together by a central hall which functioned as a covered courtyard and excluded direct access or visual intrusion from the staircase into the rooms. The staircase itself was separated from the hall by a door, which emphasized the independent "apartment" character of each floor and allowed for easy division between male and female social activities. It thus became a sort of "vertical access corridor", entered by the main gate of the house, which was followed by a vestibule. Often an enclosed forecourt in front of the main gate was provided as a buffer between the house and the street.

In contrast to other types of Muslim houses, the male reception space could also be located at the top of the house. The relatively recent habit of building a pavilion-like "mafraj" on the roof, with windows offering generous views of the city skyline, has in effect marked the townscape of Sana'a. The mafraj has become the preferred place for the men's social ceremonies, including the popular qat sessions in the late afternoon and evening. Beneath the recessed mafraj, most houses had protected roof terraces, enclosed by 2-metre high brick walls. These made up for the lack of an open courtyard and could be used by the women for all sorts of domestic activities.

With its outward looking rooms, window openings became a critical issue for the tower house, especially with regard to the Muslim ethics of pri-

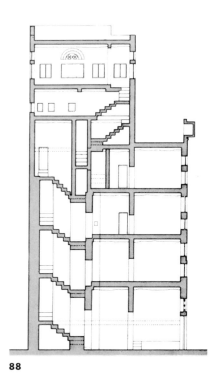

88

88 Section of a typical tower house in Sana'a (after R. Lewcock).

89 Kitchen of a tower house in Sana'a.

vacy. While the tower houses of Jedda and Mecca adopted the "roshan" system to protect the interior by wooden lattice screens, the traditional Yemeni mountain house, which was not exposed to the hot and humid climate, shows a different approach: openings were reduced to a minimum (except on the mafraj) and often camouflaged by an ornamental web which covered the body of the house. The oldest surviving houses of Sana'a, presumably from the 18th/19th century, show an ingenious fenestration system which allowed for a minimum permanent lighting, combined with possibilities of individual daylight regulation. The flexible element in this system was a small window with double shutters just above floor level, so that people sitting on the floor could look out by opening the main shutters or by manipulating a minuscule hatch built into the shutter. About two to three metres above, there was a fixed light source consisting of two circular eyes filled with an alabaster disc which excluded any visual intrusion, while permitting the sun to penetrate and maintain a dim daylight in the room, even with closed window shutters. In more recent times, the openings tended to become larger, and the "oculi" were replaced by semi-circular frames containing two layers of stained glass mosaic which fulfill the same purpose. The plastered ornamental grid into which the openings were integrated helped dissimulate the windows through a highly decorative pattern which was periodically renewed – not unlike a ritual tattooing intended to protect the female body of the house.

Components of Urban Form II: The Mosque and Related Welfare Buildings

The Arab word "masdjid", the basic term for the mosque, literally means the place of prostration, where the community worships the Lord and performs the prescribed prayer rituals. As already stated, the mosque building is not sacred in itself, nor does it contain sacred objects of liturgical importance. Its distinction is established by the state of ritual purity which the believers observe within its walls and by the orientation of the prayer space towards the Ka'aba of Mecca. The essential architectural requirements are therefore a clear demarcation, or an enclosure, and a front line perpendicular to the qibla direction, behind which the believers can stand in rows facing Mecca in order to communicate with the spiritual centre of Islam across time and space. The ritual purity of the prayer space is secured through mandatory ablutions of the users of the mosque, and must be maintained throughout the day, regardless of other activities occurring in the mosque between the five daily prayers. The prayer sequence was scheduled by the Prophet at fixed intervals, i. e. before sunrise, at noon, in the middle of the afternoon, at sunset, and an hour and a half after sunset.

In Islam, prayer can take place either individually or as a collective ceremony, involving small or large numbers of people according to circumstances. However, joint prayer is encouraged and is mandatory for men at Friday noon, when it coincides with a civic assembly of the community. On this occasion, the inhabitants of a township or a region are addressed by their political leader, his representative or another trusted member of the community who acts as their "imam", i. e. the leader of the collective prayers. The mosques where this civic congregation takes place are designated as "Friday Mosques" and usually offer not only the largest prayer halls but also rely on historical tradition established by their founders. In addition, they often serve as centres of a Qur'anic university.

Whether performed individually or collectively, prayer always involves a ritually defined sequence of bodily movements, based on a model established by the Prophet. The movements start with a standing invocation of the Lord followed by repeated recitations from the Qur'an, interspersed with a series of bows and prostrations which culminate in touching the floor with the forehead. Kneeling on the floor is the recurrent intermediate position between the prostrations and concludes the sequence of prayer movements. It

90 Street front of the 19th-century Sultan Hassan Mosque and madrasa, as seen by D. Roberts in the 19th century. The level of the mosque is raised to allow for ground floor shops, the income of which paid for the maintenance of the mosque.

leads naturally to the more relaxed sitting posture which follows the prayer itself and which is also used for meditation, for individual or collective remembrance of God ("dhikr"), for teaching and learning in the mosque, or simply for social gatherings. This type of sitting or squatting on the floor is a ubiquitous habit in Muslim societies, whether in the tent, in the mosque or in private living rooms, whether eating or chatting inside a shop. Therefore, it illustrates strikingly the smooth transition between prayer and daily life which characterizes Islamic customs.

For individual prayer, a small mat or carpet is often folded out to provide a clean prayer space and to indicate the qibla direction. In the case of community prayer, be it within the mosque or in large open spaces outside the city (for instance on the occasion of the Eid festivities), the believers align shoulder to shoulder in long rows following each other at a distance of less than one metre, so as to allow the collective performance of prayer movements. The rows of people facing Mecca are parallel to the "qibla wall" in the front of the place of prayer, which defines the orientation of the assembled believers. According to traditional customs, each row first tends to extend laterally to the full width of the available space before a new row is added behind.

The qibla wall thus is the primary architectural element of the mosque, defining the position and the proportions of the prayer hall which, at least in the early times, tended to opt for width rather than for depth in its layout. The other significant architectural elements of the mosque which complement the qibla wall are: first, the "mihrab", a niche in the centre of the qibla wall pointing towards the Ka'aba, second, the "minbar", a raised seat with a few steps leading up for the imam, from which he can address the community at the Friday noon ceremony and, third, the minaret, a tower from the top of which the prayer call can be pronounced by the muezzin. The development of these basic functional and architectural features of the mosque was marked by two major prototypes, the first one being the house of the Prophet in Medina and the second being the Umayyad Mosque of Damascus, to which we shall refer in the following paragraphs.

The large courtyard of the Prophet's house was the first congregation space of the early Muslim community. On the east side it contained the private apartments of the Prophet, while the north and the south sides of the enclosures showed simple portico structures built of palm trunks. The northern portico served as a shaded prayer place when the qibla was still oriented toward Jerusalem, while the southern one was built after the qibla had been turned towards Mecca. This southern arcade, where the Prophet also used to teach his followers, was enlarged immediately after his death to become the prototypical Muslim prayer hall. The original structure of the

91

92

91 Rows of believers sitting on the ground after concluding the community prayer in an open-air precinct (Sudan).

92 Individual prayer in front of the qibla wall of the Umayyad Mosque in Damascus. The picture shows people in various postures of the prayer sequence. Mihrab and minbar are seen on the left side of the picture.

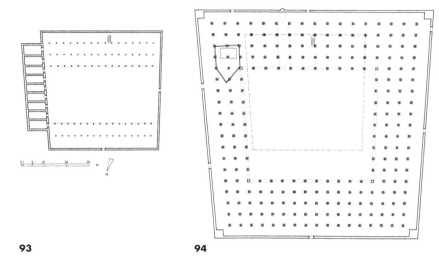

93   **94**

Prophet's house was completely replaced under the Umayyad caliph Walid II (705–715 AD) and transformed into a memorial building. This first "monumental" mosque structure has not survived in physical terms (except for the tomb of the Prophet), but its features were described by many writers and travellers during the early centuries of Islam. So were the first reactions of contemporary Muslims, some of them regretting that the new mosque was built "in the manner of the churches", i. e. using Byzantine craftsmanship for the architectural decoration.

Although the Umayyad building is not preserved, a diagrammatic reconstruction has been attempted on the basis of written documents, and we know that the builders were keen to preserve religiously a number of references to the original layout and to the way it was used by the Prophet. The location of the tomb thus corresponds to the room in which the Prophet passed away. The position in front of the qibla wall, from which the Prophet used to lead the prayer, was marked by a niche – the prototype of all future mihrabs. Traditionally, the niche, a recurrent iconographic motive, was used to enhance a memorable object or person by framing it in a dignified manner. In the context of Islam, the void of the mihrab can be seen as symbolizing the presence of the divine, which is not to be grasped in any material sense, except by the reverberation of the Qur'anic verses, as reflected by the semi-circular shape of the niche. Close to the mihrab, the new Medina mosque featured a raised chair, accessible by a few steps, with the intention of reproducing a similar structure to where the Prophet sat teaching before or after prayer. From then onwards, this chair became the exemplary minbar from where every caliph, ruler or imam addressed his community during the Friday ceremony in his capacity as "lieutenant" of the

93 Plan of the Prophet's courtyard house in Medina, reconstructed after contemporary descriptions (see also page 59).

94 Reconstructed plan of the first Umayyad Mosque of Medina, conceived as an extension of the Prophet's house (contour marked with dotted lines). The burial chamber and the position of the mihrab have been preserved in all later transformations (after Sauvaget).

Prophet. Initially, the Umayyad Mosque of Medina had no minaret, since the prayer call was originally performed by Billal, the black servant of the Prophet, who used to climb onto the roof of his house for this purpose. In later times, a tower was used to increase the acoustic range of the prayer call, and there was no shortage of such prototypes in the Middle East, from the Pharos in Alexandria and the Christian church towers in Syria, to the corner towers of the Roman temple district in Damascus.

This leads us to the second and more monumental archetype of the mosque, which resulted from the adoption of the "Temenos" (the enclosed temple district) of Roman-Hellenistic origin in Damascus. The interesting transformation process of the Roman city centres in Syria into Muslim centres has already been addressed on pages 54 - 57. While the Christians had replaced the temple in the centre of the open space with the Church of St. John, the Umayyad caliph Walid II (also the patron of the renovated Medina mosque) opted for a totally different approach: after reimbursing the Christians he ordered them to remove St. John's Basilica and to place the hall of the mosque at the southern end of the site. Accordingly, parts of the massive Temenos enclosure were used to form the three outer walls of the new mosque, while the added front elevation giving access to the prayer hall faced the large courtyard, which was surrounded by arcades on the other three sides and thus became the central piece of the site. One can only suppose that the Roman columns employed for the construction of the pillared prayer hall were those taken from the destroyed Church of St. John – a re-use process which was typical for many of the early Islamic mosques in the areas of the former Roman dominion.

The happy coincidence in this transformation process was that the qibla wall of the planned new mosque – Mecca being south – matched the long southern wall of the Temenos enclosure, allowing for the desired maximum width of the new mosque structure. Site conditions and functional requirements thus concurred in creating the typical laterally extending prayer hall, which responded so well to the preference for long parallel rows of worshippers established in the early years of Islam, when monumental architecture had not yet been developed.

Another interesting observation resulting from the analysis of the Umayyad mosque in Damascus concerns the common typological ancestry of the mosque and the early Christian church: both used the model of the Roman basilica, yet in quite a different manner. The Christian liturgy, being based on the procession towards the altar, highlighted the existing main axis and the higher central nave of the basilica and complemented it by the apse, thus transforming a secular structure into a sacred building and enhancing the existing axial emphasis of the basilica by giving it a new reli-

95

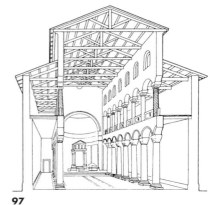

97

96

gious meaning. Islam, in turn, was interested in the basilica in terms of a multifunctional pillared hall which would accomodate the rows of believers during prayer times while allowing for all sorts of other uses in between, such as teaching, political assemblies and even socializing or relaxation. As the mihrab contained no altar, the qibla orientation did, in principle, not have to coincide with the main nave of the basilica, although this happened in the case of some early examples, such as the al-Aqsa Mosque in

95 The courtyard of the Umayyad Mosque in Damascus (705 AD) with the entry side of the prayer hall and the raised treasure house (bait al-mal) to the right (see also page 55).

96 Interior of the prayer hall, with the mihrab to the far right.

97 Structure of the early Christian basilica, showing its directional central nave.

Jerusalem. But the underlying idea of the qibla direction was different: rather than stressing a dominant central axis, it implied a field of multiple and equivalent parallel vectors, all converging on the distant vanishing point of the Ka'aba. Therefore, a bundling of spatial energies did not make sense in religious terms, although it occasionally happened for other reasons, such as the need for a royal access in the central line of the mosque. However, if this was to occur, the central aisle tended to be much shorter than the qibla wall, which gave the "Islamic basilica" different proportions and a particular character.

As can be seen in the Umayyad Mosque in Damascus, the main entry axis crosses the central nave of the building and thus creates an unresolved directional ambivalence, due to the fact that the transformation from the basilica into the pillared hall of the mosque is not as yet fully accomplished. Later buildings, such as the Amr Mosque in Cairo or the great mosques of Kairouan or Cordoba, show the progressive Islamization process which led to the typical "forest" of columned or pillared arcades juxtaposed one after the other. This concept links up with the layout of the primitive Arab palm-trunk shades, as used in the Prophet's house in Medina and in the early mosques of the first Muslim settlers. Even if later centuries employed much more sophisticated building techniques and new types of artistic decoration, prompted by the absorption of late-Roman and Byzantine architecture, the original archetypes have emerged again.

Functionally and architecturally, the mosque of the early Islamic centuries is therefore the result of a two-fold heritage. On the one hand it continues the tradition of the first religious community centre shaped by the Prophet, combined with that of the early inter-tribal assembly and meeting spaces. On the other hand it has, at least in part, absorbed the typology of the Roman basilica and, even more so, the tradition of Greco-Roman public squares, i. e. the Agora and the Forum, in both the political and the social sense. In this respect, it is enlightening to read a passage from the accounts of Ibn Jubayr, an Andalusian traveller who visited Damascus in the 12th century AD and described the evening life in the courtyard of the mosque in such a way that one cannot help but being reminded of a Mediterranean square: "Here people congregate, for it is their place of care-dispelling and recreation, and here every evening you will see them, coming and going from east to west, and others you will see talking to their friends, and some reading. In this manner they will go on, coming and going, until the end of the last evening prayers, and then depart". His words depict the synthesis of an old civic tradition and a new religious framework, which took place for the first time in this Islamic capital.

As already pointed out, the structure of political institutions in Islam was fundamentally different from that of Greco-Roman antiquity and Renaissance Europe, mainly due to the existence of a religiously defined social and legal order provided by the shari'a. Therefore, the mosque in a way combined the functions of temple, city hall and public meeting place, and these institutions did not develop as separate entities. The mosque was also the seat of the kadi (judge) who acted as the trustee of the Qur'anic law on behalf of the urban community. Together with his assistants (among them the

98

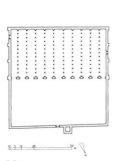

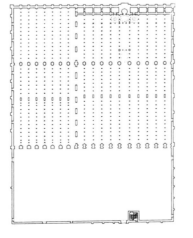

99

98 Interior of the Umayyad Mosque in Cordoba (785–961 AD).

99 Plans of the Umayyad Mosque in Cordoba showing its three phases of construction and extension (after Stierlin).

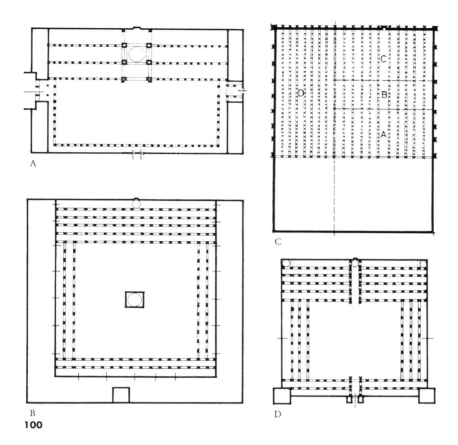

A

B

100

C

D

muhtasib or market surveyor), he was in charge of "advising the good and preventing the evil". The prayer hall could equally serve as teaching space for the Qur'anic sciences, where the sheikhs would lean against a column surrounded by groups of students sitting on the floor. Its political function was highlighted during the Friday noon assemblies, when the ruler, his representative or a religious leader would head the prayer and address the community. This weekly ceremony involved the implicit (but not less obligatory) confirmation of the social contract between the ruler and the ruled. It implied both the acceptance of the executive authority of the ruler by the community and the adherence to the given religious laws by the ruler.

During the early times and well into the Umayyad period, the mosque was connected with the seat of power. In Kufa, one of the early garrison settlements, the "dar al-imara" (seat of the government) was directly attached to the mosque, and eventually the "bait al-mal" (treasure house), originally part of the dar al-imara, was erected in the courtyard of the mosque to protect it from being plundered. In Damascus, the original palace of the

100 Typology of the early type of pillared hall mosques with arcades and an incorporated courtyard (after Vogt-Göknil).

A Umayyad Mosque in Damascus (705 AD)

B Ibn Tulun Mosque in Cairo (876 AD)

C Umayyad Mosque in Cordoba (785–961 AD)

D Al-Hakim Mosque in Cairo (991 AD)

Umayyad caliphs, of which no physical evidence has survived, is said to have been built adjacent to the great mosque, with a direct connection to the prayer hall. The same must have applied to the central palace and mosque of the round city of Baghdad, built by the Abbasid caliph al-Mansour (762–775 AD). In such cases, and especially in Damascus, it is likely that the prayer hall also served as an audience and reception hall for the caliph – a function which was in tune with the tradition of the Prophet's house and which was later continued on a more modest scale by the regular justice sessions of the kadi, as held in the Friday mosque of major Muslim cities.

While in the early times the mosque was the exclusive public facility representing the complete range of social and civic affairs in the city, it later experienced a certain reduction of its scope and a greater concentration on social and religious affairs, at the expense of its political functions. This was due to the fact that the ruling dynasties, being involved in military power games and less concerned with religious legitimation, preferred to live in palace cities or citadels detached from the settlements of the local bourgeoisie. A dual system of political leadership was thus established, which did not dissolve the original unity of spiritual and worldly matters cherished by Islam, but brought about a de facto division between state leadership (or military power) and local urban government.

On the level of the urban communities, one can almost speak of a sort of local autonomy, inasmuch as they were governed by the commonly accepted rules of the Shari'a and customary law, to a point that a simple "monitoring" by the kadi was sufficient. In case of internal conflicts, the ulema, led by the mufti and the kadi, and the sheikhs of the various social groups (whether ethnic groups, religious brotherhoods or trade corporations) were bound to settle them by internal negotiations and, if possible, by consensus. A more critical issue was the potential conflict between the military and the local leadership; in practice it led to a permanent search for balance between often divergent interests and motivations, and in most cases compromises had to be found which required skillful bargaining and a good portion of realism on both sides. From the urban management manual by the Andalusian kadi Ibn Abdun to the "Book of Governance" by the Seljuk wazir Nizam al-Mulk (not to mention numerous "Mirrors for Princes") and from the travel accounts of Ibn Battuta to the stories in Jallaluddin Rumi's "Mathnawi", Islamic sources abound in vivid descriptions of such situations and how they should or could be resolved.

Parallel to the progressive reduction of its political importance over time, the mosque also experienced a certain differentiation of functions, which resulted in the establishment of a number of related building types of com-

101

101 Miniatures from an Iraqi manuscript of the 13th century, showing the use of the mosque: above, a religious or political discussion between the imam and the community members; below, teaching and studying in the library corner of a prayer hall.

102

bined social and religious character, but of narrower functional scope. The most prominent of these new public welfare buildings was the *"madrasa"*, offering special teaching halls, combined with attached dwelling units for students, similar to a religious college. Its rise in the 11th/12th century AD was due to the desire of the Seljuk dynasty to promote orthodox Sunnism and to train new generations of loyal teachers and civil servants, who would serve not only religious, but also political functions.

The function of the madrasa halls could occasionally overlap with that of the mosque, and in fact the architectural typology of the madrasa was so successful in Syria, Iran and Egypt that it challenged and influenced mosque architecture in these countries during the 12th to the 15th century AD, giving rise to a new mosque typology which started competing with the traditional pillared prayer hall. The dominant architectural features of this typology were the four iwans built into the centre of each courtyard front, thus producing a cruciform arrangement – a lay-out known from Abbasid palaces in Samarra (9th century AD) and going back to Sassanian and Parthian precursors. Although simultaneous teaching in the four orthodox schools of Islam was a rather rare event in most places, the existence of the four schools of law gave a justification to the cruciform madrasa scheme. Its merits are, however, to be sought on aesthetic grounds, as it allowed the

102 19th-century view of the courtyard of the Friday Mosque in Isfahan (11th century AD with later additions and transformations) dominated by two pairs of iwans facing each other across the courtyard (after P. Coste).

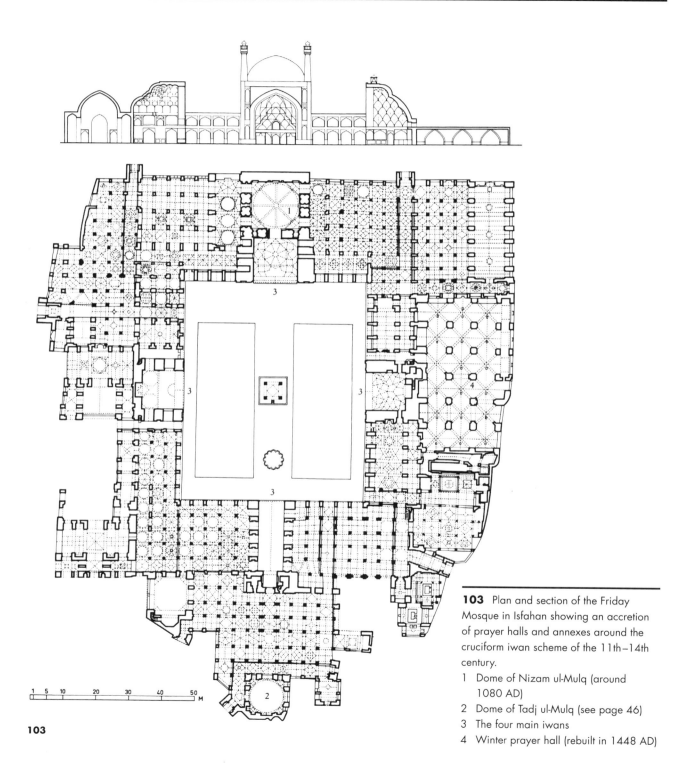

103 Plan and section of the Friday Mosque in Isfahan showing an accretion of prayer halls and annexes around the cruciform iwan scheme of the 11th–14th century.

1 Dome of Nizam ul-Mulq (around 1080 AD)
2 Dome of Tadj ul-Mulq (see page 46)
3 The four main iwans
4 Winter prayer hall (rebuilt in 1448 AD)

104

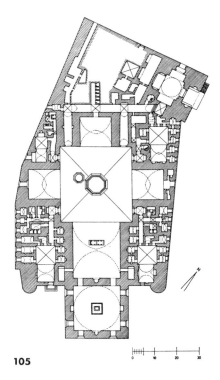

105

architects to indulge in their predilection for centred internal spaces by taking advantage of the four magnificent iwan portals facing each other around the central courtyard. While the cruciform layout of iwans contradicted the continuous flow of space of the traditional pillared prayer hall, it was sometimes inserted to enhance its courtyard. One of the most impressive cases is the Seljuk Friday Mosque in Isfahan, which was built and transformed in several phases starting in the 11th century, and reached its final shape in the 14th century AD.

The most homogeneous and most accomplished example of the cruciform iwan-madrasa is probably the Sultan Hassan Mosque in Cairo (1362 AD). One of its four iwans is orientated towards Mecca and used as the formal prayer hall. However, all four iwans could be used for teaching and individual prayer. The building shows the typical concern for composing a totally balanced and self-contained interior space in the courtyard, while the more flexible student units are used to fill the intermediate spaces between the perfectly regular shape of the courtyard and the irregular outer boundary of the site – a typical design attitude already encountered in a number of residential buildings. Smaller examples of Egyptian madrasas from the later Mamluk period (14th/15th century AD) show a reduction from four to two iwans and a courtyard covered by a dome, which created affinities with the reception room of contemporary private palaces. Some of the early Ottoman mosques of Anatolia (14th/15th century AD) also absorbed the iwan scheme of the madrasa, using only two iwans facing each other in the qibla axis and connected by a central dome.

104 View of the central courtyard of the Sultan Hassan Madrasa in Cairo with the mihrab in the iwan to the left (after David Roberts).

105 Plan of the Sultan Hassan Madrasa (1362 AD) showing the iwans, the tomb of Sultan Hassan south of the iwan with the mihrab, and the student accommodation in the corners between the iwans (see also page 98).

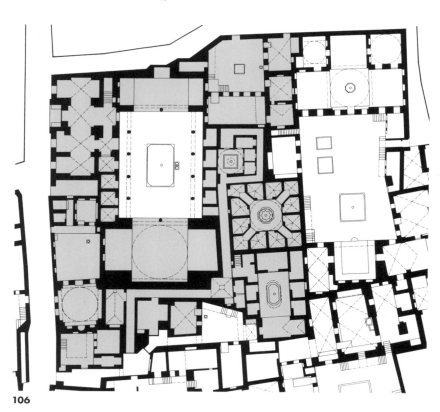

106

107

Being a lodging facility combined with a religious purpose, the madrasa served as a model for a number of comparable welfare buildings, where temporary or permanent accommodation was required. Such is the case with the derwish compound or "*khanqa*" which was used to accommodate and support members of religious brotherhoods or mystic orders (sufis), whether residents or travelling visitors. Often a khanqa (or "*zawiya*" in the Maghreb) was built in connection with the tomb of a venerated spiritual leader. Similarly to the madrasa, it also consists of a combination of one or several prayer halls and a multitude of cellular dwelling units, arranged around the central courtyard or additional side courtyards. This basic combination also applies to the "*maristan*" (hospital), which completes this group of social welfare buildings. The large Mamluk maristans of Cairo were also equipped with iwans facing the central courtyard and with a number of dwelling units resembling those of a madrasa. Occasionally they were built in combination with other social welfare structures. An early example of such welfare compounds is the group of buildings erected by the Mamluk sultan Qalawun (1285 AD), including a famous maristan with a central courtyard and two iwans, a madrasa and the tomb of the patron (see page 118).

106 Plan of the Maristan Arghun (12th century) in Aleppo, built around a nucleus formed by a central courtyard and a prayer hall (south of the courtyard). The interior corridor, bending around the prayer hall, gives access to three smaller independent units with their own air shaft, two containing cells for the sick, and one containing washrooms (see also comprehensive plan on page 151).

107 View of a small independent unit with the individual rooms around a tiny courtyard.

108 Section through Sinan's Shehzade Mosque in Istanbul (16th century), a typical example of the later Ottoman mosques.

MOSQUE AND WELFARE BUILDINGS

Other such examples are the Ottoman "külliyes" in Istanbul which formed complete welfare centres around the main mosque of the ruler and thereby created powerful new nodes of urban life.

Before entering in greater detail into the structure and the economic basis of such welfare compounds, it is necessary to address the third stream of mosque architecture, which complemented the earlier typologies of the pillared wall and the iwan scheme by the variant of the domed prayer hall. The model of this later typology was the Hagia Sophia Church in Constantinople, which must have impressed the Ottoman conquerors of Istanbul. Later, their architects (and foremost the great Sinan) set out to adapt it in accordance with Islamic aesthetics.

The transformation process can be followed by looking at the various mosque buildings of Sinan and his successors in the 16th/17th century AD. It involved the departure from the directional space of the Hagia Sophia (which had itself stretched, so to speak, the earlier Roman models in order to accommodate the Christian liturgy with its procession to the altar), and it resulted in a perfectly balanced interior space based on rotating symmetries. Thus a perfect equilibrium was established between the four sides of the building annihilating all directional trends. The two longitudinally placed conches of the Hagia Sophia were repeated and differentiated in such a way as to achieve a cascade of multiple vaultings around the central prayer hall and establish a seamless transition between the underlying square and the crowning dome structure. The only directional element added to the prayer hall was the enclosed open forecourt in front of the

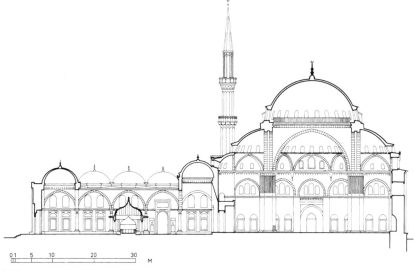

0 1   5   10   20   30
                                    M

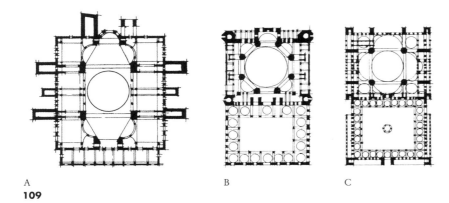

A
109

B   C

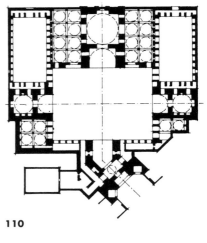

110

main entrance and opposite the qibla wall to accommodate the overflow of visitors during religious holidays.

The new typology of the domed prayer hall spread over the whole Ottoman empire between the 16th and the 19th century and was, at least to some extent, identified with its political supremacy. However, outside Turkey, it did not completely overrule earlier typologies, which continued to be applied in their regions of origin. The Maghreb, in particular, remained faithful to the model of the pillared hall, which had been introduced by the Umayyads in Andalusia and has since dominated the so-called "Moorish" mosque architecture up to the present time. Egypt and the Middle East continued to apply the Mamluk versions of the madrasa mosque while Iran, during the Safawid period (16th/17th century AD), experienced another renaissance of the iwan scheme. One of the masterworks of Safawid architecture, the Shah Abbas Mosque, succeeded in synthesizing all three typologies: its main entry and courtyard are marked by monumental iwan structures, while the prayer hall is dominated by a central dome and features two pillared halls as a lateral extension of the central prayer space.

In addition to their combined religious and social orientation, all the social welfare buildings mentioned, including the mosque, had a common economic base: as a rule, their construction and their subsequent maintenance were ensured by a religious endowment established by the ruler, a member of his family or another generous sponsor in favour of the community. This endowment was called "waqf" (plural awqaf), and its possessions and the regular revenues (which, beside the sponsored building, could also include the rents of donated grounds, private houses or commercial facilities) became the inalienable property of the local community. This accumulating body of self-sustaining public properties, administered by the kadi,

109 The transformation process from the Byzantine church to the late Ottoman mosque (after Vogt-Göknil).
A Hagia Sophia
B Selim Mosque in Edirne by Sinan (1574 AD)
C Sultan Ahmed Mosque in Istanbul (1609 AD)

110 The Shah Abbas Mosque in Isfahan (1610 AD), a harmonious synthesis of pillared hall, iwans and main dome. The bent entrance opposite the main prayer hall reflects the directional change between the square and the qibla axis, which was masterfully resolved by the architect (see page 63).

was inextricably connected with the economic base of the city and became a fundamental factor for ensuring local autonomy and urban continuity. Yet its durable character, unchangeable by definition, could also generate problems in the case of much later and unforeseen developments.

Clearly, the motives of waqf donations were not always limited to philanthropic intentions, but often reflected the desire of the donor to improve his prospects for the other world, to compensate for previous misdeeds, to be remembered by later generations and to benefit from their prayers, or simply to document his status and prestige. This eventually led to the much-cherished concept of donating memorial welfare complexes including a mausoleum of the sponsor. Although certain purist religious movements in Islam have rejected the idea of funerary monuments because of the inherent danger of idolatry, *mausolea* became an important category of buildings in Islamic architecture, especially in Egypt during the Ayyubid and Mamluk period and in Iran, Turkey, Central Asia and India under the rule of Turkoman dynasties. The origins of funerary architecture are certainly rooted in religious motives, as is the case with the Prophet's tomb and with the Shi'ite shrines in Egypt, Syria, Iraq and Iran, or with the Maghrebi zawiyas built around the tombs of holy men. Almost inevitably, this privilege reserved for spiritual leaders was then claimed by powerful political leaders who wanted to link their name to prestigious buildings and works of art – much to the benefit of master builders and craftsmen entrusted with corresponding commissions. Although not a funerary building, the Dome of the Rock in Jerusa-

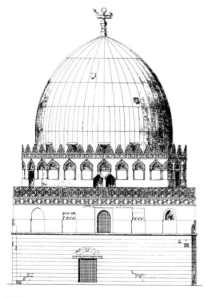

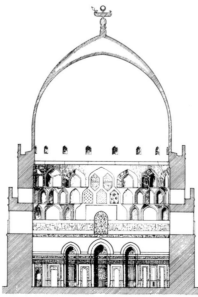

111/112 Elevation and section of the early 13th-century mausoleum of Imam Shafi'i in Cairo (after K.A.C. Creswell).

111   112

113

lem (688 AD), inspired by the Byzantine model of the "martyrion", was the earliest architectural model for this typology and had a deep influence on Muslim mausoleum buildings. These could be either free-standing or combined with a mosque, a madrasa, a khanqa or even with a large garden (as in Moghul India), to form large social welfare complexes.

An extremely important facility was the public bath, or *"hammam"*, which together with the mosque and the suqs constituted the triad of essential urban facilities in the Islamic city. Like the mosque, it combined religious and social functions, since it allowed easy accomplishment of the great ablutions while also serving as an alternating meeting place for both male and female society. Some public baths were integrated into the central market system, often close to the main mosques, and were conceived for predominantly male use, while others were integrated in residential districts, offering a very popular entertainment for women and children in the afternoon and allowing for male use in the evening.

113 The endowment compound built by Sultan Qalaun in 1285 AD in Cairo on the site of the former Fatimid palace.
1 Main entry
2 Mausoleum
3 Madrasa
4 Hospital (destroyed)

114 Entry hall of the 13th-century Hammam Nahassin in Aleppo, with a series of raised alcoves around the central space for changing and resting of visitors.

In principle, the hammam adopted and continued the system of the Roman thermae, providing three successive stations: the ante-room (which could be used as a dressing room and for resting, drinking and eating after the bath), an intermediate room, and the hot steam room, which was mostly provided with a water basin or central pool. Usually the steam room was covered by a pierced dome, which could be quite monumental in certain cases and generated the dim and relaxing ambiance of a grotto. The sequence of the three rooms allowed for graded transition between cold and hot, and the intermediate buffer space could also be used for relaxation, washing and massages. In order to ensure the necessary water provision, hammams had to be connected to the urban irrigation system or be posi-

114

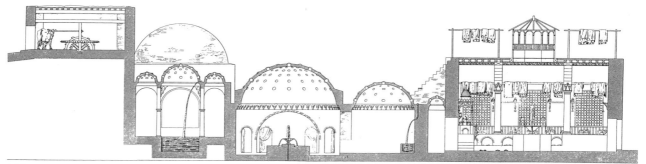

115

tioned close to a natural source of water. The heating section of the hammam was often combined with a public bakery to make economic use of the furnace and the firewood.

As traditional Muslim cities were not always equipped with a complete irrigation system reaching every single house, *"sabils"* (public fountains) were constructed in the main streets and in important residential alleys, which became important visual references and social meeting points. Apart from providing comfort, their trickling added a reminiscence of the cool oasis and the heavenly realm evoked by the Qur'an. In certain cases, the sabils were combined with an upper balcony which served as a children's school. Such composite structures, called *"sabil-kuttab"*, were extensively

115 Section through a hammam in Cairo, showing entry hall to the right, followed by the intermediate room and the steam-room towards the left (after P. Coste).

116 Inside a Turkish bath in Istanbul (after R. Walsh).

117 Late 19th-century view of the gateway to the welfare compound of Sultan Qalaun (see page 118), with "sabil kuttab" attached to the left. The fountain on the ground floor is partly hidden by encroaching shops. The upper loggia was used for teaching children.

116

117

used along the main streets of medieval Cairo, often in conjunction with mosques, madrasas or mausolea, and marked important corners or bifurcations of the public street network. Sponsored by the local rulers or rich notables, they were to provide a service to the local community and to keep the name of the pious sponsor alive.

Components of Urban Form III:
Trade and Production Structures

Stretching from North Africa to Turkestan, the Islamic world soon assumed a key position in intercontinental trade, which remained unchallenged from the 8th into the 16th century AD. Many luxury products, such as spices, incense, fine clothes, rugs and precious stones, which were increasingly coveted in medieval Europe, had to be transported through the Middle East or were processed there by local craftsmen. The "Silk Road" through Transoxania and Iran, as well as the frankincense trail through the Hejjaz, served these intercontinental transactions. They were complemented by the sea routes through the Indian Ocean, the Gulf and the Red Sea – all leading to major Muslim port cities, where commercial exchange could take place. The radial caravan routes of the Hajj, passing through intermediate stations such as Tunis, Cairo, Baghdad and Damascus before eventually converging in Mecca, established an equally important network, which performed both religious and economic functions.

Thus Muslim countries held the monopoly on international East–West trade until Europe, during the age of discovery, started building up its own overseas trade network. The decisive event was the discovery of the sea route to India around the southern tip of Africa, which provided Europe with an alternative connection to the Far Eastern markets, bypassing the Muslim dominions. But even after the establishment of this new route in the early 16th century, the old trade centres of Damascus, Aleppo, Cairo, Istanbul, Isfahan or Samarkand remained important turnover points of international and inter-regional commerce, benefiting from their strategic geographic location. Many of these ancient cities were convenient stations on the age-old caravan routes crossing the vast Middle-Eastern desert areas. Their central markets, besides serving as an outlet for local production, were also equipped for stocking merchandise and for wholesale and retail trade in imported goods. Several European nations or city states had permanent missions residing in these places, in order to manage and supervise their intercontinental trade activities.

Since the early days, commerce was a vital component of Muslim urban life, and the markets always occupied a prominent position in the city centre in conjunction with the Friday mosque and related social welfare buildings. The strong interaction between religious and commercial activities was

118 Inside the covered suqs of Aleppo.

explicitly endorsed by the Qur'an, and it became one of the hallmarks of traditional Muslim cities. The roots of this tradition can be seen in the history of Mecca, which was not only an ancient place of pilgrimage but also a striving centre of caravan trade.

While the central market of the big capitals provided the outlets for the international trade network, there was also a system of more modest local markets, anchored in age-old exchange customs and operating since the earliest times of Islam. The local markets could function within a city, a village or even on the edge of the desert. In the country, they were usually held on a weekly basis and provided meeting opportunities for a dispersed Bedouin population. Sometimes they were enclosed by walls; yet in general, their setting was rather informal. The merchandise was displayed on the ground, leaving a number of free lanes between the open-air "shops", which could be covered by improvised tents. These informal market patterns could also extend into the urban realm, with ambulant vendors benefiting from the pedestrian flows around the gates, on the main arteries and close to the main mosques. Up to the present time, this habit is very much alive in many Muslim cities, including Mecca and Medina, where pilgrims sell specialities from their home country around the Haram in order to do business and recover some of their travel costs.

The right of temporary occupation of available public ground for trade purposes relates to the old customary law of Bedouin societies and was practised since the early times of Islam in Medina, as well as in the first garrison towns in Mesopotamia such as Kufa and Basra. The formalization of these early informal market structures and their conversion into permanent urban suq structures first occurred during the Umayyad period. We know for instance that the caliph Hisham (724–743 AD) ordered his governor in Medina to construct a walled double-floor structure with arcades and gates in order to accommodate the central market. The Roman provinces offered many opportunities for such commercial compounds, and it is not surprising that Syria offers the most interesting examples of the formation of early Muslim suq structures. When the square of the old agora in Aleppo was vacated to construct the Umayyad Mosque, the resident merchants were shifted to a separate enclosed structure near the western gate – a building which must have been a precursor of the later caravanserais or khans. Simultaneously, the colonnaded main avenue was invaded by street vendors who started occupying not only the bays of the lateral arcades but also the central part of the avenue, which was no longer used by carriages and therefore offered abundant space for pedestrian circulation. This vigorous new commercial activity must soon have led to the construction of parallel rows of little stalls and huts, which eventually grew together and split the

119 Vernacular ways of setting up a rudimentary suq structure continue up to the present day: rural market near Mulay Idris (Morocco).

120 Improvised booths on a large public open space between the old and the new city, in Marrakesh.

119

120

121

large avenue into a number of parallel smaller lanes. Later, the informal arrangement was replaced by vaulted architectural structures which "monumentalized" the original pattern, retaining the additive structure of small cellular shops and the constituted pedestrian flows.

The typical formal structure of many later suqs was thus achieved by the progressive architectural accretion of hundreds of small niches bracketing the most busy sections of the public street network. Most shops resembled simple cupboards, which had to be opened from the alleyway and could accommodate just the shop owner and his basic stock. Often the shop owner would sit on a raised bench, from where he could easily scan the stream of potential clients, and he would encroach upon the public space to display his merchandise and receive his customers. Usually, each shop had an awning projecting into the street to create a small protected ante-room, where people could meet, sit down, negotiate or chat under the "umbrella" of exposed merchandises, while passers-by would use the median section of the street. The suq therefore transformed the street into a (predominantly male) social meeting place which, beyond its commercial purpose, became the major centre for exchanging all sorts of news. In many Muslim cities, this major public function was acknowledged by covering the central sections of the market and converting the most important suqs to generous halls and arcades (see pages 122 and 131).

121 Temporary occupation of public ground in front of a city gate (Fez).

122 Plan of the old city centre of Aleppo (after Gaube/Wirth). The Umayyad Mosque occupies the former agora while the parallel suq spines, running from west to east, occupy the former Roman avenue and its lateral arcades (see also page 57). South of the main suqs, framed by a number of north-south alleyways, are located several large "khans" constructed during the Ottoman period. The Hammam Nahassin (see page 119) is interspersed between the suqs and the khans.

123 The transformation process from the Roman colonnaded avenue to the later suqs (after Sauvaget).

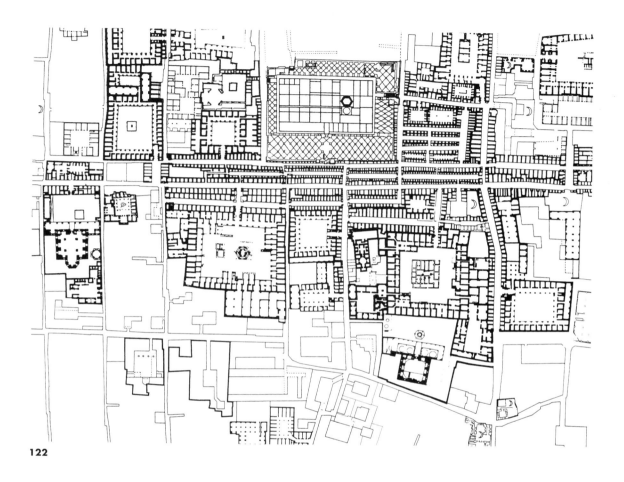

122

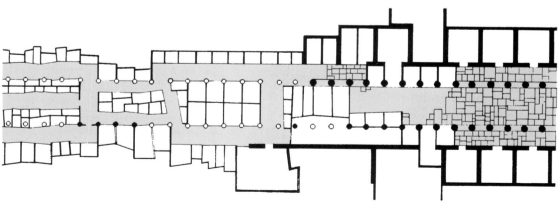

123

The single cells of the suq corresponded to the highly individualized pattern of the traditional economy, which operated on the basis of a multitude of small enterprise units. Yet at the same time, the system also favoured the integration of individual cells into larger units of commerce and production which corresponded to professional and social entities and reflected the corporate organization of commercial and industrial activities. In spatial terms, there was the possibility of either forming linear series of individual shops along both sides of pedestrian thoroughfares or providing angular compositions around an enclosed courtyard, accessible by a single entry/exit point. In both cases, the framed open space was controlled and maintained by the respective trade or production unit, which had to concede public access to the occupied space.

The linear arrangement produced the ubiquitous suq structures of the Islamic city – long shopping alleys, which could easily be subdivided into interconnected individual sections. The spatial integrity of each suq section was safeguarded by gates which could be closed at night, so that accessibility to the central market sector could at times be interrupted, much in the same way as in the residential clusters. Individual suq sections could also be duplicated by parallel units placed "back to back" or enlarged into wider systems by conjunction with perpendicular units, in order to form more complex market units in the inner city.

The angular composition produced spatial "pockets" instead of linear sequences and led to the formation of the typical caravanserai structure, which usually served storage, wholesale, production and accommodation purposes rather than retail trade. The names given to those structures varied from region to region: the term of "khan" was used in Persia and most of the Middle East, "wakalla" in Egypt, "funduq" in the Maghreb and "samsara" in Yemen. Due to their tight enclosure walls and the central courtyard, the caravanserais were independent structures and could either stand on their own (as in the case of the isolated khans offering shelter along the major caravan routes) or be integrated into the urban fabric. There they often filled the "meshes" in the grid of the suq, being located right behind the lines of shops, with only the entry projecting into the front row of suq shops. The entry gate of major khans could be connected with a dome covering the alleyway in front of it, which often led to the formation of strategic nodes punctuating the suq network.

Usually the khans consisted of a double or triple floor structure with a lower portico and upper galleries, allowing for a variety of functions: on the ground floor they offered compartmentalized storage space for local wholesalers or visiting merchants and, if needed, stables for the animals of their caravans. Offices and workshops could be located on the first floor,

124

124 Example of an isolated 13th-century khan in inner Anatolia (after A. Gabriel).

125 Khans included in the suq network west of the Umayyad Mosque of Aleppo, as seen from the top of the minaret.

while the uppermost levels were mostly reserved for rooms and apartments which could be rented by visitors and merchants. Thus the khans provided an essential backup for the suq, with all the necessary support facilities. But their most important contribution to the city was perhaps the integrated open space which, within a few steps from the crowded streets, provided a welcome change of environment. As many of the central suqs tended to be roofed by permanent vaulted structures, gabled roofs or more improvised shading devices, the contrast between the enclosed main sections of the market and the islands of open space offered by the courtyards of the khans was a source of considerable enrichment for the townscape.

A special element of many cities, which could be interpreted as a hybrid between a covered caravanserai and a grouping of closed suq units, was the "qissariya" complex (called "bedestan" in Turkey). It was always located within the network of the central markets. Its name is derived from the imperial hall of the Roman and Byzantine markets ("Caesaria"), and like its predecessor it formed a specially enclosed and protected district – either a pillared hall or a series of contiguous suqs – accommodating the trade in the

125

126

most precious articles such as silk, gold and jewelry. It thus became the "treasure house" of each central market complex and was often located close to the most prestigious mosque of the city. During the night it was locked and guarded by watchmen.

As the public space of the city centre was always dominated by the Friday mosque, it is not surprising to observe certain trade hierarchies in relation to the mosque, which were reflected in corresponding locational preferences. While there were no formal rules in this respect, it was natural that the required ritual cleanliness of the prayer space excluded all transactions

126 19th-century view of the main north-south spine of historic Cairo, which was framed by a series of important public buildings and mausolea sponsored by the rulers of the Ayyubid and Mamluk dynasties. Most of these endowed buildings were erected to provide integrated commercial facilities on the ground floor and to generate income for their maintenance. The stairs leading up to the main floor are hidden behind a second line of informal market activities with booths occupied by ambulant vendors and artisans. To provide shade, a timber roof was fixed over the street (after D. Roberts).

127

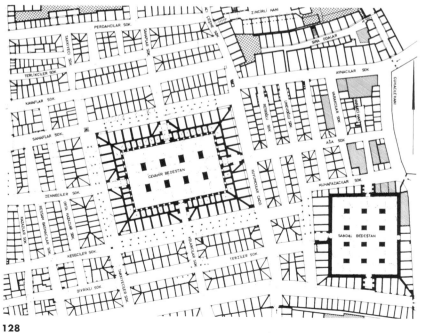

128

127 View of one of the main lanes of the covered bazaar in Istanbul (after R. Walsh).

128 Detail of the comprehensive plan of the covered bazaar in Istanbul, showing two bedestans integrated into the network of covered markets.

involving polluting products in the immediate surroundings of the mosque. The preferred trades in this area were those dealing with noble matters such as perfumes and spices, or those related to the mosque's academic function, such as manuscripts and book binding. Precious imported goods and the finest locally produced articles also gravitated towards the Friday mosque or the qissariya. A certain basic retail geography was thus established in the city centre, which did not greatly change from one city to another, allowing for easy orientation within the manifold compartments of the central suqs. Most trade branches were concentrated in specific locations, and although the respective corporations (comparable to the medieval guilds in Europe) did not develop an institutional profile, they existed as a social reality and had a clear impact on the land use of the city. (An example of the location of various trade branches in relation to the mosque is given in the map of the city centre of Fez, on pages 144/145.)

The distribution of production activities was dictated by the sequence of manufacturing processes, from the raw material to the finished product, and by space requirements and circulation constraints within the city. Raw materials such as timber, agricultural products and livestock were sold in special open markets at the periphery of the city, within or outside the gates, and then underwent a first stage of processing or storage in areas close to the

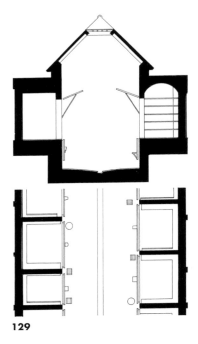

129/130 Section, plan and view of a typical covered suq with integrated booths and projecting shutters (shoemakers' suq in Marrakesh).

129   **130**

131

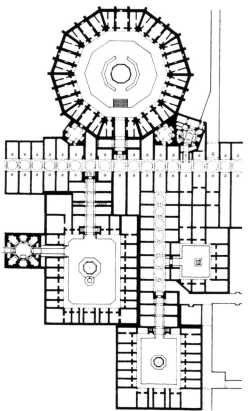

132

131 Courtyard of the caravanserai of Sultan al-Ghuri in Cairo (around 1500 AD), with commercial and storage space on the two lower floors (under the arcades) and a series of multi-floored apartments for rent above.

132 Combination of linear suq structure with enclosed khans in the central bazaar of Kashan, Iran (after Ardalan).

133

134

gates, where sufficient open space or large storehouses and manufacturing places could be made available. Each step of further refinement in the chain of artisanal production meant easier transportation, processing, stocking and selling, and thus facilitated the absorption of goods by the dense and crowded central suq system.

Some materials needed by the craftsman, such as clay and lime, were often available within the city walls, but the potters and their kilns had to remain at the periphery. The chain of wool and textile production, as well as that of leatherwork, depended on raw skins which had to be tanned, trimmed and dyed. These processes were subject to the availability of abundant water supplies, which often meant that compromises had to be made with other users or with adjacent residential areas. The stages of the various pre-industrial production chains called for repeated intermediate transactions, which could include wholesale, special auctions, or retail to craftsmen and private users. At some points, home production would interact with these commercial activities, as families sold their surplus production or acquired materials for additional crafting by the ladies of the house, which could later be sold back to the market.

The interchange between the different manufacturing chains shaped the complex sequence of production and trade, which culminated in the retail of refined goods in the central markets. The suqs were grafted on the main spines connecting the city gates and the heart of the city, complemented by a number of parallel alleys and cross-links in the central area. They were subdivided into specialized sectors, allowing customers to review the avail-

133 Cloth market in the old suqs of Aleppo.

134 The covered street of the carpenters in Ouezzane (Morocco).

135 The tanners' district in the old city of Fez, located in the heart of the city due to the availability of a natural spring.

135

able retail choice in one single location. Walking from the periphery to the centre, a visitor could thus find a cross section of locally available goods in increasing degrees of refinement. The shops of the main streets were the visible outlets of this production, but behind them there were several layers of wholesale and manufacturing, sometimes immediately behind the screens of shops (in the case of the big khans and wholesale stores), sometimes in more remote production areas, immersed in the urban fabric. However, the transport of semi-finished goods from one station to another gave clear evidence of this commercial network and constituted a major activity in the streetscape of traditional Muslim cities.

The Deep Structure
of the Traditional Urban Fabric

Historic Muslim cities in the Arab World show a variety of origins and growth patterns. These were conditioned on the one hand by *external* factors such as pre-existing settlements, deliberate locational choices and prevailing dynastic evolutions and changes, and on the other hand by *internal* factors such as the morphological principles implied in individual architectural components and in the genesis of the urban fabric.

In our context, morphology refers to the underlying shaping forces of urban form which, drawing on related, deep-rooted human attitudes, constitute the real agents of physical manifestation and are the source of the non-material qualities transpiring through material expressions. While the ultimate objective of this chapter, rather than tracing the evolution of individual cities, is to shed light on these internal structuring processes, it may nevertheless be appropriate to first summarize the external factors of historic urban development, before venturing into the more complex morphological issues.

It has often been claimed that Islam, due to its Arabian origins, was not an urban civilization; yet its ethics and social order favoured a strong community life and in fact resulted in an almost instant revival of pre-existing urban traditions under changed spiritual auspices, specially in the Near Eastern area, which became the first target of early Arab-Islamic immigration. As pointed out in chapter 3, the surviving physical structures of late Roman-Hellenistic cities in Syria (such as Damascus and Aleppo) became the setting for the cultural encounter between the Arab immigrants and a local sedentary population that was gradually converting to Islam. By the same token, these cities were to serve as melting pots for a novel urban civilization which, being strongly imprinted by Muslim community ideals and highly ritualized daily living patterns, eventually led to the progressive transformation of pre-Islamic urban structures.

The locational choices of historic cities in the Arab world generally depended on prevailing trade routes and geopolitical considerations, the availability of natural resources (such as perennial water supply and an agricultural hinterland) and, in some cases, on the religious significance of certain places. In most cases a combination of several of these factors was involved in determining the city's site and growth: the holy city of Mecca

selecting location for a city.

136 Aerial view of the medina of Fez, with the traditional city centre around the Qairawiyin Mosque and the funeral mosque of Mulay Idris.

was already a centre of pilgrimage and trade before the advent of Islam, benefiting from a famous spring which added to its attraction. Medina grew in an oasis and was a welcome station on the frankincense trade route. Damascus and Fez relied on rich water resources and were located at crossing points of important regional trade connections – an advantage which had already been exploited in Roman-Hellenistic times in the case of Damascus. Cairo and Baghdad were founded at strategic geopolitical locations, benefiting from the Nile and the Tigris rivers. Local crafts and commerce, especially if supported by a strong local dynasty and its court, boosted the importance of emerging urban centres, as did the presence of venerated saints and holy men, who often provided legitimation to ruling dynasties and created an additional stimulus for city growth.

Whereas most of the above-mentioned locational choices are generally applicable to pre-industrial cities, the impact of the ruling class, and particularly the development patterns resulting from the succession of individual dynasties, produced distinct characteristics representative of the urban history of Muslim societies. The distant tribal origin of many conquering dynasties, for instance, meant that these rulers were not really rooted in the local population. The same applies to the chain of Mamluk rulers which was not of dynastic character, since it involved a military hierarchy based on the selection and the eventual rise of slave-soldiers brought in from Central Asia. Furthermore, once the ideal caliphate of the early days had passed away, the actual holders of power, as stated by Ibn Khaldun, were seen as a "necessary evil" needed to support and protect the religious community, rather than being acknowledged as the legitimate peak of an organic social hierarchy. This explains why the camps, residences, palaces and citadels of the ruling dynasty were mostly set apart from the city of commoners, the latter structure being much more marked by local crafts and trade, by the religious institutions, by the traditional community facilities and by a strong intellectual and spiritual life of its own. In most instances and particularly in the case of military dynasties, the ruler was not considered as an integral part of the ideal Muslim "civitas", which found its more appropriate reflection in the vernacular town, as developed under the influence of the local bourgeoisie and its notables.

Accordingly, the rulers' residential cities were usually founded outside, or at best adjacent to existing urban nuclei and implied separate functional systems and often different, more formal and highly abstract layouts. A prominent example is the plan of the Abbasid "Round City" of Baghdad (762 AD), which was strongly influenced by Iranian cosmological concepts – ideas no longer pursued in Muslim town-planning of later periods. Although no archaeological traces of the "Round City" have survived, its

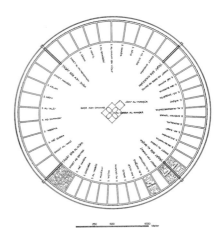

137

137 Schematic reconstruction of the plan of the "Round City" of Baghdad, with its four main gates and accessways leading to the central palace and mosque complex. On the periphery, close to the walls, are the residential quarters, divided into 45 segments.

plan was related by contemporary authors in such detail that a diagrammatic reconstruction could be attempted. Another example is the Fatimid foundation of Cairo (969 AD), laid out as a fortified palace city with a central north-south axis, not unsimilar to Roman-Hellenistic city plans. The Marinid city of Fez-Jdid, founded in the 14th century, although less formal in plan, is a good example of the attachment of a palace and administration town to an existing urban nucleus. It is significant that it was situated uphill in a dominant position, controlling all of the water resources flowing into Fez al-Bali (the old Fez). In Cairo, Granada and Aleppo, the 12th-century citadels, although within or very close to the existing urban structures, were vertically separated from the city of commoners.

Looking at the development of Baghdad and Cairo over the centuries, another interesting phenomenon can be observed, which became typical for many Muslim cities: as certain dynasties were ousted or substituted, the old residences were abandoned or replaced by new palatial settlements or citadels, with the result that the city's centre of gravity started shifting and

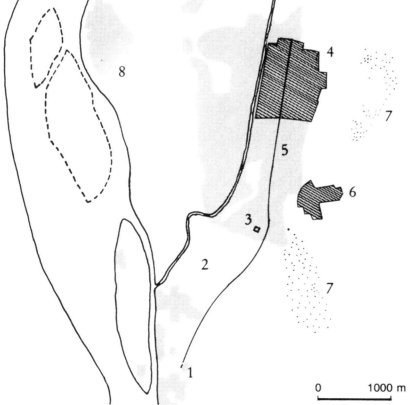

0   1000 m

138 The various successive or simultaneous components of historic Cairo around 1800 (After J. Abu-Lughod).
1 Location of the first Arab settlement of Fustat (7th century)
2 Former site of the Tulunid city of Qata'i (late 9th century)
3 The mosque of Ibn Tulun
4 The Fatimid city founded in 969
5 Main spine of the Fatimid city
6 Ayyubid citadel
7 Cemeteries
8 River-port district of Bulaq (17th-18th century)

often continued to do so over long periods. In the case of Cairo, the 10th-century Fatimid palace was built two kilometres north of the earlier origins of the Muslim city located at Fustat, the first encampment of the military force which had set out to conquer Egypt in the 7th century. In the 8th century, Ibn Tulun, a governor of the Baghdad-based Abbasid dynasty, had already founded his own palace north of Fustat, whereas the original settlement extended into an important city of trade called Misr, which burnt down in the 12th century. The rise of the Ayyubid dynasty saw the construction of Saladin's citadel, started in 1176 AD, while the old Fatimid palace city was left to the local bourgeoisie. The site of the destroyed palace itself became the building ground for the splendid social welfare complexes constructed by the Ayyubid and Mamluk sultans between the 13th and the 15th centuries, combining mausolea with madrasas, prayer halls, hospitals and public fountains. While these royal "waqfs" fostered new focal points in the urban system, the rulers themselves lived in separate locations outside the city, which increasingly took on the character of military strongholds, especially during the period of the Crusades.

It is worth mentioning in advance here that the segregation of the ruler's palace and the military establishment from the vernacular city anticipated similar choices related to the siting of colonial cities, as created by the Ottoman and the European powers during the 19th and early 20th centuries.

139 Aerial view of the mausolea and welfare complexes of the Ayyubid and Mamluk sultans, built on the plots of the former palaces on both sides of the surviving main axis of the Fatimid city of Cairo. In the centre, the complex of Sultan Qala'un completed in 1285 AD (see page 118), further left the tomb and madrasa of his son Sultan an-Nasir (1304 AD) and the madrasa of Sultan Barquq (1386 AD). Above the Qala'un complex, on the other side of the street, the tomb and madrasa of the last Ayyubid sultan as-Salih (1242-1250 AD).

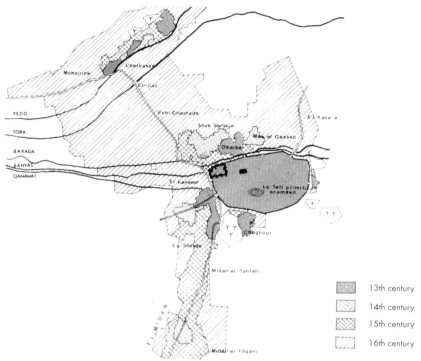

140

This later development – the first step to an either evolutionary or abrupt modernization – could thus build on a pre-existing logic of urbanization patterns although, in the case of colonialism, the corollary introduction of an alien cultural system did not favour a smooth integration.

Ethnic migrations, not infrequent in the Muslim world, could also lead to the foundation of separate town units, or to the informal growth of new suburbs "extra muros". Such new quarters often clung to one of the main gates of the walled city and developed along major routes of caravan traffic, whose loading and unloading point was, obviously, at the city gates. The plans of Aleppo and Damascus illustrate this phenomenon with their extensive informal additions to the walled city, going back to the 15th century. The location and the development patterns of such suburbs often reflect the geographical direction of their rural catchment area or, in the case of Midan (the southern suburb of Damascus), the district's function as a turn-over and departure place geared to the caravans leaving for and arriving from Mecca.

Accordingly, the historical development of large Arab cities often shows a shift of gravity centres, with old quarters being abandoned or re-used by different populations. This went hand in hand with a complex aggregated

140 Plan showing the historical development of Damascus and its suburbs between the 13th and the early 20th century (after J. Sauvaget).

Legend:
- 13th century
- 14th century
- 15th century
- 16th century

structure, based on the juxtaposition of self-contained and largely auto-nomous community units of different ethnic, religious or functional character. The Jewish quarters of Muslim cities are no exception to this; they reflect the deliberate autonomy granted to discrete ethnic and tribal groups within a pluralistic and multi-focal urban development pattern, rather than the modern "ghetto" concept.

From an urban design point of view, it has been stated by several authors that historic Arab cities show either "spontaneous" or "planned" urban patterns, the former being related to more vernacular urban confi-gurations (sometimes of rural origin), the latter being defined by the formal layouts of palace cities. While there is some truth in this distinction, one could also argue that the planned palace cities were a response to military concepts and to princely representation needs which were not typical of the common Muslim city. Here, the strong social order of Islam (practised in con-junction with equally strong customary laws), the conspicuous absence of formal civic institutions and the ensuing empowerment of self-regulating pri-vate communities and social groups resulted in a particular type of space management which was reflected in "organic" growth processes, i.e. an urban form grown from within, so to speak, and conditioned by incremen-tal decisions at grass-root level, rather than obeying imposed external schemes. Thus the orthogonal grid system, where it existed, was gradually overgrown by a vernacular pattern, based on the common appropriation and transformation of public space by the various social groups, as can be seen in the 19th-century plan of Fatimid Cairo recorded by the Napoleonic expedition. This resulted in an overlay of often tortuous residential access lanes and cul-de-sacs reflecting the prevalent "spontaneous" urbanisation mode – not unsimilar to the mutation of the Roman-Hellenistic grid pattern in Damascus and Aleppo.

Since the intention of this book is to present and to analyse the incre-mentally grown morphological patterns of Arab cities, rather than focusing on the architecture of power and its formal expressions, we shall now con-centrate on the more vernacular aspects of urban form, as encountered in the surviving structures of historic cities such as Aleppo, Damascus, Fez, Tunis or Baghdad. These urban structures, admittedly, represent a late stage in the evolution of urban form, stretching over the last three or four centuries, and yet they reflect perennial principles and attitudes firmly rooted in tradi-tional community life and in certain tribal customs, which can be traced back to the "khittat" system, as practised in the first centuries of Islam. The following remarks therefore relate to this ubiquitous archetype of traditional Arab urban form, with a view to understanding its dominant functional

141

model, as well as the inherent concept of order which produced its singular physical character. In doing so, we will rely on the previous typological descriptions of the various architectural components, showing how they interacted to form a comprehensive and coherent urban fabric without ever losing their individual spatial identity.

The main land-use patterns of the historic Arab-Muslim city are usually focused on a multifunctional core structure enveloping or at least partially surrounding the central mosque by different layers of interconnected suqs. As a rule, these are interspersed with a number of hammams, madrasas and

141 Map of Cairo recorded around 1800, during Napoleon's campaign in Egypt. (The dashed lines indicate the boundaries of the former Fatimid city.)

1   Tomb and mosque of Mulay Idris
2   Qairawiyin Mosque
3   Mosque library
4   Former residence of the judge (kadi)
5   Hall for mortuary prayer services
6   Former stand-by place of notaries
7   Ablution room / toilets
8   Attarin Madrasa
9   Mesbahia Madrasa
10 Seffarin Madrasa
11 Sherratin Madrasa
12 Public bath (hammam)
13 Private residence formerly used as
    marriage house
14 Former hospital (maristan)

15 Spice market, with specialised parallel
    and perpendicular branches of the suq
16 Former booksellers' suq
17 Perfumers' suq
18 Qissariya complex (precious fabrics
    and jewellery)
19 Jellabah suq (traditional dresses)
20 Carpet suq
21 Pottery suq
22 Carpenters' suq
23 Square of the coppersmiths
24 Caravanserai (funduq)
25 Former residences now converted to
    exhibition rooms, restaurants and
    shops

142 Plan of the traditional city centre of Fez al-Bali, showing the close interrelation existing between mosques, madrasas, suqs, caravanserais and residential districts.

caravanserais which constitute the support system for the mosque and the retail shops. The unique symbiosis between religious, educational, social and commercial functions is expressed in the volumetric assimilation of the mosque building into this complex central compound. Indeed, the pillared halls of the mosque and its roofing system often show striking analogies to the arcades of the covered suqs, the only difference being that the mosque is a permeable structure, thus allowing for multiple uses and large congregations. The minaret, and possibly one or several larger domes, are the only elements emerging from the continuous roofscape which extends like a blanket above the aggregated volumes. The large central courtyard at the heart of the friday mosque becomes the primary public open space of the central compound and, to some extent, of the city as a whole. As the central mosque is often enmeshed in a system of surrounding alleyways or suqs, it is usually accessible from different sides through a number of entry gates. Once one has passed the threshold which protects the ritual purity of the mosque space, the central courtyard is easily entered from the suqs, either directly or through the prayer hall.

Whereas the compactness of this central compound, based on its exclusively pedestrian movement mode, clearly compresses the available public space within the suqs, it is balanced by the courtyards of the ancillary or satellite buildings, such as madrasas and caravanserais. They are meant to

143 Oblique aerial view of the centre of Fez al-Bali, from the east.

provide compensatory public space off the covered main alleyways and are allocated to more specialized functions and social needs. When moving through this highly articulated complex, the visitor experiences a distinct feeling of spatial continuity transcending the limits of individual buildings and connecting the various realms of public life. Yet at the same time, he receives clear physical guidance with respect to the differentiation between different sectors. A subtle visual reference system relates to accepted (and expected) codes of social behaviour within the given urban compartments. Each individual realm carefully retains its specific spatial character, while interacting with neighbouring units through distinct architectural devices, such as intermediate gateways, internal passages, thresholds and communicating doors. Hence the impression of meandering through a seemingly endless series of interconnected chambers within a highly articulated and yet homogeneous urban universe.

In such urban structures everything seems to be "under one roof", and thus the city can be compared to a spacious but coherent single mansion. By analogy, the mosque would be the main living room, the madrasas and caravanserais would correspond to the teaching room, guest rooms and utility rooms, and the suqs, equipped with long rows of cupboards, would represent the connecting internal corridors. The residential districts, as will be shown below, provide the private quarters of this collective urban

144/145 Contrast between a central market spine in Fez (left) and a secluded dead-end access to a residential cluster (right). Beyond the threshold of individual houses, a bent and fully private interior corridor leads to the courtyard, the hub of each house.

144   145

146

"house" and are structured along similar principles as the public places but with greater emphasis on the articulation of intermediate passages.

The multifunctional central compound of the town is linked with the outer gates via a number of main spines, ensuring communication between the interior and the exterior of the walled city. The main gates constitute important secondary centres of the urban system, inasmuch as their traditional function is to act as turn-over points for the loading and unloading of wholesale merchandise and materials brought from the rural hinterland, which could not enter the fine-grain system of the inner city without prior stocking, processing and distribution to retailers. Accordingly, the gates had to sift the flows of people, animals and goods in such a way as to avoid excessive congestion in the inner circulation system. For this reason they offered more abundant (and less structured) open space, surrounded by caravanserais with convenient lodging and storing facilities, wholesale markets and large workshops.

As a rule, the centripetal main spines leading from the gates to the city core became narrower as they approached the central markets. They were lined with a multitude of shops, framing the primary pedestrian flows and taking commercial advantage of potential clients. Besides establishing a functional continuity between the central suqs and the gates, these lines of shops (and the occasional rows of caravanserais behind them) accomplished a second, less obvious purpose within the logic of this urban system: they served as protective shields, hiding the adjacent residential districts and keeping them free of undesirable intrusions. Small gates, discreetly placed

146 Open market in the buffer space behind the the southern gate (Bab Yemen) of the old city of Sana'a.

147 Former orchards on the periphery of the walled city of Fez, partially overgrown by the expanding fabric of the old residential districts.

148 Bird's-eye view of the Bab Qinasreen district in Aleppo (see plan on page 151) showing interacting solids and voids within the residential clusters.

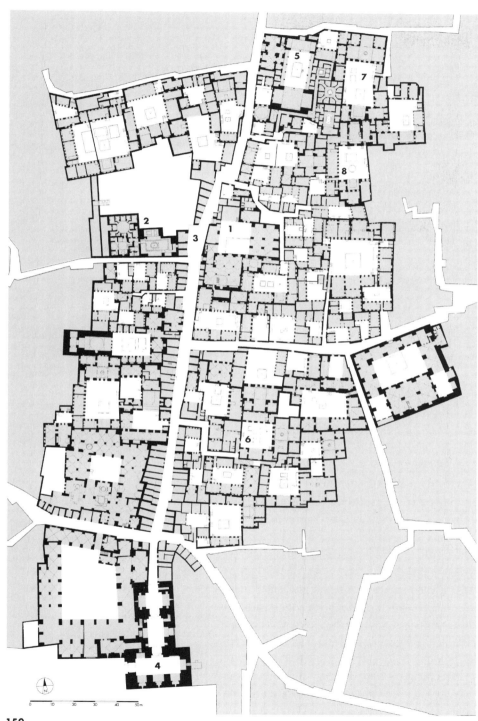

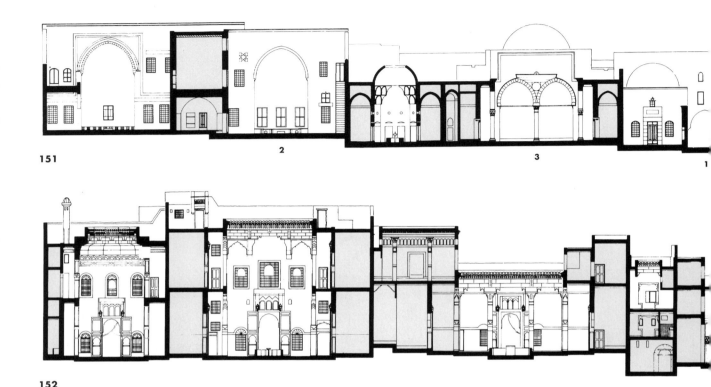

151   2   3   1

152

crossing the city, everything being contained by the outer city walls. As a rule, the housing units tended to stay as close as possible to the central area, in the vicinity of the Friday mosque, where the oldest and most prestigious families used to settle. In the remaining open area towards the city wall, there was a fringe of private orchards, which provided the residents with part of their sustenance. This agricultural space tended to diminish over time, as it was occasionally used for cemeteries (though most of them were located "extra muros"), for certain crafts, such as potteries, or for the needs of the expanding housing clusters. In their gradual growth process, housing clusters would often absorb the pre-existing agricultural pathways and irrigation systems which, once internalized, became subservient to the residential units. By the same token, the former undifferentiated open space reappeared in a fragmented manner within the residential units, in the form of enclosed garden courtyards belonging to the newly built individual houses, which were often much more spacious than the houses in the crowded inner city.

As described in chapter 4, the structure of the residential quarters was generated and sustained by strong micro-communities, often sharing the same tribal origins. These neighbourhoods were largely self-reliant in the

151 East-west section through the upper part of the plan on page 151 (Aleppo), looking southwards. The section shows on the one hand the volumetric coherence of the urban fabric achieved through coinciding enclosure walls shared by adjacent housing units, and on the other hand the subdivision of urban space into independent, largely autonomous residential units, focused on their own courtyards. Streets and alleyways are virtually swallowed by the residential clusters, being transformed into a series of internal corri-

sense that each one formed a virtually autonomous social unit, embracing a representative cross section of society and establishing, controlling and maintaining the basic shared facilities, such as a local mosque, one or several small hammams and public ovens (the latter tended to be built side by side with a shared heating system), and a number of street fountains. The irrigation networks and the internal access system connecting the houses with the major public thoroughfares were also controlled and managed by the neighbourhood communities. The public space of the central suqs, by contrast, were controlled by the trade and craft corporations and supervised by the muhtasib.

In most cases, the identity of each small residential cluster was physically defined by more or less hidden enclosures, composed of the contiguous outer walls of the group of houses laid out around a shared dead-end alleyway (see page 39). The impasse itself could be closed by a gate, thus transforming it into an interior space. This access system was the preferred solution at the residential micro-scale, as it allowed for selective gradual privatization of public space and direct control by the owners of the adjacent houses. By mediating in a subtle manner between the "inner" and the

dors. The houses can only be seen and experienced from within and do not depend on external open spaces. The self-contained character of each housing unit and the vertical orientation of its courtyard thus enables lateral merging of different individual structures.

1   Public alleyway
2   Maktabi house (nr. 7 in plan)
3   Maristan Arghun (nr. 5 in plan)

152 Composite north-south section through the plan on page 150 (Fez).

"outer" world, it enabled the self-contained units of individual houses to merge and to become components of a coherent residential cluster, which in turn was entrenched within a larger multi-cluster unit representing a complete neighbourhood. At the respective hierarchical level, each residential unit of the urban structure had its own inbuilt circulation system, the individual sections and ramifications being separated *and* connected by interior gates that preserved the territorial integrity of the various sub-communities. Joining individual units, whether houses or clusters, was not a matter of loose juxtaposition but implied a structural assimilation which would step by step absorb and incorporate entire building blocks into the larger urban system.

This progressive integration process would not have been possible without the consistent use of an omnipresent cellular composition system of attached, interconnected or overlaid precincts with enclosed circulation systems, repeated in various sizes and at various hierarchic levels of the urban structure. The merging and overlapping of discrete architectural shells into more complex patterns created the extraordinary sense of inner unity and homogeneity which becomes apparent from the bird's-eye views of the residential fabrics of traditional Arab cities – and even more so from the closer analysis of corresponding ground floor plans. Interestingly, such patterns

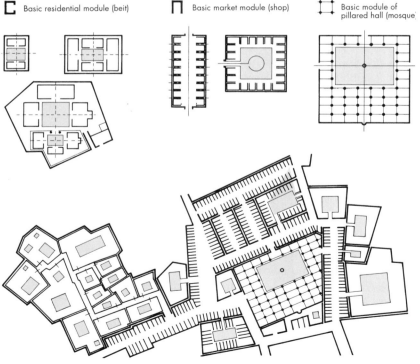

⊏ Basic residential module (beit)

∏ Basic market module (shop)

⊥⊤ Basic module of pillared hall (mosque)

153 Diagram exemplifying the consistent cellular composition of the urban fabric in the Maghreb. The repetition of similar patterns of enclosure and inclusion, throughout various hierarchic levels of the complex built form, results in complete structural integration.

154 Schematic plan identifying the main enclosures or "containers" of the urban system of Fez, which traditionally could be locked by gates and separated from the main circulation paths. Among these containers are the main mosques, the closed sections of the central market and the many residential clusters around collective dead-end alleyways or "darbs". The partition lines between the residential clusters, composed of the walls of the outermost housing units, form a series of invisible enclosures within the city walls.

154

allow for multiple interpretations, since the continuous cellular structure blurs the division between individual components, with the effect that architectural units transcend their original definition and can be read differently at different levels and scales of the urban structure. The incrementally ("naturally") grown urban fabric thus produces structural effects not unsimilar to those encountered in the much more crystalline, deliberately designed geometric patterns of Islamic art. In both cases, the secret of cohesion and inner unity within a rich variety of individual formal expressions relies on the presence of vertical chains of analogies and correspondences as the main principle of either inductive or deductive structural compositions.

Looking at the urban fabric as a whole, and remembering the earlier chapters on architectural typology, one discovers the great affinities between public and residential buildings, relating to both the vocabulary of complex individual structures and the way in which the composite elements are interconnected and incorporated into larger compounds. The main difference in the mode of connection appears when it comes to the shift from the public to the private domain. Here it was necessary to insert appropriate resistances and retardation effects. The transition was often achieved by extended, deliberately tortuous access lanes and by buffer spaces controlled by gates and thresholds. Market compounds and residential clusters could be placed in adjacent locations, sharing their enclosures "back to back", but without direct communication – a system which enabled both functional division and volumetric interlocking.

Thus the typical urban form of historic Arab cities grew as a compact aggregation of smaller and larger precincts, each one equipped with the appropriate cellular infill, as well as inbuilt open spaces, access systems and shared facilities allocated to the respective groups of collective and individual users. The fact that all these micro-elements of urban form shared the same structural principles, in spite of different functions, made them fully compatible. Their largely self-centred and self-contained character, due to the vertical orientation of interior courtyards and air shafts, facilitated horizontal cohesion, favouring their integration into larger urban components which were complete in themselves at each stage of development, in space and in time.

By a series of centring, enclosing and incorporating processes through ascending hierarchic levels of the urban structure, this remarkable system of space management produced a differentiated and yet totally homogeneous type of urban form, where the divisions provoked by isolated public open spaces and an incisive street network were avoided or overcome. Since the adopted circulation system made it possible to select and regulate the desired degree of seclusion within a continuous and extremely dense urban fabric, it was the ideal tool for neutralizing the antagonism between open and closed spaces, public and private zones, and male and female realms. The polarity between opposite qualities, while balanced and resolved within the overall structural pattern, remained the spring of the urban system, producing the pulsations which kept the organism of the city alive.

In his perceptive morphological studies, Johann Wolfgang von Goethe wrote that the main driving forces of growth and metamorphosis in nature are polarity and gradation ("Polarität und Steigerung"), through their mutual interaction. Looking at our analysis of traditional Arab urban form, we

155   **156**

realize that it is precisely the combination of these two forces which bestows life, unity and an "organic" quality on its vernacular urban patterns. It is indeed striking to observe how the polarizing force implied in the nuclear cellular structures (i. e. their articulation by division of space into "included" and "excluded" portions) provides clear separation between neighbouring buildings, while simultaneously exerting a strong contraction at the next structural plane of urban form. The "push-forces" at a lower level are so to speak transformed into "pull-forces" at an upper level, allowing the existing dualities to be absorbed by progressive integration into a higher order. This hierarchy occurs on virtually every plane of the urban structure, from the single room to the house, to the residential cluster, the market compounds, the enclosed street sections and the walled city as a whole. Potentially conflicting units can therefore be placed side by side and integrated into a highly articulate and cohesive overall system of urban form.

155/156 A typical example of "polarity" within the old city centre of Fez: the transition from the compressed street space of the spice suq (nr. 15 of the map on page 144), where all the streams of public life mingle, to the relaxed and contemplative open space of the Attarin Madrasa (nr. 8 on the map).

The result is a breathing and "animated" urban structure, projecting a radiant inner unity which is fundamentally different from the sterile uniformity produced by more mechanical modes of addition or subdivision. It is indicative of the higher (one could even say spiritual) nature of such a type of unity that it is capable of spreading and multiplying itself without ever losing its essential qualites. As it is present in every single "seed" of the complex cellular urban structure, the entire urban fabric down to its smallest particles is so to speak impregnated with the attributes of wholeness and unity. The city turns into a vibrant multi-focal pattern, embracing scores of self-contained sub-centres, which all share the "wholeness" of the overarching system. This structural order translates into a paradoxical physical experience which is characteristic of most traditional Arab cities: one always has the feeling of being at the centre of things, in whatever sub-unit of the composite urban structure it may be.

It can be concluded that the inner unity of the urban fabric is predicated on the capacity to express and articulate different needs in a consistent language of affiliated forms, based on the variation of cellular patterns at different hierarchic planes. The integration of individual components is sustained by multiple structural analogies and by ascending correspondences within the deep structure of the city. Thus the urban fabric gains access to a symbolic dimension, since small elements can reflect the structure of the whole in the same way that the human microcosm can mirror the universe. It is this hidden vertical reference system which gives depth and unity to the urban fabric, instills spatial quality to its individual components, and grounds man in his environment by inscribing his temporal urban existence within a timeless order.

PART II
The Clash between Tradition and Modernity

The Impact of Western Models on the Contemporary Development Patterns of Historic Muslim Cities

"The traditional vision of things is above all 'static' and 'vertical'. It is static because it refers to constant and universal qualities, and it is vertical in the sense that it attaches the lower to the higher, the ephemeral to the imperishable. The modern vision, on the contrary, is fundamentally 'dynamic' and 'horizontal'; it is not the symbolism of things that interests it, but the material and historical connections." (Titus Burckhardt, "Cosmologia Perennis")

Having dwelt on some of the key features of traditional Muslim cities, we shall now address the factors of change to which they were exposed during the past century. It would be hard to enter this topic without touching upon the forces and processes which generated the modern Western cities of the Industrial Age, since they had a delayed but massive impact on the Islamic world. In the West, industrialization reached a first climax in the second half of the 19th century, after a long incubation period. The transmission of this new civilization to other parts of the world was filtered through Europe's colonial development activities. As colonialism in its conventional form came to an end after World War II, the impact of Western technology, fuelled by economic factors, demographic growth and political ambitions, grew even stronger in the fifties and sixties of this century, at a time when politically independent national governments in the various regions of the Islamic community were established. Nationalism, a by-product of the 19th-century political revolutions in Europe, penetrated into the former colonies together with many other ideological, economic and technological influences, and the retardation effect could not but increase the explosive force of the shock, generating a turmoil of rushed and often ill-controlled development.

To shed more light on the origins and consequences of this complex cultural conflict, and particularly its urban aspects, it will be useful to first point out the factors governing the rapid development of secular industrial societies and corresponding political systems in Europe, as well as the rupture they caused within Western cultural traditions, and then to describe the penetration of modern Western concepts, ideologies and urban models into the Islamic world from the imperialist colonial expansion of the late 19th century up to the present time. Following this, we will trace an outline of typical contemporary problems affecting historic cities in the Islamic world.

Europe's Break with Tradition and
the Growth of a New Industrial Society

Looking at European cultural history in a wider context, one discovers that its more recent development, starting with the "Renaissance", continuing with the "Enlightenment" and culminating with the 19th/20th century, displays unique features which are unparalleled in the whole history of mankind. The singularity of this development process is due to the concept of secularization, i. e. the increasing separation of human existence from its natural roots or, spiritually speaking, from its divine origins and the corresponding deeper reality. Man no longer saw himself as an integral and responsible part of a sacred universe but as the free master of his own destiny. On the one hand, this new attitude facilitated "progress" as a way of gaining better control over an isolated material dimension of development. On the other hand, it ceated a serious legitimacy gap, since the references to the permanent sources of truth were lost. This explains the aggressive expansion of modern Western civilisation during this period, as well as the absence of shared higher standards and principles, which became manifest in the repeated social and political upheavals of modern Europe.

During the Middle Ages – the period of European history best comparable with Muslim and other traditional cultures – wordly leadership and spiritual authority, represented by the kings and the nobility on the one hand, and the Pope and the Church on the other hand, were kept in a state of fragile balance. In fact, the duality of material and spiritual realms was inherent in the Christian religion from the beginning, in contrast to the Islamic way of thinking which always stressed the integration and interaction of both levels within a complete social order. To some extent, the Christian dichotomy was overcome by mutual interaction, since medieval kings originally had to be invested and sanctioned by the religious authority, while the Church often enough intervened in worldly matters. However, the precarious union of opposites broke apart with the rise of the Renaissance, when political leadership became emancipated from spiritual objectives and constraints, as did arts and science, while the Church gradually retrogressed to a separate religious institution administering the believers' welfare but exerting less and less real influence on social and cultural matters.

The power released by this cultural disintegration process was similar to that of a chemical fission and ignited most of the dynamic processes of modern Western civilization: suddenly man saw himself as the sovereign ruler of the universe and discovered the physical world as a seemingly inexhaustible and purely "material" resource for unrestricted exploitation. Although already implied by the Renaissance, this new trend did not emerge to full power until the 19th century, when science was productively linked with technology and industrialization. The basis for the ultimate "explosion" was the French Revolution in 1789, when the last remnants of the aristocracy, by now devoid of its original function and legitimation, were swept away together with the authority of the Church, which had lost credibility in its perverted form of a privileged religious bureaucracy. This final stroke of secularization was the ground on which all the major intellectual, social, political, economic, scientific and technological changes of the following century took place, giving birth to modern Western civilization and the related physical and non-physical structures.

As a result of these events, the human intellect was converted into a rational instrument for increasing man's control over the earth. Engineering and the natural sciences started playing a dominant role and the rationalized intellect eventually became a tool for creating an independent man-made world, using the elements of the divine creation as raw material for its own limited objectives. The subsequent industrialization processes, based on the discovery of new energy resources, the practical application of electricity, and the invention of new modes of transportation (such as railways, steamboats, motor cars, airplanes), eventually resulted in a radical transformation of European civilization. The changes generated in a few decades by industrial means exceeded the changes that had taken place before over centuries. Far from being mere technical innovations, they shook the whole set of social and cultural parameters, and the vacuum created by secularization, combined with a frantic departure towards new horizons where everything seemed possible and feasible, created a climate of permanent revolution, as it were.

The new intellectual and physical mobility indeed stirred speculation in every sense: ideologically, in terms of alternating scientific or philosophical systems and political theories which struggled for power among themselves and often ended up being more dogmatic than the religion they had replaced – without ever gaining access to the sources of authentic and universal truth; materially, in terms of worldwide commercial transactions based on the newly discovered monetary wealth, which was to become the dominant measure of human achievement. In fact, the disrupted connections between man and earth, as those between man and heaven, now permitted everything to be converted into quantitative values. The resources of the soil, accessible by potent methods of exploitation and processed in large industrial plants, allowed the invested capital to work and to accumulate, producing previously unknown concentrations of economic power. Modern means of transportation encouraged the independent setting up of manufacturing facilities, fostered demographic and economic segregation, created urban development pressures and fuelled real-estate speculation.

The resulting capitalist economy privileged the newly established bourgeoisie which in a sense occupied the vacuum left by the former nobility, while a new working class, the proletariat, mainly uprooted rural immigrants flocking to the booming urban centres, served as a convenient human resource for sustaining industrialization. In this major socio-economic transformation process, century-old patterns of local identity and human solidarity were loosened and destroyed. Eventually, centralized government structures had to make up for the disrupted social network, since society was progressively atomized and the old structures of mutual responsibility and self-regulating social units lost their former strength. This in turn led to the rise of modern state bureaucracy, which had to perform a social function as well, by preventing excessive disparities in the distribution of wealth. The increase of state control often went hand in hand with new nationalist tendencies, and it is not by chance that most European nations sharpened their identity, their ambitions and their conflicts during this period.

The demographic concentration, combined with the accumulation of capital and with new industrial technologies, changed the aspect of the large European cities, which grew from a few hundred thousand to several million inhabitants within a few decades. At the same time, conventional war and defence techniques had become obsolete, which led to the elimination of the walled-city concept and initiated a new type of urban sprawl, resulting in the development of large new suburbs. The social cleavage between the bourgeoisie and the proletariat was expressed in distinct land-use patterns: the lower classes and rural immigrants occupied the declining quarters of the medieval city centres or settled in the industrial suburbs, where factories, industries and poor housing facilities mingled in a haphazard and disorganized way, sometimes producing even worse environmental conditions than in the crowded historic centres. Meanwhile, the upper classes started major urban redevelopment projects, appropriating and adapting the prestigious architectural language of the "ancien régime" for their privileged areas.

The transformation of Paris by Baron Haussmann between 1853–69 is probably the best example of this process: the concept of the boulevard, which was to become the major feature of European town planning in the second half of the 19th century, was inspired by the axial layouts used in the earlier palaces, gardens and residential cities of absolutist monarchs, and clearly exploited their architectural symbolism for representational purposes and affirmation of class status. In many European cities the new boulevards filled the now useless moats of the medieval city, but often they were cut into the historic fabric, thus generating a polarization between the new upper class streetfronts and the districts to the rear. These were left to themselves

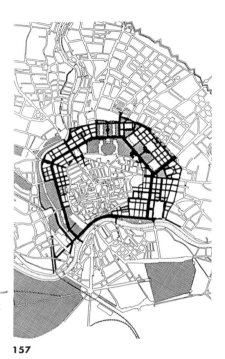

157

157 Plan of Vienna, showing the medieval inner city, as well as the Ringstrasse (constructed on top of the former moats) and the adjacent network of representative new streets (in black).

158

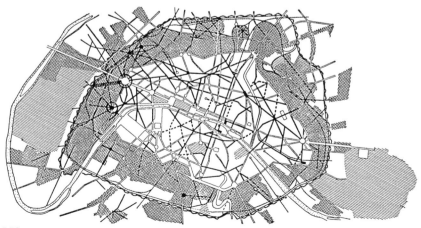

159

158 Demolition in the inner city of Paris during the construction of a boulevard, around 1860 (contemporary engraving).

159 Plan of the transformation of Paris through Haussmann's "Grands Travaux".

160

and gradually turned into slums, in expectation of forthcoming redevelopment projects. An additional and not unimportant function of the large boulevards was to allow for easier military containment and governmental control in case of social unrest in the proletarian districts.

Apart from the boulevard, the 19th-century European bourgeoisie gave birth to a number of new representative building types, such as railway stations, department stores, museums and exhibition halls, which complemented the traditional public buildings such as the church and the town hall. The architectural language used in these new typologies was highly eclectic, drawing from the classical repository of previous periods and accommodating different vocabularies in rather superficial ways. Revivals of previous historic styles, from Gothic to Renaissance and Baroque, were staged in much the same way as fashion trends – an attitude which was later to provoke a strong reaction by the Modern Movement.

At the end of the 19th century, most of the important European cities had put in place this new urban framework based on boulevards, representative public buildings and a series of focal squares, celebrating the intersection of major boulevards. This system of public spaces became the pride of the

160 View of the Vienna Ringstrasse in 1873 (contemporary engraving).

161 Hall of Vienna's railway station in 1865.

162 Square in front of the Zurich railway station (around 1880). The gate faces a new boulevard (Bahnhofstrasse) constructed on the former moat of the old city.

new bourgeoisie. Yet, impressive as it was, it meant a loss of urban quality when compared to the central urban squares of medieval cities which, although more modest, carried out a much more comprehensive and integrated civic function. With the advent of the motor car in the 20th century, the boulevards, originally intended for the use of horse carriages, for walking, promenading and for leisure, were increasingly taken over by the single function of vehicular transportation, whose impact multiplied with the further advance of technology. While the problems of social and economic disparities were gradually mitigated as a result of political struggles, the boulevard now became an indispensable functional element of modern cities. Increasingly, town planning was identified with transportation planning and parallel clearing of decayed historic quarters. Regular grids of roads with combined infrastructure and sanitation networks became the new structuring elements of urban form. The most telling examples are the checkerboard plans of the new American cities, such as Manhattan or Chicago, where few or no pre-existing historic structures had to be taken into account.

However, increasing mobility and growing emphasis on centralized urban functions resulted in extremely crowded modern city centres, which lowered the quality of the residential districts; hence the subsequent movement towards more salubrious "garden cities" outside the city centre, as promoted since the early 20th century. Decanting the crowded city centres became a necessity, and the transportation-driven arguments which had earlier

161

162

been advocated for creating heavy urban concentrations were now used to implement the idea of vast new residential districts on the periphery of the city, or new dormitory-type cities at some distance from the historic centres. This in turn led to the concept of segregating urban functions and allocating specific spaces to housing, industry, leisure and recreation, the only link between them being the transportation system. The result was a dramatic loss of social and physical coherence of urban form.

The Impact of European Colonialism on the Islamic World

Europe and the Islamic world have a long history of encounters, exchanges and conflicts, which saw the two opponents in changing roles. During the early Middle Ages, Europe had much to learn from the highly developed Islamic culture, and it has often been said that the Renaissance would have been impossible had the Arabs not served as agents for the transmission of the Greek and Roman heritage as far as literature, philosophy and sciences were concerned. The age of the crusaders, apart from generating the first military and religious conflict of interests, was also an important period of cross-cultural communication, and at that time the Middle East was definitely more on the giving than on the taking side. It is no exaggeration to say that it was the Islamic world which provided Medieval Europe with more refined patterns of civilization. Commercially, Europe depended on the Middle East to provide it with many rare and desirable luxury goods such as spices, fancy textiles, silk, rugs, jewels etc., some of them originating in the Far East, but transiting through Muslim countries.

During the Renaissance, Europe started drifting towards different horizons of cultural development and discovered other spheres of interest, leaving Jerusalem and the Muslim world to their own fate. Perhaps the main reason for this change of attention was that the age of discoveries, initiated in 1492 (the very year of the fall of Granada), suddenly gave Europe the possibility of bypassing the core regions of Islam. Its energies were thus diverted to other goals, all the more so as the search for the sea route to India had (by mistake, as it were) resulted in the discovery and colonization of the Americas. Likewise, the resources of black Africa offered further fields of activity for European conquerors. At that time, i. e. between 1500 and 1800, the Islamic expansion had already come to a halt and the former empire of the caliphs had disintegrated into a number of regional dominions and sultanates, of which only the Ottoman Empire (the last attempt to resurrect the Islamic Caliphate) still exerted some pressure on the eastern borders of Europe during the 17th century.

The period of apparent mutual disinterest came to a rapid end with the awakening of European imperialism in the 19th century. Clearly, the idea was not a new invention, since it had already governed the age of discoveries in the 16th/17th century. But only now, in the age of industrialization, did Europe develop the tools and leverage needed to impose its technical supremacy and to sustain its colonial expansion deep into other continents, beyond the easily accessible coastlines. Missionary zeal for the "civilized" European way of life (rather than for Christianity), curiosity for exotic folklore, obvious commercial interests and hunger for resources and new markets went hand in hand to produce a second and much more violent wave of colonialism, with the result that by 1920 large parts of the globe were in European hands.

With the exception of India, which had already fallen under British rule in 1764, most of the Islamic world, and particularly the Middle East, managed to escape colonial status during the 19th century. In 1798, Napoleon made an attempt to conquer Egypt and to establish himself as an emperor in the footsteps of Alexander the Great and Caesar, ruling over both West and East. The only lasting result of this expedition was the "Description d'Egypte" composed by the accompanying group of geographers and scientists – a significant mark of Europe's resurgent interest in the Orient, which was followed by many other orientalist writings, engravings, paintings and even operas. Politically, the expedition was a failure, as much as Napoleon's Russian expedition. Thirty years later, however, France succeeded in the conquest of Algeria, which became the first European colony on the Islamic shores of the Mediterranean.

One of the most important factors explaining the resistance of the Islamic world to European colonization during the 19th century was the survival and relative strength of the Ottoman Empire, the heir of Byzantium. Yet the Ottoman Empire played an ambivalent role. On the one hand, it served as the last military bastion of Islam against the West and was proud of continuing – at least nominally – the tradition of the Caliphate. On the other hand, it acted as a filter and transmitter of Western influences which penetrated into Muslim countries via Istanbul. This process had already occurred in the 15th century, after the conquest of Constantinople, and resulted in the innovative assimilation of Byzantine elements into the new Ottoman architecture, as witnessed by the unique skyline of Istanbul. Now it was to happen again in the 19th century, but under less fortunate circumstances which led to a creeping "Westernization" of Ottoman architecture, without much local creativity going into the transformation process.

Decorative features borrowed from Classical and Rococo architecture were indeed abundant during the late-Ottoman period in Istanbul, and

163

163 Orientalist painting showing a carpet dealer in a traditional house (late 19th century).

164
165

Western-type apartment houses started lining the streetfronts of new districts. French and Italian architects were commissioned to do important architectural and urban projects. To a somewhat lesser degree, this trend also influenced provincial capitals such as Aleppo, Damascus or Baghdad, where the Ottoman administration established new Western-type municipalities around 1870 to supervise urban development. The new Rasheed Street in Baghdad, a shopping street with lateral arcades of Mediterranean character constructed before the first World War, is reminiscent of European colonial architecture. So is the small boulevard north of the walled city of Aleppo, built around 1900 after filling in the former moat. In both cases, the new street elevations screen the dissected urban fabric, but their modest building height (usually three floors) does not exceed that of the traditional houses behind them.

In the provincial capitals, the Turks also built new suburbs for their governmental employees, which strangely resembled the residential quarters of colonial Western administrations. In some places, such as Baghdad, the medieval city walls were demolished in an attempt to allow for easier urban extensions, in a way not unsimilar to European examples, but under much less virulent development pressures. Also, a number of important railway connections were built to connect the provinces with the capital and to ease the pilgrimage. The new railway stations in Istanbul, Damascus and Medina combine Western architectural models with orientalizing details and again provide interesting parallels to Western colonial architecture, consonant with contemporary revival trends in Europe.

However, the most interesting transformation of an Islamic city along Western lines in the 19th century happened in Cairo, at that time the second-ranking city within the Ottoman Empire. After the revolution under Muhammad Ali, Egypt had established relative independence from Istanbul under

164 Streetfront of the late-Ottoman Rasheed Street in Baghdad.

165 Streetfront of Moat Street in Aleppo.

166

the dynasty of the Khedives, before it was eventually forced to acknowledge British supremacy. Muhammad Ali and his successors, the Khedives, began the modernization of Egypt, which led to the construction of the Suez Canal and the transformation of Cairo. The champion of these planning projects was the Khedive Ismail, who visited Paris in 1867 on the occasion of the preparations for the World Fair. There he became acquainted with Haussmann's new schemes for the French capital which had reached their climax by that time. The "Grands Travaux" impressed him so deeply that he decided to adopt them for his own new capital. This was the origin of the "European" part of Cairo, to be built southwest of the old Fatimid and Mamluk city on vacant land which had been gained by the progressive move of

166 Planned new urban development in Cairo under the Khedive Ismail, around 1870 (after J. Abu-Lughod). Hatching marks the old Fatimid nucleus.

the Nile riverbank to the west, away from the existing city. The Khedive's new town plan was a small-scale replica of Haussmann's schemes, with several axes extending from the new city centre into the old city and thus cutting through the historic urban fabric. Eventually, only one of the planned axes through the old city – the Muhammad Ali Avenue linking the Esbekiya Square with the Citadel – was actually built.

It is interesting to note that a contemporary European critic (Arthur Rhoné) commented rather sarcastically on this urban redevelopment scheme, especially concerning its impact on the historic fabric. His reaction may have been, at least in part, based on romantic conceptions, yet it recognized the dangers of a technocratic instant modernization, which does not consider the physical, social and economic impacts of its schemes. In this sense, the modernization of Cairo anticipated a number of problems which were to become virulent all over the Islamic world by the middle of the twentieth century. Not the least of these problems was the growing social rift between a new local bourgeoisie choosing to live in a Westernized environment and the population accumulating in (or confined to) the old city, which was suddenly stigmatized with backwardness and a lower social status.

The mediating role of the Ottoman Empire in the 19th century characterizes the first stage of the penetration of Arab countries by modern Western influences. The second (and more dramatic) stage followed after the disintegration of the Ottoman Empire in World War I and its reduction to a national state, confined to the Anatolian Peninsula. This process not only provoked the rise of modern Turkey, modelled on Western examples by the secular movement of Kamal Atatürk, but also opened up the Middle East to the political interference of Western nations. During World War I, the Arab tribes of the Najd, who had resented the Turkish dominance imposed on the Arabs, cooperated with the allied European powers in abolishing Ottoman rule in the Arabian peninsula and eventually succeeded in forming the independent Kingdom of Saudi Arabia (1926), after unification with the Hejjaz. In the other areas of the former Ottoman Empire, and in North Africa as well, the victorious European powers, i. e. France and England, resorted to a distribution of the remaining booty according to their national interests. Syria, Lebanon and the whole Maghreb, including Tunisia and Morocco, became French protectorates, while Iraq, Palestine and Egypt fell under British rule. For one last time, the European powers were in a position to impose their "divide et impera".

The political subdivisions which resulted from the colonial power game were rather arbitrary and had little or nothing to do with geographical, social and cultural realities. Yet they foreshadowed the borders of future political entities and therefore already contained the seeds of later conflicts which were to erupt with the advent of nationalistic ideologies passed from the West to the Islamic world. Thus the long cherished Islamic concept of the "umma" was forever relegated to the realm of wishful thinking as the political map of the Arab world was drawn by the European powers during the last decades of the colonial age. Today, the problems induced by this subdivision are appearing in their full dimension, as exemplified by the presumptuous and short-sighted "solution" of the Palestine issue by the colonial powers.

The third phase of Westernization started after World War II, when European nations, weakened by their internal struggles, had to abandon all imperial aspirations and yield their position to the newly emerged Western superpower, the United States of America, which had then entered the theatre of world politics. Imperialism now took a more subtle guise, based on worldwide economic, financial and technological dominance rather than political and military rule, and yet increased in actual strength.

This turning point in European history coincided with massive political struggles for independence everywhere in the Third World. Around the 1950's, most countries of the Arab and Islamic world managed to establish their political autonomy, either through revolutionary actions or through peaceful agreements. The problem was, however, that political freedom did not automatically bring about cultural independence. In fact it is a significant paradox that the last (and most violent) phase of Westernization should have started with the establishment of independent national governments. The main reason for this was the previous conditioning of Muslim societies by Western models during the colonial period: governance structures and procedures were already as much in place as the artificially created national borders. The fact that the foreign officials and civil servants were mostly substituted by indigenous ones, without questioning the system itself, means that more fundamental problems were eluded. The question of what revisions, in both philosophical and practical terms, would be required in order to adapt imported Western tools and methods to local needs, potentials and constraints thus never became an explicit issue.

Eventually, the new "independent" nations were more or less forced to continue their pre-established economic patterns, which had become dependent on international trade structures and were geared to the application of modern Western technology. Rapid industrialization may not have been the only alternative at the time, but it was hard to escape its pressures, considering the superior living standards of Europe: even more so, since Western education unquestionably became the prerequisite of success and prestige for the new local elites, which were transformed into internal agents of

Westernization. The cleavage between "West and East" was thus introduced into the very social body of new Muslim nations, setting the seeds of a growing cultural dependence. It may be exaggerated to state that Western ideologies could only fully succeed after Europe's political retirement from the Third World. But it is undeniable that the mentality which drove colonialism suddenly spread to an extent which would not have been possible before, when it was still curbed by political resistance.

The unfiltered adoption of alien development modes in the former colonies carried the risk that the new leaders would misuse Western tools and instruments for securing their own privileges, rather than for the sake of a sound evolution of the community as a whole. A ruling class – unless inspired by higher ideals – will hardly be inclined to question the soundness and appropriateness of an imported civilization when its tools can be used as an instrument of social and political control. The colonial "divide et impera", once applied within a nation's own ethnic group, started producing a dangerous rift between a new "elite" and the "masses". This internalized dichotomy was bound to weaken the precious solidarity bonds of traditional societies and hamper the potential emergence of new concepts of civic sense and responsibilities, on which a sound social and political evolution must depend. Moreover, it provided a breeding ground for ideological controversies between traditionalists and modernists, which tended to become increasingly dogmatic and unproductive, as neither "fundamentalist" or "technocrat" ideas are firmly rooted in social and cultural realities.

Contemporary Conservation and Development Problems in Historic Cities

The dynamics of the socio-economic changes produced by the Industrial Age found their physical expression in the radical transformation of existing historic cities. Whereas during previous centuries, changes in the architectural fabric had always occurred as part of a natural evolutionary process, the new development was of a different nature: first, because of the unprecedented speed and the massive scale of new construction; and, second, because the underlying philosophy no longer implied a holistic concept which could bring together spiritual, social and material concerns within a meaningful cultural framework.

The result of this disruption was the vanishing of a concentrated, all-inclusive sense of presence from man's daily life. Suddenly, an everwidening chasm between past and future opened up, which pulled the present apart and emptied it of many of its essential qualities. The past became a matter of history, science, curiosity or romantic nostalgia, but was considered a defunct state of being. The future became the target of new hopes and projections, with utopian ideas of progress succeeding each other but never reaching the elusive goal. Concordant with these new mental patterns, the built environment was subject to the polarization between, on the one hand, conservation of historic elements, and, on the other hand, aggressive technology-driven modernization and development. Although highly antagonistic, both attitudes actually condition each other, being different expressions of the same fact: the broken unity of human vision and action, translated into the realm of man's physical world.

It is interesting to note that the earliest attempt to introduce an organized and comprehensive conservation effort in Europe dates from 1798, when the first committee for the preservation of national monuments in France was formed as a reaction to the deliberate destruction of castles and churches during and after the French Revolution. This committee, which was to be followed by similar institutions in other European countries, recognized the salvaging of the architectural heritage of past periods as a new task to be fulfilled by the government, in order to safeguard and to manage artistic, historic and educational values. While this was certainly a positive attempt, without which Europe would probably have lost its "cultural memory" within one or two centuries, it was also an implicit recognition that this heritage was now considered as something no longer directly related to the daily life of society, making it a "museal" patrimony. The rising antiquarian interest, which expressed itself in the conservation movement, was also instrumental in the development of the 19th-century revival styles and, more generally, in the genesis of the new historic sciences and the incipient exploration of foreign, i. e. non-European civilizations. Orientalism was one of these branches, in the sciences as well as in the arts, and satisfied the hunger for the exotic and the picturesque.

Since the 19th century, the conservation movement in Europe passed through various evolutionary stages: from the inventive "restoration" of Violet-le-Duc to more careful, discreet and scientific preservation techniques, and from the conservation of isolated monuments to the consideration of the physical context, culminating in the idea of protected historic districts, which began to be implemented towards the mid-20th century and gained increasing momentum during the seventies and eighties. Fighting against modern redevelopment, the conservation movement succeeded in salvaging and enhancing much of the physical shells of European historic cities, which might otherwise have disappeared. It thus greatly contributed to maintaining the cultural identity of historic cities such as London, Paris or Rome (not to speak of countless cities and villages of smaller size; and interestingly, the image of these large metropolises, in spite of extensive new development, is still identified with their historic core. Two centuries of modern construction have not succeeded in producing architectural, urban and environmental qualities which match those of pre-industrial cities.

It is quite telling that during the past decades historic areas in Europe, apart from serving as prime attractions for foreign visitors, have become subject to increasing gentrification. Artists were the first to rediscover the intrinsic qualities of historic districts, perhaps more for the sake of escaping a totally rationalized modern environment than out of romanticism. They were soon followed and often replaced by the liberal professions (including modern architects searching for an attractive home) and by businessmen. Both gentrification and tourism, while contributing to the economic sustainability of historic centres, also posed a threat to their integrity, due to excessive commercialization and the inevitable loss of authenticity.

Turning our attention from European historic cities to their counterparts in the Muslim world, we can perceive certain similarities (mainly due to the common contrast between pre-industrial historic fabrics and modern ways of town planning), but also fundamental differences. These can be attributed to the vigour of vernacular local cultures, the specific structural composition of Muslim historic cities and finally to the delayed and more abrupt impact of industrialization. Changes which took place in Europe over two centuries caught surviving traditional cultures completely unprepared. The attempt to absorb them within a few decades explains the violence of the clash, as well as the ambivalent conditions prevailing in many contemporary historic cities of the Muslim world.

The strength of many Arab cities resides in the fact that the local communities now residing in the historic city centres, although poverty-stricken, "decapitated" by the exodus of the former bourgeoisie and exposed to the pressures of rural immigration, maintain a strong sense of social solidarity and participation, based on the affinity with the traditional cultural paradigm which had moulded the old urban structures. The weakness, however, lies in the split cultural identity and the uncritical Westernization of the new ruling class, which favours institutional structures, administration procedures, investment priorities and technical approaches which are detrimental to the rehabilitation of the historic fabric or even accelerate decay and destruction.

Paradoxical as it may appear, it is the richest Arab countries which have lost most of their traditional urban heritage, since the abundance of financial resources and the ensuing development pressures have led to the wholesale demolition of most of their historic centres in a short period of time. Other countries and cities struggle with poverty and suffer from the inability to maintain their traditional housing stock and to provide the most basic public facilities, but a fair part of their urban heritage still is in a position to be rescued. Here, however, it often happens that the few available funds are channeled to "prestige projects" in the capital cities and investments in the modern parts of the town. In both instances, the rehabilitation of historic city centres is not seen as a priority, either because of its "backward" image, or because of the lack of technical and institutional capability to get to grips with the complex mix of physical and social rehabilitation problems.

Whether the issue is wholesale demolition or rampant neglect, the common problem is that most decision makers identify themselves with a development process that is alien to the cultural traditions of their own societies, and that they are rarely provided with technical approaches and institutional tools which could demonstrate the viability of alternative, more appropriate models of intervention. In this context, the physical compactness of the old urban structures is both a blessing and a risk: on the one hand, it opposes considerable physical resistance to conventional urbanistic interventions; on the other hand, it may create the impression that only radical measures can succeed in rejuvenating the historic city.

The physical development of most historic Muslim cities over the past 50–80 years was, at least initially, predicated on the approach chosen by the colonial powers in setting out their "new towns". The decisions varied according to topographic preconditions, the geopolitical importance of the site and the cultural choices of the administrators responsible and their architects. Basically, the possible range of urban interventions was defined by two extremes. One consisted in superimposing the new city on the old historic fabric by cutting out large new roads and sites for major public buildings – an approach which entailed the progressive demolition of historic urban structures by the expanding new facilities. The other one consisted in setting up completely new colonial cities on virgin land, without seeking any interface with pre-existing urban structures. A median solution pursued by the French colonial administration during the protectorate period in Morocco, Tunisia and Syria was to create twin or parallel cities, allowing them to co-exist at a little distance or side by side. In a way, this preference resumed the previous habit of Muslim rulers of erecting new palace cities adjacent to (and often superseding) existing settlements in the event of important dynastic shifts of power. Fez, Rabat, Marrakesh, Tunis, Aleppo and Damascus are good examples of this urbanization policy.

The case of Fez is especially interesting, because topographic conditions prevented the new city from being planned adjacent to the old one. Following the earlier trend of the former Marinid palace city, it was built upstream, on the plateau dominating the original walled city, and exercised

167

167 Contrasts in the historic city centre of Baghdad: in the foreground a decaying caravanserai, side by side with a modern skyscraper.

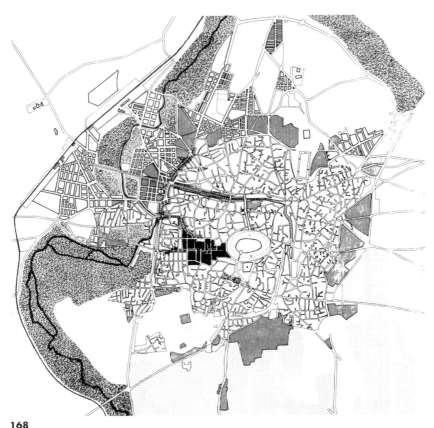

168

control over the vital natural water resources. General Lyautey and his architect Henri Prost constructed the new city around a major avenue pointing
towards the old city, but took care to preserve the integrity of the original
site. This permitted the modern settlement to expand without infringing on
the historic fabric. After the fifties, each of the two cities acquired its own
satellites, the old city in the form of a number of spontaneous (and "illegal")
popular quarters in the vicinity, built by rural immigrants, and the new
city in the form of fashionable new residential quarters spreading into the
countryside. A new middle class district (Aïn Qaddous) was planned on the
hills above the Marinid palace city, bridging the gap between the first two
urban structures.

Aleppo and Damascus are examples of the progressive indentation of
the modern city centre into the old city, caused by the abutting position of
the colonial city. In both cases, there was already a nucleus of an Ottoman
"colonial" city which had been taken over by the French. With the growth
of the modern urban system and the increasing pressure for vehicular acces-

168 Plan of Aleppo in 1930, showing
the former moats of the walled city being
converted into major traffic spines (tramways in dashed lines). Two new roads
converge at the northwestern corner of the
old city, from where the colonial Ottoman
centre, extended by the French colonial
city, started developing. North and east of
the walled city are the historic suburbs,
which have developed spontaneously
since the 15th century.

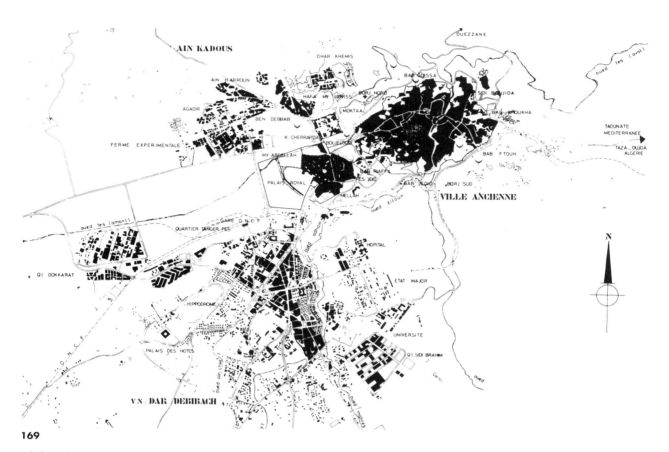

169

sibility, the desire to extend the new traffic spines into the historic core of the old city became irresistible. The Ottoman filling of the moat around the walled city was thus complemented by new roads cutting into the historic fabric. In Aleppo, the ambitious projects of André Gutton (1954) envisaged large traffic channels through the old city centre, "pour mettre en valeur le site de la citadelle", but were never fully implemented.

During the sixties and the early seventies, the French architect and town planner Michel Ecochard designed a system of new thoroughfares through the old city centres of Fez, Damascus and Aleppo. In Fez, the road scheme was based on covering the whole length of the River Boukhrareb, with a lateral branch cutting through the central market district, in order to give vehicular access to the Qairawiyin Mosque and the historic suqs. Only one third of this scheme, covering the southern part of the river, was executed, while the difficult sections cutting through the heart of the old city were first kept on hold and later abandoned (see case study on Fez in Chapter 12). In Damascus and Aleppo, Ecochard proposed reconstituting the orthogonal

169 Map of Fez in 1970, showing the components of the urban system: on top, towards the right, the first nucleus of Fez, founded around 800 AD. Southwest of it, the Marinid palace city from the 14th century, at the bottom the French colonial city, and north of the old medina the district of Aïn Qaddous, built in the fifties.

Roman street grid by undoing the century-old "organic" growth of the Muslim city, with the intention of combining improved car access with a partial archaeological reconstruction of the Roman town plan. Again, this proposal was never fully implemented, because it was difficult to enforce and to finance. It also raised violent reactions from conservationists in the early eighties which persuaded the authorities to shelve the project.

While more difficult to handle than in the medieval cities of Europe, the fine tuning of vehicular access is a key issue for preserving both the viability and the authentic character of historic Muslim cities. On the one hand, poor accessibility (coupled with other factors, such as lacking services, badly maintained facilities and the old town's "backward" image) was the reason which provoked the progressive exodus of the local bourgeoisie from the old city centre into the residential suburbs of the new town. The ensuing social segregation devalued the historic nucleus and paved the way for its conversion into an urban slum area. Overdensification, poor economic conditions, inappropriate industrial activities, lack of commitment and discontinued maintenance of buildings then lead to a rapid dilapidation of the housing stock. Similarly, poor accessibility is a handicap to commercial and administrative functions which are needed to maintain the balance and the viability of the traditional urban system. Although built as pedestrian structures, the suqs have to be supported by a supply system which has to respond to changed means of transportation.

On the other hand, the excessive impact of vehicular traffic, together with induced new development, can blow up the city's physical shell and destroy the qualities inherent in its built form. Privacy of residential units, human scale, physical and social integration, interaction between buildings and enclosed open spaces, linkages between housing, markets and social facilities are essential assets of the historic city, which need to be carefully balanced against the advantages of better vehicular accessibility.

Eventually, the viability of a historic area will depend on how its position, its function and its specific comparative advantages can be defined (and enhanced) within the rapidly growing overall urban system, particularly with respect to the modern districts. While a certain degree of centrality will support the attractiveness of the old centre, reinforce its economic basis and provide incentives for privileged residential use, too high a degree of centrality will burden it with tasks that its architectural fabric cannot absorb if it is to retain its specific character and qualities.

As shown in the following case studies, no simple and universal answers to such problems exist, but the right mix, considering the carrying capacity of the historic fabric, is important. So is the complementarity between the old and the new city centre, with a view to fostering symbiosis rather than

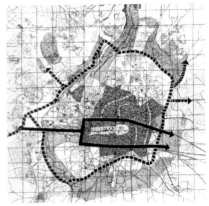

170

170 Master plan scheme for Aleppo by André Gutton (1954), proposing two highways "from the sea to the desert" cutting through the historic fabric.

171 Plan of Damascus in 1968 with the elliptical old city in the centre. South and north of the western corner of the old city, the old suburbs from the 15th–18th century, which have come under heavy pressure from the modern city centre.

172 Master plan for the walled city of Damascus by M. Ecochard (1968), proposing new roads, parking lots and demolition of a number of residential clusters for the creation of public gardens.

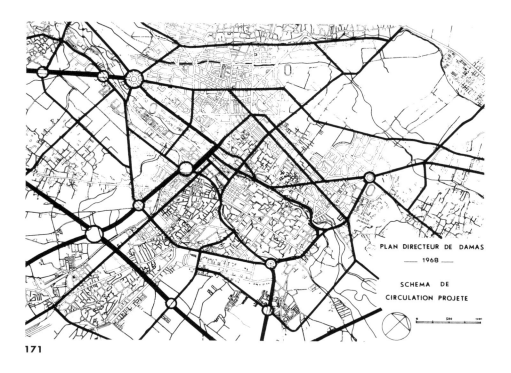

PLAN DIRECTEUR DE DAMAS
—— 1968 ——

SCHEMA   DE
CIRCULATION PROJETE

171

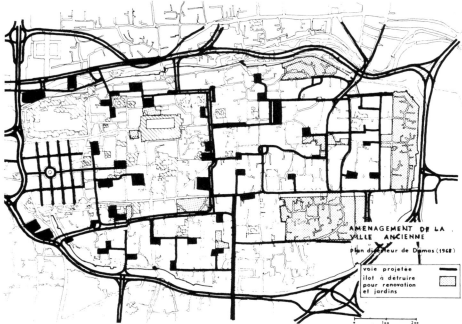

AMENAGEMENT DE LA
VILLE ANCIENNE

Plan directeur de Damas (1968)

voie projetée
ilot à détruire
pour renovation
et jardins

172

competition. This may, moreover, require sensitive planning and adjustment of the modern city centre, to make it compatible with the adjacent historic districts. Transition areas will have to be designed in such a way as to provide functional integration, while ensuring physical differentiation. The traditional physical characteristics of the historic city, such as the walls, the gates and the narrow lanes are the best means of physical protection against the impact of vehicular traffic and should therefore be strengthened, while at the same time introducing attractive new functions and easing access through attractive public transportation.

A related issue which needs to be considered is the upgrading of the historic quarters to levels not identical with, but comparable to modern districts. This implies that governmental investments in infrastructure, social facilities and enhancement of public open spaces, which so far tended to favour the new quarters, have to be redirected towards the old city, in order to ensure a more equitable treatment of both urban entities and to release catalytic effects with regard to private sector rehabilitation efforts. Yet in order to avoid counter-productive investments, careful adaption of such new facilities will be required to match the specific physical constraints of the historic fabric.

The massive rural immigration towards the old cities and their fringe areas – a phenomenon which started building up after political independence in the fifties and recalls similar demographic shifts in late 19th-century Europe – is often seen as a threat to the survival of the architectural heritage. It would, however, be erroneous to completely identify the social processes that occurred a century ago in Europe with those taking place in the Islamic world today. First of all, historic Muslim cities have always retained much closer ties with their rural hinterland and the respective tribal societies. In fact most cities perpetuated semi-rural patterns of living and production inside the walls, and there is a long tradition of rural peoples settling on the periphery and gradually building up new suburbs in continuity with the urban structure "intra muros". As remarked by Ibn Khaldun, the city, although in seeming opposition to nomadic and rural structures, nevertheless depended on them and drew much of its vigour from the regular interchange with them. The urban milieu, in turn, exerted a civilizing and educative influence on the absorbed rural immigrants but did not impose a totally new or alien way of life on them.

Moreover, it would be unrealistic to expect that recently urbanized rural societies can successfully integrate Western industrialization models within a few years. Leaving aside the question of whether this would be at all desirable, it is simply not feasible, as demonstrated by many Third World problems resulting from inappropriate and ill-digested "progress". The recent

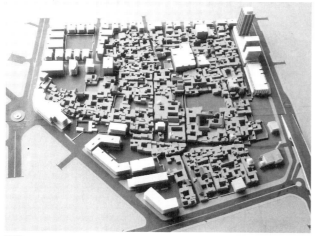

173

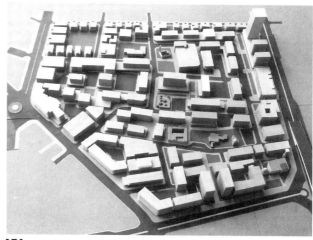

174

demographic explosion has generated a strong need for labour-intensive production methods which are at odds with present Western high-technology concepts. Therefore, alternative and intermediate ways of development have to be sought, which enable the specific resources and capacities of these societies to grow and bear fruit in their own way. Looking into the present spontaneous urbanization modes in the Muslim world, one can sense that such alternative processes are already taking place in a rudimentary form, mostly without any support and often against the will of local governments. The interesting thing is that informal development patterns reproduce, variegate and continue the traditional social structures and the archetypes of built form, which were once instrumental in generating the structure of historic cities. The spontaneous settlements on the periphery of old and new towns, as well as the individualized small enterprises occupying the niches of the modern urban system, give ample proof of this.

Over the past ten to twenty years, there has been a growing awareness that both the informal sector and emerging non-governmental organizations can react much more flexibly to the needs of the population, that they are virtually self-sustaining, and that they can assume tasks which the formal sector and the governmental administrations are unable to carry out – even if they had the financial resources to do so, which is rarely the case. Yet successful partnerships between the two parallel systems have rarely been achieved so far, mainly because conventional government structures failed to mobilize the hidden resources of grass-root initiatives.

Beyond providing substantial social and economic yields, the vernacular mode of development also constitutes a formidable cultural potential,

173/174 A typical modern redevelopment scenario: first, traffic planning cuts the traditional urban fabric into isolated fragments surrounded by vehicular roads; then massive blocks are constructed along the easily accessible and commercially valuable street edges. Eventually, the block structure spreads out, to substitute the asphyxiated and no longer viable residues of the historic fabric (Suq Sarouja district, Damascus).

175 Aerial view of a spontaneous settlement in the quarries around the old city of Fez.

175

capable of regenerating and transforming traditional cultural patterns from within. By operating at grass-root level, it will avoid the risk of superficial transfers or dependency on foreign ideologies and can eventually generate a meaningful new system of cultural references. Such processes may not always favour conservation in the museal sense, but they carry the promise of authentic and homogeneous cultural expressions which can contribute to bridging the gap between tradition and modernity.

Structural Conflicts between Traditional Islamic Concepts and Modern Western Planning Methods

"The reason we are interested in 'traditional' forms of building, dwellings and settlements is that we believe that such achievements met human needs in a more sensitive way than contemporary and/or alien methods do. It is this belief that sends us back to the past, and that sends us to the local and the specific. (...) Our respect for these undeniable achievements, and our dissatisfaction with our current mechanisms for translating human needs into the built environment are the motivations behind our renewed interest in vernacular architecture and settlement plans." (Janet Abu-Lughod, "Disappearing Dichotomies: First World – Third World; Traditional – Modern.")

As a result of the "cultural shock" described in Chapter 8, Muslim societies today are facing an ambiguous situation: in most countries the framework of surviving local traditions provides continuing cultural bonds and a strong sense of community, while at the same time Western institutional, political, economic and educational systems were adopted which, to some extent, contradict vernacular customs and beliefs. This basic conflict, though often concealed or belittled, cannot be ignored. Although it has already been addressed to some extent in chapter 8, a more specific analysis of the divergent assumptions, concepts and standards is needed in order to gain better understanding of the divide which will have to be overcome.

In doing so, we will use the term "Islamic" as a general connotation for a traditional *Weltanschauung* fundamentally different from the secular positivist approach that dominates 19th and 20th century European civilization, but not in the sense of a dogmatic religion. Indeed, Islam is more than an abstract ethical system, as it involves an entire social order and has developed pragmatic rules of conduct which permeate all aspects of daily life. It may be exaggerated to speak of uniform Muslim living patterns, but it is also clear that without concordant (or at least compatible) social practices, Islam is bereft of its cultural shaping forces. Meanwhile, Western science, technology and political systems, although claiming to provide value-free tools for development, definitely imply a philosophical system of their own, based on the belief that they can construct a different and supposedly superior social and political order by exclusively rational means. Yet their values are divorced from deeper existential realities and therefore unable to provide meaningful directions for human conduct, let alone the spiritual dimension which a civilization needs in order to project cultural identity and to sustain sensible modes of human interaction.

The interaction between modernity and tradition has yet to find its appropriate articulation, as neither extremist positions nor false compromises can get to grips with the problems involved. One current attitude is predicated on the violent verbal refusal of Westernization, coupled with de facto introduction of all its technical achievements. Another, less hypocritical attitude relies on the somewhat naïve assumption that Western concepts can be appropriated as such and that they will somehow amalgamate with traditional values. Both eschew the inherent cultural antagonisms, which tend to increase in violence if left to erupt at a later stage.

What is needed instead is a viable reconciliation between Islam as a cultural paradigm and modern civilization as an ideology of progressive technical development. To be successful, any such attempt must first uncover the intents, driving forces and hidden preconceptions of each position. While modern sciences exercised considerable ingenuity in putting traditional cultures and their achievements into a "historic" perspective, they were strangely unaware of the conventions conditioning their own perception. They were thus unable to acknowledge that their empiric approach, in spite of its alleged comprehensiveness, could never fully grasp the observed realities, because it imparted on them the limitations of a purely rational, quantitative outlook. The unshakable conviction of their own superiority led certain Western thinkers to believe that they had invalidated other, much richer and more meaningful cultural systems, while what really happened was simply a shift in interests and perspective, enforced by the power of an aggressive technological civilization.

No real dialogue between the two world views can be established unless this change of paradigms, with all its implications, is clarified and evaluated in the light of overriding cultural objectives. The following paragraphs endeavour to touch upon such issues, in the full knowledge that the very nature of the problems addressed precludes easy and immediate solutions. Before answers can be envisaged, the right questions have to be posed, without being inhibited by the constraints of modern prejudices.

It appears that the key to the required creative assimilation process is the choice of correct values and objectives which must guide the selective appropriation of technical tools, in order to ensure the consistent interaction between ethical principles and daily practice – a hallmark of Muslim civilization. The increasing awareness of the moral crisis in modern sciences and technologies, combined with acknowledgement of the evolutionary potential of local traditions, may favour the growth of a new synthesis which could make better use of the scientific, technical and architectural tools available today.

The Problem of the Modern Movement

At this point it seems appropriate to consider the origins and objectives of the Modern Movement and to evaluate them from a more disillusioned "post-modern" point of view, accepting that Modernism has now become history itself and that its somewhat utopian promise of achieving total welfare for the whole of humanity is far from being accomplished, even in the modern Western context. Founded in the twenties and thirties by the generation of Loos, Gropius, Mies van der Rohe, Le Corbusier, Hilbersheimer and others, the Modern Movement was a reaction against both social injustice and the academic style of 19th-century Europe, which had attempted to camouflage the new building typologies of the industrial age by an arbitrary revival of historic styles. This mimicry of bygone architectural expressions lacked truth and relevance, as it was no longer supported by a corresponding cultural reality. However, the Modern Movement threw out the baby with the bath water, so to speak, by rejecting the possibility of architectural forms expressing cultural identities. In its urge to conform with the Industrial Revolution, it became obsessed with functionalism and rational efficiency, which were to become its main articles of faith.

Although well-intentioned in its concern for health, safety and welfare, the alleged "humanism" of the Modern Movement was distorted by its ideological prejudices, which neglected both spiritual and social realities and therefore provided an excellent breeding ground for utopian thinking. It ignored the fact that man has vital needs which transcend the material plane and that people may be unable (or unwilling) to identify with an artificial physical environment dominated by rational criteria. It also made abstraction of man's biologically conditioned structures of mind and behaviour which were certainly not substituted by the Industrial Revolution.

One could indeed argue that the Modern Movement, though in different ways, was as "academic" as the 19th-century architecture it had set out to overcome. Most of its champions, in spite of their genuine social commitment, worked in the ivory tower of their rational dreams. The Brave New World they intended to construct was confined to abstract three-dimensional schemes that had a certain aesthetic quality but lacked deeper understanding of given cultural, social and environmental realities. The overriding concern seemed to be that architecture should fit the impending total mechanization of urban life. The alienation and loss of identity such plans and buildings would produce did not occur to their authors – yet it was anticipated by visionary contemporary writers, such as Franz Kafka, who expressed the absurdity of an inhuman universe governed by abstraction and technocratic control.

The mishap of the functionalist utopia of the Modern Movement was that it did not remain in the realm of dreams but was to dramatically change the character of cities all over the world, hand in hand with the progress of industrialization and the related economic and financial mechanisms. Geared to expeditious efficiency and helped by its abstract, seemingly neutral and easily reproducible character, it eventually became the suitable instrument for large-scale urban redevelopment driven by capitalist structures, free enterprise, and land speculation. Its massive and worldwide spread, however, was only to come after an initial retardation period caused by the depression and World War II. Megalomanic schemes such as Le Corbusier's "Plan Voisin" (1925), which would have wiped out a large portion of historic Paris in one strike, fortunately remained on paper, but the concept of the "Radiant City" was to have its impact after the Second World War.

The implementation of the Modern Movement's ideas proceeded via North America, where leading members of the Bauhaus had found a new and receptive base of operation after their emigration from Germany. A country unhampered by old cultural traditions, the United States was to provide the ideal platform for these concepts. Here, urban redevelopment schemes could easily be applied to the urban centres, supported by the pre-existing grid structure of many American cities and the already accepted idea of high-rise development. With the spread of the "American way of life" after the end of the war, the Modern Movement was re-imported to Europe, where the bombing of historic cities offered an extraordinary opportunity for wholesale redevelopment. The movement also became instrumental in promoting the "New Town" concept and had its decisive impact in the decades from 1950–1980. During that period, it also began to be exported to developing countries, where it continues to boom as a ubiquitous "International Style".

One of the major shortcomings of the Modern Movement was its disdain for the social, cultural and physical context, as expressed in its rejection of historically grown urban structures. Whether in Europe or in the Third World, the indiscriminate implementation of its town planning principles always resulted in the partial or complete destruction of traditional urban form. In some cases important monuments were kept, but they were stripped of their urban context. Wholesale demolition prevailed over conservation, repair and careful renewal. Since the Modern Movement saw architecture as being completely detached from its cultural and social matrix, it did not

176

176 Engraving from the "Caprichos" by Francisco de Goya: "El sueño de la razon produce monstruos" (The dream of reason produces monsters).

consider the dangers of the simultaneous disintegration of the underlying social network which had been instrumental in producing, nurturing and maintaining the growth and the evolution of historic cities.

It took the physical evidence – and incidentally the decay or the demolition of a number of prominent development schemes – until the fallacies of the Modern Movement and its prolific commercial offshoots began to be recognized. While the formal approach to modern architecture is now changing, the ideological debate is still open and has been enlarged in scope by a stronger interaction with the environmental sciences. Recent trends in architectural thought and practice have attempted to reinterpret the pre-industrial and the classical traditions of urban form in Europe, as exemplified by the works of Christopher Alexander, L. and R. Krier and others. Whether the "post-modern" reaction will bring a solution to the crisis in modern architecture (which is one of meaning more than one of technical issues) is an open question. But the new movement's greater sensitivity to complex cultural issues, historical continuity and the importance of regional traditions, as well as its renunciation of earlier claims to provide the ultimate solution to man's universal problems, certainly make it appear less aggressive than its predecessor.

Meanwhile, in many Third World countries the Modern Movement continues to serve as an unquestioned sign of progress, no matter how illusory or inappropriate the underlying concept of development may be. To Western observers who are witnessing the collapse of the modern utopia, it must seem puzzling that obsolete Western ideologies should exert such an influence in areas which can muster a strong cultural background of their own. This is even more surprising, considering that a new generation of Western architects is now showing a growing interest in the timeless values of vernacular architecture, sometimes to the point of acknowledging them as a resource for reforming current Western planning methods. Yet many decision-makers in Muslim countries still take for granted the "superiority" of the foreign paradigm and neglect to question both the validity of the imported principles and the alleged obsolescence of their own traditional urban heritage.

During recent years, large-scale development projects have been exported to many Arab countries, where they were implemented as complete "packages" – without recognizing the fact that the physical forms of these projects have grown out of an alien ideological matrix and imply different codes of behaviour and different environmental conditions. Basic facilities in terms of housing, transportation, schools or public buildings were not re-assessed in the light of the traditional patterns and local customs, but simply identified with the physical structures these needs and facilities have assumed in the West. Many imported structures, from high-rise buildings to over-dimensioned transportation schemes, may not have been chosen for their supposed functional advantages but merely for the prestige these icons of modernity seemed to convey. Yet much of the new hardware is far from being functionally and culturally appropriate (or even necessary), and a closer analysis may often reveal that its side-effects, which had not been reckoned with, outweigh the anticipated positive factors. As a result of such development processes, many traditional urban structures have been left to decay or were deliberately wiped out, while modern Western-style development has spread at a rapid pace. Since most imported schemes no longer reflect surviving traditional customs and values, they deprive the inhabitants of a consistent, meaningful architectural setting and interrupt the intimate interaction between man and his built environment – the very source of cultural identity. Consequently, the faculties of self-determined cultural regeneration are at risk, because instead of organic innovation being fostered from within, alien structures are adopted which work against the native cultural genius and suppress its creative resources.

In order to gain a better understanding of these internal conflicts, one needs to go beyond the closed circle of conventional formal and aesthetic debates and examine the values and motives which underpin the genesis of the built environment. Such factors are rooted in deep human convictions which relate to man's metaphysical existence and may therefore involve religious issues as an expression of spiritual concerns. The following paragraphs are an attempt to analyze some of the main cultural conflicts, starting on a conceptual, rather philosophical level, and descending gradually into more physical matters of planning and architecture. The author may be forgiven for accentuating the dialectics of this controversy for the sake of a sharp and clear-cut understanding of the basic issues.

Different Concepts of Development

The Industrial Revolution in the 19th century marked the first climax of a secular development concept, as it had never been known before in the whole history of mankind: man no longer saw himself as part of a meaningful creation (of which he was the custodian) but declared himself independent of it. Thus he began to regard the world around him as a mere object, the raw material, so to speak, for the production of a new and autonomous "second-hand" reality, to be achieved by rational methods and technical tools. The hypothesis of man being divorced from the larger universe and becoming the only master of the world engendered the corresponding ideology of technological progress. Since everything appeared to be feasible (or only a

question of time and further development) under the new technical imperatives, the best of all worlds seemed to be within reach. Technology was seen
as a means of anticipating the traditional eschatological notion of paradise
on earth, which was usurped and perverted by a new secular ideology. In
the dissolution process that followed, spiritual concerns were eliminated
from the real world, with reality being alienated and reduced to its mere
material dimension. The human intellect, traditionally considered as the
organ for reflecting the divine macrocosm in the human microcosm, was limited to its rational faculties, which were obviously strengthened by this
restriction of scope and purpose. The result was a fixation on the quantitative
aspects of reality which had an almost hypnotic effect on man.

Accordingly, development could only be understood in terms of a new
type of "progress", leading in a direct line of ascent towards eternal bliss
for mankind – again a concept based on secularized religious concepts.
The firm belief in the absolute success of a self-induced linear development
eventually assumed the status of an ecclesiastical dogma, as it were, the fal-
lacy of which resided in the very fact that realities of a higher order were
ignored. Most traditional cultures, regardless of their religious orientation,
were much more realistic in this respect, as they accepted the given cyclical
development of life, death and transformation that operated in nature, in
man and in whole civilizations. Moreover, they were able to accommodate
the darker components of life, whereas modern civilization, precisely by
attempting to suppress them, is an easy prey for the powers of evil.

Today, the illusory character of this single-minded type of progress and
the eventual collapse of the ideology of linear development has become
only too obvious: it is sufficient to mention the ever-increasing environmental
problems of modern civilization, which have their origins in the false
conception of man being independent from the overriding laws of creation.
The devastating exploitation of nature as a dead raw material, including the
rapid depletion of natural resources accumulated over millions of years, has
been a direct consequence of this attitude. Inevitably, the present tendency
to cope with the emerging environmental problems by further intensification
of technological means will only aggravate the situation, as long as the
basic attitude is not revised.

From the point of view of Islam, there is no reason why science and
technology should be incompatible with religious creeds. The history of science gives ample evidence of Muslim endeavours in this domain, which
were to provide the basis for modern Western achievements. The problem
starts when technology is no longer subservient to higher purposes but pur-
sues its own goals. In strictly ontological terms, the total dependence on
technology is unlawful, because it places man in the role of a seemingly

almighty creator, and therefore contradicts the basic tenet of "La ilaha ill'Al-lah" – no divinity except God alone. Furthermore, Islam has always stressed man's role as God's responsible vice-regent (khalifa) on earth. This view is clearly opposed to the concept of man as the sovereign exploiter of nature, an attitude which must appear as sheer human arrogance, if judged by traditional values.

The above argument does not impute that Islam, or any traditional culture for that matter, should renounce the benefits of modern technology to preserve its identity. But it makes it clear why careful selection and adaption of technical innovations is so important in order to absorb and to integrate them into a meaningful cultural system. Otherwise society is in danger of being caught by a secular ideology, which saps the roots of much more comprehensive and legitimate concepts of reality. An unfiltered and uncontrolled impact of technology can conflict with man's traditional duty, which is to enhance the divine creation, ensure its natural balance and protect its wealth and beauty. The Qur'an is quite explicit in this respect, admonishing man to admire the miracles of nature and to reflect on the "signs" of the divine creation. In more practical terms, the environment of traditional cities demonstrates how people, even in difficult climatic conditions, were able to live in harmony with cosmic laws for thousands of years.

Different Concepts of Economy

Modern Western economies are based on the capital-intensive industrial production that emerged in the middle of the 19th century, when a new technological civilization began disrupting age-old bonds between man, earth and cosmos. The transformation of all goods and resources into mere "objects" allowed for full convertibility into abstract monetary values and thus provided the basis for the rising importance of capital as the main driving force of modern development. Due to improved transportation and processing technologies, production no longer needed to be linked to individual places, human skills or social units. Hence raw materials can now be exploited anywhere in the world, and processing and production may take place wherever cheap labour is available. As environmental strain is not taken into account in production costs, materials and goods can be easily shifted, taking advantage of new transportation means and playing with income disparities and other market factors. Following the rules of general mechanization, worldwide industrial production becomes increasingly standardized and obeys the imperatives of technology and marketing more than actual consumer needs. A dwindling cultural identity allows for manipulated "fashions", which are introduced with the help of special publicity techniques to speed up the obsolescence of the products and to spur consumption rates.

For traditional cultures, economic benefits never constituted a goal in itself, but were a means of sustaining a society committed to principles and objectives of a higher, non-material nature. Accordingly, traditional production processes were not intended to generate and accumulate capital as the principal tool of development but to maintain and reproduce a meaningful social order. Within this system, the raw materials were part of a given natural resource, i. e. God's creation, which man was allowed to use without destroying. The production processes were predicated on the existence of specialized crafts and trades rooted in cultural traditions and in cooperative social structures of their own. Human skills and resources played a major role, and anybody could enter and remain in business without high capital investments. The market was mainly local and, with the exception of imported luxury goods, production proceeded in closed cycles. This is true not only for the consistent use of locally gained and processed materials (which meant a minimum environmental impact) but also for the financial flows: commercial benefits, revenues and taxes were recycled in the local economy, and in spite of differences between rich and poor, the favoured classes sustained the disadvantaged members of the community.

When it comes to Muslim societies, it must be added that Islam has never accepted the idea of capital possessing an intrinsic value of its own. Its attitudes in this respect are clearly expressed by the interdiction to charge interest on lent money, which confirms the low status of capital. Commercial gains are by no means condemned, but they need to be achieved by human skills and supported by the help of fortune, not by the productivity of an abstract capital. Money, seen as a convenient tool of exchange, was never meant to be accumulated as a measure of success, but rather to be reinvested for meaningful purposes. The same principles governed the establishment of religious endowments (waqf), which were meant to provide continuous and shared benefits to society without engaging in capitalist procedures.

In the modern world economy, pre-industrial production systems are judged according to the criteria of industrial models which establish the basis for the notion of "underdeveloped" or "developing" countries. The predominant yardstick of this type of development is the gross national product, which measures progress in terms of monetary values, related to industrial production and corresponding consumption processes. This was, however, meaningless in a pre-industrial economy, where people were still capable of producing for their own needs or exchanging goods without going through Western market mechanisms.

In their search for exploitable resources, inexpensive labour and new markets, the colonial powers pursued the integration of Third World countries into their own economic order. It is only fair to say that they invested important funds in providing the colonies with modern infrastructures, such as roads, communication networks and factories, but these were from the beginning geared to the prerogatives of modern Western societies rather than to local needs. The colonial powers' declared intention of raising the living standards of their subjects was a pretext for imposing their own patterns of production and consumption, which would make traditional societies more and more dependent on the industrial economy and its corollary structures, while keeping them on the lowest echelons of the income ladder. The new hierarchies established by industrialization thus stressed the parasitic character of modern Western economies, introducing the well-known polarization between "centre" and "periphery" and the corresponding drainage of local wealth. This happened not only on an international scale, with the Third World countries becoming the periphery of the First World, but also on a local scale, with the capital cities of developing countries (usually the footholds of Western-type economies) becoming centres with regard to the rural hinterland.

Given the contagious effect of this cleavage, it is clear that local communities within the boundaries of historic cities could not escape it. As a Western lifestyle became synonymous with "upper class", the high-income strata of the society detached themselves from the more popular districts, while these quarters (including many historic centres) in turn attracted a large number of rural immigrants who constituted an uprooted "proletariat" at the lower end of the new social spectrum. The result was a rapid loss of local autonomy and self-sufficiency followed by a social disintegration process, which had a strong impact on historic urban structures. Many old cities are now marginalized with respect to the modern districts. The moving of the social "elite" from the historic quarters into modern Western-style suburbs abolished old community structures based on social solidarity and deprived the old city of a major source of income. With the simultaneous massive immigration of rural populations, the supporting social fabric was torn and old cities became prone to social and physical decline. Moreover, new production modes put stress on the functional and occupational patterns which had shaped the traditional structure of the urban centre with its production areas, khans and markets. Many of the marketed products are no longer locally produced; craftsmen are substituted with shopkeepers, who in turn tend to lose their independence as they become employees of rich entrepreneurs. The remaining local production changes from the traditional crafts to semi-industrial manufacturing processes, using imported machinery and raw materials; polluting industry spreads into former housing districts or occupies vacant areas at the fringes of the old city, confusing traditional land use patterns, causing congestion and creating precarious environmental conditions. While these processes are to some extent unavoidable, they need to be managed and controlled in a way which allows the historic centres to gain a new equilibrium.

Housing is probably the domain where the loss of traditional skills and the disappearance of self-sufficient local modes of production are most dramatically felt. Expensive imported building material and industrial construction techniques tended to replace traditional processes and thus no longer engaged the capabilities of local communities in providing their shelter by their own efforts and with easily available local building material. Often the overt or hidden coalition between a speculative construction market and a rigid administration, keen to maintain full control over the housing sector, stifled peoples' capacities to cater for their own needs, without ever solving the housing problem of the masses. For the disadvantaged low-income strata of the population, modern industrial housing is not only hard to afford but also much less appropriate in environmental, climatic and social terms. Far from being an improvement, it often is the direct cause of social and economic misery. Thus new modes of interaction between the formal and the informal sectors need to be developed in order to harness the resources of surviving vernacular modes of production.

Different Concepts of Community Structures and Institutions

In keeping with the logic of their rational development concept, modern governmental institutions have to crack the closed circuits of traditional social units and subdivide society into "functional" components which can be recomposed according to the rules of a mechanized system. The corresponding new structures tend to become highly artificial and never attain the vitality of organically grown social entities. The lack of internal cohesion then calls for compensation by external control mechanisms which expand their grip on individuals, thereby further reducing the self-regulating capacities of formerly autonomous social units – a vicious circle with no end to it.

In most cases, the modernization of traditional societies thus results in the destruction of existing informal networks of social bonds and mutual responsibilities and in their replacement by a costly and highly formalized administrative system, imposed by a distant governmental authority. The existing codes of social interaction and mutual commitment are largely substituted with anonymous abstract institutions, to which the individual can no longer relate. While the new institutional structures may intend to provide "total welfare" to their recipients, they in fact often become bureaucratic straitjackets inflicting previously unknown restrictions on human activities. Such constraints may eventually press more upon people than the rules and conventions of old traditions ever did, yet they lack the legitimate authority, in terms of ethics and moral principles, from which the traditional social order used to draw.

Moreover, the abstract control mechanisms of modern societies have an evident potential for abuse by totalitarian forces, which make them an easy vehicle for abusive manipulation by ambitious political leaders. In theory, this risk can be reduced by democratic rules, but even the merits of a well-functioning democracy (relatively rare in present Third-World countries) cannot obscure the basic fact that the new technocratic and bureaucratic forces have deprived man of more direct and more human types of social self determination. In this regard, it could be argued that most pre-industrial societies, even in the case of despotic regimes, managed to maintain a higher degree of autonomy than is the case under highly bureaucratic government institutions.

In traditional Muslim communities, institutional control in the modern Western sense was largely absent, because it was "interiorized" through the common acceptance of a set of unquestioned ethical rules, both in terms of spiritual principles and in terms of everyday patterns of behaviour. Social structures were enhanced by shared values and sustained by direct human relationships, such as kinship and neighbourhood solidarity. Administration and bureaucracy could be minimized, because the various social groups functioned as responsible and self-supporting cellular units within a larger framework, which had developed its own system of checks and balances. This is mainly due to the fact that the traditional Islamic law (which could be labelled the only Muslim institution) was created with the intention of shaping an ideal, spiritually rooted way of life rather than establishing a penal code to punish violations of man-made prescripts. Since the divine origins of the Qur'an were collectively acknowledged by society, there was no need for a large administrative machinery to enforce law. At any rate, it was understood that the ultimate control and punishment was vested in God, the supreme Lord, and not in man – a fact that went a long way in encouraging tolerant attitudes.

The recent adoption of Western legal codes and administrative systems in various Muslim countries has often created an ambiguous situation. On the one hand imported administrative institutions tend to destroy the self-regulating social structures which have survived from the traditional order. On the other hand, the new system cannot work properly on its own terms, because residual habits and customs, like those of personal commitments or tribal solidarities, obstruct its smooth implementation. Therefore, there is a risk that the values of traditional communities may be abolished without the efficiency of the modern system ever being achieved – which can cause blockages in the institutional system, due to inconsistent governmental policies. Furthermore, the indiscriminate adoption of Western institutions could weaken the intimate connection between material and spiritual spheres of life, one of the essential concerns of Islam.

The ultimate goal of Islamic law was to provide the believers with a "path" which would allow them to shape their worldly living patterns in accordance with timeless religious principles. Given the very nature of temporal life, this objective implied the need to react to changing outer conditions. In the early centuries, Islam was indeed successful in developing the "Shari'a" (religious law) in such a way as to respond to arising new circumstances without betraying the supreme principles. Its achievements in this respect were due to the creative individual search of trusted members of the community and to the consensus established among them. The drawback came when the "door of individual search" was closed and the legal system was frozen, as it were, in its medieval condition. To be sure, this did not invalidate the original references of the Shari'a, but it caused increasing problems in applying them to changed outer conditions. Today, a major effort in interpreting and adapting its principles to present circumstances would be required, if Islamic law were to fulfill its function again.

Different Concepts of Planning

The methods and standards of modern physical planning were established as a corrective to the shortcomings of the new development concept described above and are an outcome of the administrative and institutional framework produced by secular industrial civilizations. It is therefore not surprising that they should fail when transferred to the context of traditional societies which obey different prerogatives. While modern planning is often seen as the miraculous instant solution to arising development problems in the Third World, it appears to be even less viable there than in the Western context, unless its objectives, methods and procedures are rigorously controlled. For its implicit value system, consciously or unconsciously imposed on a different cultural context, can induce internal conflicts which end up paralyzing the internal control mechanisms of the community.

In philosophical terms, the most controversial aspect of modern planning is probably its claim to be able to predict and fix future conditions to an amazing degree of precision, leaving no room for unforeseen needs and developments. Indeed, the Cartesian approach of modern planning intimates that man is the full master of his future and that all influences unforeseen by his mind can be excluded. One does not have to share the Islamic belief in divine providence to realize that this illusion is the cause of the collapse of so many planning schemes around the world. Over the past one or two decades, such failures have been acknowledged in professional circles in the West, and in general the trend is now towards more flexible planning methodologies, which allow strategic overall guidance to interact with spontaneous trends, benefiting from the greater participation of the social groups involved. Nevertheless, conventional master plans continue to be applied all over the Muslim world, with ambiguous results. For besides being based on debatable assumptions, Western planning methods cannot be correctly implemented, as the municipalities of most Arab cities today do not have the institutional structures, the human resources and the technical experience which are required for the successful implementation of such complex master plan schemes. This holds true for both the initial decision-making process and the important follow-up phase, which may extend over 10–20 years. Foreign technical assistance is often seen as a solution to this, but is not sustainable (and hardly desirable) in the long term.

In terms of implementation, planning schemes tend to be detached from social realities and to exclude the vital human resources which are essential in shaping the built environment. Master plans are mostly too abstract to be understood by the population concerned and thus do not generate the necessary personal commitment and identification. Their long-term directions are easily contradicted by spontaneous day-to-day decisions made by both governmental agencies and private land owners. Personalized decision making, which was the strength of Islam within its own cultural premises, turns out to be a major handicap once the system of references is changed. Furthermore, the introduction of modern planning instruments, together with the corollary governmental control mechanisms, can disturb the subtle balance between commonly accepted licences and matching social constraints. The shared architectural language which previously provided the common ground for individual expression, ensuring the homogeneous character of the collective urban product, is threatened by incongruent regulations, and a random new vocabulary of foreign elements and forms starts competing with indigenous expressions. Individual liberties, originally sanctioned by the Islamic concept of private property, are stressed in an abusive way and speculative trends are no longer contained by the idea of public welfare. All these factors have contributed to the conflictual and sometimes chaotic situation which characterizes modern cities in the Muslim world.

177

177 Allegoric representation of the deified geometry – the goddess of Cartesian planning, as it were (Dutch painting from 1650).

In traditional Muslim societies, the shared values, the social consensus and the interdependence between the members of the community were strong enough to hold together the mosaic of individual decisions in a natural and flexible way. The inbuilt social constraints allowed for a certain amount of "laisser-faire", while still producing an organic whole out of the sum of individual acts of building. There was no formal scheme which would pre-define forthcoming developments in terms of rigid and comprehensive structures. Nevertheless, the collective patterns of life and the given range of the traditional architectural vocabulary, consistently applied over several generations, ensured a balance between the parts and the whole at each stage of urban development. "Planning" was thus limited to a simple act of consultation, in order to prevent possible individual infringements on the rights of neighbours and on the interest of the community. Due to the strength of customs and of self-evident tacit agreements, there was no need for the explicit building codes, which are now governing the life of modern cities.

In the city of the industrial age, a formal planning framework is usually imposed from outside, relying on external coercion rather than encouraging internal forces of human commitment and social solidarity. This diminishes the scope for self-regulating processes, and the resulting gradual disintegration of traditional communities calls in turn for increased governmental control and restrictive building regulations. Regrettably, very few attempts are being made to adapt the planning instruments to the local customs prevailing in Muslim cities. Most codes and prescriptions merely replicate Western models and are therefore likely to provoke conflicts with traditional social conventions. This is true for many new residential districts, where the street plans and the corresponding by-laws violate the Islamic concept of privacy and neighbourhood. Without the planners being aware of it, inappropriate master plans often act in a repressive manner, obstructing or destroying essential community forces.

The contrast between the socially integrated cybernetics of traditional cities on one hand and the bureaucratically controlled planning processes of modern cities on the other hand transpires in the visual appearance of the respective urban structures. The first mode has produced a distinct type of "organic" order, where the variety of individual components by no means precludes, but indeed sustains and enhances the overall unity of urban form. The second mode oscillates between a sterile uniformity (if its prescriptions are strictly followed), and sheer chaos (if the formal rules cannot be enforced), without ever being able to attain a lively urban form, which could reflect the collective creativity of the society. In the present transitional period of urban development, skillful compromises are called for, as planning cannot be totally dismissed, but needs to engage internal social control mechanisms and responsibilities, instead of imposing rigid constraints derived from alien cultural models.

Different Concepts of Land Use

Conventional Western master plans tend to differentiate urban space along isolated functional criteria, singling out areas for housing, commerce, recreation, industrial activities and governmental use. The objective is to break up the city into sectoral components and to fit the loose parts into an artificial (and supposedly more efficient) urban system, according to mechanical and technological criteria, rather than to human needs and social considerations. The ensuing functional segregation first disconnects related human activities and then calls on modern communication means to make up for the lost social interaction. Overdimensioned roads, highway and transportation systems are thus introduced to artificially reconnect what has been broken by zoning schemes. The corresponding traffic channels cause further disruption in the urban fabric, cutting through residential areas and transforming formerly coherent zones into isolated pieces of urban form.

By singling out and lumping together functions with similar operational needs, the rationality of the "machine" is seemingly increased, as is the control of planners, administrators and governments, but all relations to human scale and to interaction are lost. Looking at the various functions one by one, each may work perfectly in theory, yet their interrelation within a meaningful overall concept is totally neglected – not to speak of the waste of energies and resources or of the loss of social and environmental qualities. This is why, in spite of obvious functional improvements, so many modern cities paradoxically no longer work, quite apart from losing many of their human and environmental qualities. As many contemporary examples in the West demonstrate, the search for extreme rationality of the urban system has often turned to the opposite, producing outright irrational, if not chaotic results. One cannot help being reminded of Goya's vision: "The dream of reason produces monsters" (see page 188), which illustrates with admirable conciseness the dilemma of excessive single-minded development.

Whereas modern planning is based on massive concentration of disaggregated sectoral functions, traditional Muslim cities have always applied the reverse principle of creating decentralized but integrated sub-units. This implied that each part of the whole had to be whole and viable in itself, and that the close interrelation of various aspects of urban life should operate at each hierarchical level of the urban structure. Clearly, the Muslim city had its own internal subdivisions, but they were organized in such a way as to allow individual components to act as complete entities fitting into a comprehensive urban system. There was, for instance, the recurrent separation between various ethnic or religious groups – a differentiation which encouraged each individual group to follow its own way of life and build up integral, almost self-sufficient social cells. There was also the clear division between public and private realms, which reflected the Islamic concern for privacy in the residential quarters. However, this never resulted in a disruption of the urban fabric, for each architectural sub-unit was complete in itself and could easily be clustered with others into overarching urban compounds.

178

Looking at the conditions of contemporary Muslim cities, one can easily see how the functionalist concepts of modern planning, combined with a penchant for dubious replicas of modern Western architecture, have led to a progressive disintegration of the urban fabric. In the residential areas, the stratification of society according to economic and functional criteria works against the survival or the formation of coherent, self-sufficient urban quarters. In the central business districts, the new separation between "sacred" and "profane" realms has evident spatial consequences. New mosques are often designed in complete isolation from the physical and social urban context, and their potential for acting as focal points of aggregated community facilities and other public spaces is ignored. A strange fact when one considers that in the West a new generation of urban planners is deploying considerable efforts to regenerate downtown areas as active meeting places and to bring back to them some of the lost urban density and richness which is still so appealing in the surviving medieval centres of European cities. Historic Islamic cities provide even more striking evidence of the desired interaction between all domains of public life, and there is no reason why the principle of integrated commmunity centres should not be applicable under present conditions.

Different Concepts of Circulation

Since the age of the Renaissance, the perspective view, a new instrument for representing the physical world in seemingly objective terms, became the basis of spatial concepts in both painting and architecture. This new world view, singling out man as the dominator of the universe, was celebrated in the display of monuments, royal palaces and prestigious urban sceneries which were to claim man's total control over nature. As illustrated in Chapter 8, the concept was resumed and further developed in the 19th century by the promotion of the boulevard as a major planning device of developing European cities. It was used to cut through decaying medieval quarters, often on

178 Classical perspective scenery by Sebastiano Serlio (1545).

sanitary and aesthetic grounds, but equally for reasons of better governmental and military control. Since then, town planning in Europe, with rare exceptions, became equivalent with road planning, and urban form with an addition of isolated blocks dissected by a rectangular grid of streets and avenues.

Traditional Muslim cities, on the contrary, were built on a pedestrian scale and provided an extremely dense townscape, showing a high degree of complexity. Available open spaces were allocated to and often integrated with specific architectural units, such as mosques, khans or private houses and therefore detached from the public circulation network. The streets became subsidiary to the cellular urban structure and were often transformed into narrow internal corridors. The city was conceived as a closed universe, and man was enveloped by multiple architectural shells embodying and reflecting his cultural values. Given this strong identity between containing structures and the human life contained in them, architecture became a second body, as it were, which also means that the artificial division between an independent observer and a neutral architectural object (as postulated by the perspective concept of space) did not apply: man was always *within* his comprehensive universe, in both ontological and physical terms.

In the constitution of the urban fabric, priority was given to the clear definition of well-marked territories and space compartments for various private and public uses. As the various sections of the ramified street network were absorbed by the corresponding architectural units, the main thoroughfares were integrated into the suqs, secondary lanes into the residential quarters, and the dead-end alleys into the clusters of private houses to which they gave access. The sequence corresponded to a well-established hierarchy and was punctuated by gates and thresholds announcing transitions and required changes of social behaviour. The circulation system therefore helped implement increasing degrees of privacy, ensuring that every section of the network matched the character of the space it served and the social needs of its users. Instead of splitting up the volumes, it tied together and interrelated the various components of the urban fabric, similarly to the arterial system in an organic body. Beyond providing mere movement patterns, it offered a complete and integrated communication system.

Modern planning interventions in historic Muslim cities tend to disregard the traditional urban system and to emulate the Western approach, cutting axial road systems into the organically grown city and dividing the formerly coherent fabric into isolated blocks. Such operations brutally disrupt the cellular order of the traditional fabric and expose the introverted precincts of secluded residential areas to the immediate impact of functions and activities

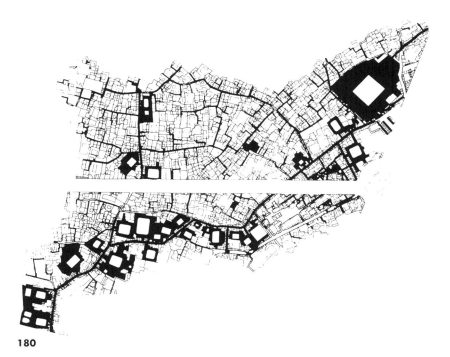

179

180

from which they were carefully screened off. Apart from the physical destruction, this also affects the function of the social rituals linked to the spatial qualities and visual codes of the traditional environment. Occasionally, large new roads and squares are not only advocated on the grounds of traffic improvement, but on the pretence of enhancing important monuments such as mosques and sanctuaries. However, nothing could be more erroneous in

179 Avenue de l'Opéra in Paris – one of Haussmann's boulevards cutting through old Paris.

180 A new road in Isfahan cutting through the cellular tissue of the old city and the main bazaar spine.

terms of traditional Islamic architecture than separating individual public buildings from their urban matrix and exposing them as if they were isolated architectural sculptures.

As a rule, modern highway schemes are just the first step of a much wider erosion process and trigger off a number of subsequent steps of destruction. Once new traffic channels are carved out from the compact urban structure, the old city is confronted with a new scale of transportation, while being bereft of its traditional protecting devices that allowed for gradual filtering of circulation flows by corresponding buffer zones. The following step is fuelled by the redevelopment opportunities arising from increased vehicular accessibility (see page 183): speculative pressures develop along the fringes of new roads, and new street-oriented blocks are built according to a foreign typology. The modern buildings often overshadow the ancient structures, curtailing their privacy (an important concern of traditional societies) and changing their micro-climate by preventing the flow of cool breezes. As a result of such interferences, the remaining fragments of the historic fabric lose their physical, functional and semiotic context – and thus their raison d'être, which resides in being part of a larger and significant whole. Dangerous social changes are instated or accelerated, and final decay and total disintegration are only a question of time, if no suitable countermeasures are taken.

New traffic schemes are often planned with the declared intention of upgrading the old city and preserving its viability. It is true that the historic districts, in order to survive, need infrastructure improvements, as well as the injection of new economic forces, which require improved accessibility. Such interventions, however, must rely on an intimate knowledge of the cellular structure of the historic fabric and its inner meaning; they can only be successful if they proceed with the necessary subtlety and take into account the induced reactions and side effects. Unfortunately, what happens most of the time is closer to careless carnage than to conscientious surgery, as witnessed by countless historic Islamic cities from North Africa to India, which have become victims of such fatal cures.

181

Different Concepts of Urban Form

It has been said that the two most reliable indicators of good urban form are the degree of integration of individual architectural components and, corollary to that, the successful interaction between buildings and open spaces within the overall built environment. A closer look at the characteristics of pre-industrial cities, be it in Europe or in the Arab world, confirms the importance of a differentiated treatment of open space for the genesis of lively

181 Interaction of solids and voids in the medieval Italian city of Siena.

urban textures. Well-defined and judiciously placed open spaces can constitute walled outdoor rooms that serve as precious townscape components. Such voids may either be shaped by surrounding solid volumes or, inversely, stand out as nuclear core areas which define and organize by themselves the plastic architectural masses around them. The mutual interaction between active and passive (or "positive" and "negative") qualities of space can be seen as the spring, so to speak, of lively urban form. The perpetual dialogue between related indoor and outdoor spaces within a complex urban fabric holds together the various architectural components and produces what man perceives as an attractive built environment.

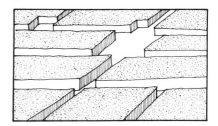

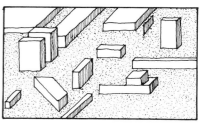

182

Often skillfully applied by outstanding individual architects, these formal qualities have deep collective roots, which appear in most suggestive manner in the products of the vernacular architecture of different periods and places. Looking at them, one can easily understand that the basic urban form qualities are a natural outcome of distinct human attitudes, cultural conventions and synergetic living processes which create a consistent built environment and by doing so define the connections operating between the parts and the whole. Such interrelations can work at various levels – for instance between man and society, between man's world and the universe, or between individual buildings and the city as a whole. The multiple affinities and correspondences between the different levels are a prime source of cultural richness. Pre-modern cultures (including Europe from the medieval times to the baroque period) abound with examples demonstrating how a specific urban form became a consistent image of a corresponding cultural order, of a "cosmos", with which the actual users could identify. In this respect, modern Western architecture has a serious handicap, as it is no longer guided by holistic concepts relating man, society and the universe. The price paid for the obsession with mechanical functionality was the loss of emotionally and biologically rooted responses which, although not "measurable", are essential ingredients of human culture.

The effects of the one-sided approach of modern Western civilization have already been discussed in the previous paragraphs. Here, it is important to add that with the rise of the Modern Movement, urban form in the traditional sense ceased to be a concern. Many of its urban design schemes resemble mere blow-ups of abstract master plan diagrams, and therefore transmit the corresponding limitations to the built environment, producing seemingly functional but mostly lifeless shadow-schemes of urban form. Perhaps the most emblematic expression of this impoverishment can be seen in Le Corbusier's concept of the "Radiant City" which was to find many followers all over the world. Its characteristics are deceiving in terms of urban form qualities: contextual values and human-scale interrelations between

182 Comparison between traditional and modern urban form in European cities. Above, the traditional rapport between architecture and open space. Below, the fragmentation of urban form into isolated structures and the resulting confused structure (after Rob Krier).

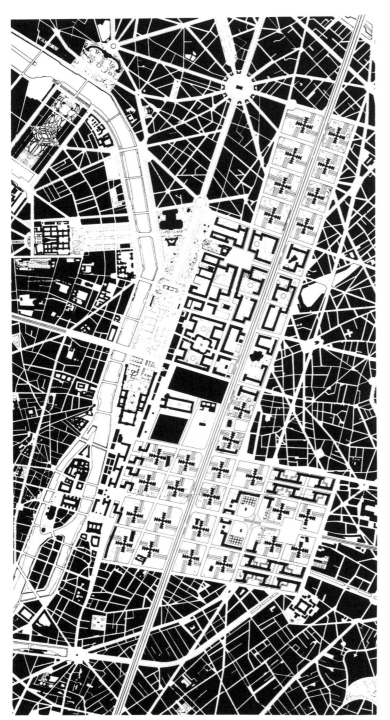

184

183 Le Corbusier's "Plan Voisin" for Paris (1922).

184 Bird's-eye view of Le Corbusier's "Radiant City" blocks.

buildings (or between buildings and open spaces) are neglected in favor of a rigid "functional" separation of housing, public facilities, traffic and open spaces, single functions being isolated and inflated to a point where they become meaningless. High-rise housing blocks dissolve the ground floor pedestrian scale, prevent the differentiation of attractive "inside" and "outside" sequences and produce anonymity, crowding and alienation. The concentration of central and commercial facilities in special downtown areas destroys the interface between various facets of social and public life, undermines the quality of public spaces and generates a fatal increase in traffic volume. Massive traffic arteries disrupt potentially connected urban components, generate heavy pollution and produce a kind of urban wasteland. Geometrically arranged skycrapers float as unrelated "objects" in this loose open space which is too unstructured to be of any real social use and too aseptic to be of any environmental value.

While the architectural or social merits of such schemes are limited, it is easy to see why they appealed to investors in terms of commercial potential. By its simplistic rational approach, functionalism became a springboard for speculative development trends, which were not in the least concerned with social and environmental qualities. This explains the rapid international

185

185 Urban tissue of the city of Salé (Morocco).

spread of the "Modern Movement" after World War II, starting with the United States. American cities today still suffer from the concentrated application of the Radiant City concept in their downtown areas, as well as from the reverse but correlated phenomenon, the sprawling suburbia. Both are "no-man's-lands" in terms of social interaction and urban form, and therefore symptomatic of the atomization of cities brought about by the functionalist approach. Interestingly, American architects of the post-modern movement were also among the first to feel these deficiencies and to advo-cate the re-invention of classical features such as the urban plaza, as a counterweight to the anonymous modern townscape.

The urban form of most traditional Muslim cities follows rules which are diametrically opposed to those of the "Radiant City". The formation of the urban structure is not subject to the purely quantitative division of large space into smaller fragments but based on an incremental or "organic" aggregation process, originating in the definition of socially relevant micro-spaces which are then connected into larger units. The enclosure of voids by correlated solids, repeated in countless variations, is the generating princi-ple of urban form. Open spaces and pedestrian movement systems are inte-grated into the various components of the urban structure from the very beginning, which prevents the disruption of built form by the circulation net-work and excludes the emergence of anonymous wasteland ("lost space") within the urban system. Structures are not conceived as abstract graphic forms, but as vibrant shells of human activities, reflecting and conditioning the activities of their occupants. Down to the smallest components of the urban fabric, such as the stall of a suq, all architectural envelopes are tai-lored to the needs of human beings, granting them protection and identity. Due to the interdependence between actors, activities and space definition, every place has its specific significance within the semiotic system of the town. The questions of how to sustain such urban form qualities, how to translate and integrate them into a contemporary design language and, most importantly, how to achieve the conditions which enable their imple-mentation are far from being resolved, but pose a challenging task to archi-tects in the Muslim world.

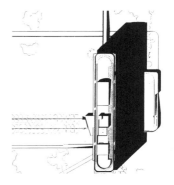

186

Different Concepts of Architectural Form

The foregoing paragraphs have already touched upon some of the basic differences between the Modern Movement and the traditional approach. The Modern Movement tended to design buildings in a vacuum and to produce isolated blocks floating in an abstract urban space emptied of all its essential qualities. Individual buildings do not contribute to a meaningful

186 Isolated block structure versus inte-grated courtyard structure in Western architecture. Above Le Corbusier's Unité d'Habitation and below the Uffizi complex in Florence (after C. Rowe).

187

definition of public open space, as related to corresponding community activities. Moreover, the elevations of single structures are mostly reduced to repetitive grid features echoing the graphic subdivisions of corresponding planning schemes and no longer convey any symbolic content in terms of cultural identity. There have been reactions by creative modern architects to this stereotypical design practice, aimed at greater aesthetic variety, but the results are often arbitrary and have difficulty in transcending the limitations of personal fantasies or mere fashions.

Traditional Muslim architecture used to work on different premises altogether: buildings were not conceived as detached "objects" but as living architectural shells, shaped according to the internal needs of distinct social micro-units and responding to the enclosed activities. Each individual enclosure incorporated the necessary amount of open space and the required access system within its respective boundaries. It therefore constituted an integral and virtually autonomous entity with its own resource of air, light and open space, independent of the street space. Yet close linkages with other buildings ensured the integration of single units into larger clusters, producing a cohesive urban environment. The layout which most perfectly matched the ambiguous requirements of autonomy and integration was the

187 New pavilion-type blocks rising above the semi-destroyed traditional urban fabric outside the walled city of Aleppo.

introverted courtyard house. With many local variations, it became instrumental in producing the dense and totally interwoven urban fabric which is so typical of most historic Arab cities.

The introverted character of such integrated architectural containers creates a sense of space which is very different from that of Western architecture. Each enclosed area is focused on the centre of its courtyard, and the elevations of the building are turned inward, facing each other instead of looking onto the street. The central void determines the shape of the solid structures around it. The outer walls are often blind or do not appear at all, as they are shared with attached neighbouring buildings. Instead of flowing out in every direction or being channelled into linear avenues, the spatial energies are contained and concentrated in a multitude of open vessels, as it were. The city thus becomes a multi-focal system excluding any dominant axial orientation, with the sole exception of the qiblah direction of religious buildings. Street elevations are of secondary importance or vanish altogether. To experience a building, one has to enter and to apprehend it from within, which corresponds to the Islamic concept of sacred privacy and relative autonomy of each social unit. Being enveloped by omnipresent architectural enclosures, one always feels being at the centre, wherever one may stand. Buildings exude a definite sense of place and identity, and provide the users with a feeling of security, peace and equilibrium.

Conventional modern building technologies almost invariably fail to provide the type of built environment which could match the sophisticated visual reference system of traditional Muslim architecture. Their shortcomings become apparent once new buildings are inserted into the historic structures of Arab cities. Since the design criteria, starting with access, street orientation, contextual factors, etc., are fundamentally different, the replacement of traditional courtyard houses with modern blocks inevitably leads to disruption and the progressive destruction of the traditional urban fabric. Apart from the typological incompatibilities, modern Western architecture also shows a lack of consideration for local building technologies, due to its bias towards heavy industrial means of environmental control. It thus tends to exclude cheap and easily available local materials in favour of costly, mostly imported industrial products, which in turn demand highly sophisticated and expensive building and maintenance technologies. This makes little sense in countries which have a long tradition of inexpensive and environmentally appropriate construction techniques, not to speak of millions of capable and willing hands who still know how to build their own houses. New models of built form and of direct interaction with the traditional modes of building need to be established in order to sustain and take advantage of the traditional know-how.

Different Concepts of Aesthetics

Accepting the traditional notion that beauty should be "the reflection of truth", one will find that different ideals of beauty correspond to different concepts of truth. In Modern-Movement architecture, truth is mainly sought with regard to material factors, and therefore the goal is to display the construction system, to express the dynamic of structural forces and to expose building materials in a straightforward way. Much of this attitude is influenced by the ideal of the machine and its functional features, to the point that many modern design products, for the sake of "purity", are less practical, less comfortable and even less functional than many of their traditionally crafted predecessors. An artificial geometry is often imposed on objects of daily use, as if the flawless lines of cubes and squares automatically correlated with functional qualities and social benefits.

As long as they remained faithful to the spiritual dimensions of beauty and truth, traditional Muslim architects and craftsmen were immune to the simplistic equations which produced the crude architectural "realism" of the Modern Movement. They were aware that physical forms need to refer to non-material contents, but also that any attempt to freeze spiritual principles in material forms and shapes was bound to fail from a metaphysical point of view. This very attitude, which marked the artistic creativity of Islam for centuries, was also the main factor which fostered the alliance between architecture and the fine arts. In Europe, a divorce between the various crafts has been taking place since late medieval times, and the substitution of symbolic images with increasingly naturalistic representation went hand in hand with the progressive isolation of the different branches of fine arts, i. e. painting, sculpture and architecture. Because Islam was more cautious with regard to the autonomous power of images and to issues such as naturalism, it could prevent the loss of symbolic references and the disintegration of the arts as long as the corresponding traditions stayed alive.

The intimate connection between Islamic architecture and fine arts was supported by the fact that the main means of artistic expression, i. e. calligraphy, geometric patterns and the arabesque, were surface-related and therefore suitable to fully merge with the planes of floors, walls or ceilings which were to carry their message. The decorated architectural surfaces performed a function which was quite the opposite of what Western functionalists would expect: the intention was not to display material qualities or structural forces but to transform the physical structure to a point where it could reflect the supreme reality to which calligraphy and geometry referred. The effect was a deliberate de-materialization of architectural structures – a paradoxical process which implied the veiling of the physical substance in order to unveil the invisible forces of creation. The rich orna-

188

mental tapestries of many Islamic buildings therefore follow a logic which goes far beyond superficial decoration and has nothing to do with the "horror vacui" often quoted in this respect.

While limited to the wall surface and subtle relief structures, Islamic art was able to gain a new dimension through its marriage with architectural structures. This is due to the specific sense of space generated by the dominant courtyard typology. The main elevations being introverted and therefore facing each other, the central enclosed open space became totally detached from the outside world. This enabled the courtyard to be deeply imbued with and transformed by the imprint of the ornamented walls. Accordingly, the de-materialization process was extended into the third dimension and the core of the building acquired a timeless quality, often sustained by the interaction with fountains and gardens evoking the image of paradise. As pointed out in Chapter 2, architecture thus achieves a paradoxical function, since it first defines a clear-cut central space, while at the same time it de-materializes and transfigures it, abolishing the limits of time and space by artistic means. This vertical layering of meanings is characteristic of the Islamic philosophy of life, which was realistic in its attitude towards worldly matters, and yet always conscious of the non-material realities working above and within them.

The introduction of Western building typologies and the corresponding aesthetics threaten to reduce the vital role of the arts in Islamic societies and thereby impedes a significant visual expression of the synthesis between material and spiritual concerns. Since the colonial period, there have been

188 The courtyard of the Attarin Madrasa in Fez (14th century).

many attempts to combine modern Western building structures with Islamic ornamental features. Most of them, however, have failed because they used Islamic art out of context, that is, without considering the interrelation between the artistic decoration of walls and the corresponding concept of space, which calls for a specific architectural approach. Deprived of this correlation, traditional decoration loses its deeper meaning and is reduced to a shallow ornamental feature. All attempts to capture or resuscitate the spirit of Islamic art and architecture therefore need to consider their complete philosophical and environmental implications, rather than dealing with certain isolated stylistic aspects.

Towards Reconciling Tradition and Modernity

The above paragraphs were intended to clarify in schematic terms the basic philosophical contradictions between what could be defined as, on the one hand, the "traditional approach" and, on the other hand, the "modern approach" to the planning and design of the built environment. It must be acknowledged that this distinction is not necessarily (and no longer) identical with an opposition between "Muslim" and "Western" concepts. Yet while these labels are admittedly simplistic, they can hardly be avoided if we are to analyze the reasons underlying the current breakdown in the management of the built environment in most Muslim countries and in the developing world at large. Be this as it may, the ultimate objective of such an analysis cannot be to deepen the rift between East and West or past and present, or to anathematize specific contemporary attitudes and approaches. What is urgently needed is a thoughtful and creative bridging of the gap, but this can only be achieved if the existing divide is candidly acknowledged and not ignored or camouflaged.

Today's political discourse in the Islamic world is still tainted by the dogmatic and unproductive controversy between "modernists" and "fundamentalists". The cultural domain, having access to spiritual resources and to the power of creative imagination, may offer the best chance to overcome such sterile dichotomies. For the shadow-boxing between extreme but equally limited ideologies can only result in obscuring the real issue, which is how the present clash between different civilisations, mentalities and ways of behaving can be replaced by a more constructive interaction, drawing on all available potentials and strengths. It will hardly be possible to achieve this without on the one hand distilling the essential values from the local traditions and on the other hand scrutinizing Western technologies and architectural concepts with regard to their underlying ideologies and social implications.

189

190

Any attempt to achieve a new synthesis would have to adapt and transform foreign concepts and tools to meet the specific needs of contemporary Muslim societies under changed outer conditions, thereby sustaining cultural continuity in creative ways. It would, furthermore, have to demonstrate how the abuses and mistakes of a single-minded industrial development, as implied in modern Western civilization, can be avoided under different and possibly more propitious circumstances. And above all, it would have to explore the innovative potential of traditional structures and the underlying social processes – acknowledging their achievements with regard to basic human needs and braving all fears of "looking backwards". Fundamental issues of this magnitude cannot be resolved overnight; they need to be nurtured through patient dialogue, based on clear perspectives, shared values and the strong participation of involved local groups.

To be viable, the desired reconciliation between tradition and modernity can hardly be constructed at the theoretical level of the previous conceptual analysis, although ideological implications clearly have an impact on social and economic change. Thus synthetic approaches need to be worked out at the level of concrete situations, as encountered in specific case studies. Testing pragmatic solutions and abstracting the lessons gained from actual field work may well be the best way to explore the possibilities of a new intermediate approach. Accordingly, the following case studies seek to illustrate in more concrete terms the general problems outlined in this chapter. Examples from various regions of the Arab world, including the cities of Mecca, Medina, Baghdad, Fez and Aleppo, are intended to document the hazards and losses that can be occasioned by inappropriate interventions and, to some extent, to provide examples of possible mitigation or resolution of respective conflicts.

Considering the range and the complexity of the problems raised in chapters 8 and 9, it should not be expected that such limited case studies can provide miraculous instant solutions. However, they may be able to give a better insight into the dynamic nature of the change processes which need to be accommodated, and to demonstrate that the two extremes, i. e. either fossilizing historic structures or erasing all pre-existing cultural references by a deliberate "tabula rasa" policy, are both equally disastrous. Accordingly, it would seem that the present challenge is to manage urban change in a meaningful and appropriate manner, maintaining, adapting or re-interpreting traditional urban structures where possible, while responding to emerging new needs and enabling local resources to respond vigorously and authentically to changed conditions.

As will be seen in the individual case studies, conservation in the strict sense may be a solution for individual monuments, but cannot be sensibly

189/190 Views of a model of a project for the new campus of the King Abdul Aziz University in Mecca, by Skidmore, Owings and Merrill. Developed with the help of a number of advisors specialized in Islamic architecture, this project was an interesting attempt to identify key principles of traditional urban form and to translate them into a contemporary design language.

applied to complete cities. Therefore it needs to be complemented and supported by other modes of intervention, such as adaptive re-use, careful urban renewal and even substitution of elements which are no longer viable or need to be replaced by new functions, under the condition that the new infills will contribute to the survival of the historic city. In other cases, precipitate wholesale demolition may call for subsequent repair of the disrupted urban fabric – a repair which in most cases would not restore the previous historic conditions, but may remain faithful to traditional typological and morphological principles. By re-interpreting tradition in the light of modern needs, while at the same time making modern development processes subservient to an overarching idea of cultural and urban continuity, it should be possible to resolve the present antagonism between "progress" and "tradition" and thus overcome the conventional dialectics between seemingly contradictory forms of urban development.

The rehabilitation of historic Muslim cities, including the introduction of adapted new building structures, can play a pioneering role in this reconciliation process. As a laboratory of practised cultural continuity, it could set examples which would have much wider application, even in modern parts of the city and particularly in the areas of housing, neighbourhood centres, university compounds and recreational spaces. Admittedly, this would not cause the current duality of urban vocabularies to disappear, but it would offer the society new opportunities and choices and, above all, it would remove the stigma of "backwardness" from the historic districts, which through their centrality and environmental qualities are potentially valuable residential areas. Brought back into the mainstream of the development discourse, a renewed local building tradition may then emerge which would offer valuable alternatives to the current worldwide confusion of architectural idioms.

PART III
Case Studies: Interventions in the Historic Fabric

Case Study I:
The Holy Cities of Islam – The Impact of Mass Transportation and Rapid Urban Change

Historic Background and Project Context

The case studies in this chapter exemplify the pressures which urban transportation can exert on the urban fabric under extreme conditions, such as those produced by the annual pilgrimage (Hajj) in Mecca and Medina. Conservation of the historic city structure around the holy mosques has proven to be practically impossible under these circumstances, and the extension of the prayer halls and the surrounding open spaces, as well as the planning of adapted structures around them, have posed complex urban development problems.

Mecca, city of the "House of God" (the Ka'aba) and the hub of the spiritual cosmos of Islam, has always remained the major religious centre of the Muslim world. The second holy city, al-Medina, comes close to it in importance, as it is the place where the earliest Islamic community took shape under the leadership of the Prophet Muhammad, and it still houses the tomb of the Prophet. During the reign of the first caliphs, Medina remained the political centre of Islam, but with the rise of the Umayyad dynasty (661–750 AD) and the expansion of the empire into the Fertile Crescent it was replaced first by Damascus and later by Baghdad, the newly founded capital of the Abbasids (750–1258 AD).

Thus in the course of the Islamic history, various urban and cultural centres such as Damascus, Baghdad, Cairo, Isfahan and Istanbul overshadowed the holy cities in the Arabian peninsula, which in spite of their religious eminence lost political and cultural importance. Although the major Muslim dynasties used to endow the religious sites with important buildings and social welfare institutions, Mecca and Medina remained provincial cities compared to the leading Islamic capitals. Their relatively modest urban development was, however, counterbalanced by their international character, since once a year, during the pilgrimage month (Hajj), they became the meeting point for Muslims arriving from all directions of the Islamic world to fulfill their religious duty.

Islam prescribes that the believer should once in his lifetime perform the pilgrimage to the holy Ka'aba if he is physically and economically able to do so. In the early times, the pilgrimage was just a journey within the Arabian homeland and thus relatively easy to undertake. In later centuries,

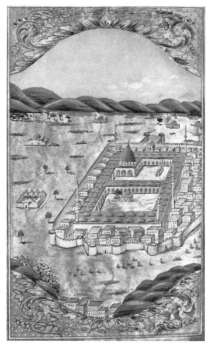

191

191 Miniature from an 18th-century Ottoman manuscript showing a simplified typological representation of the fortified city of Medina. The Haram with the Prophet's tomb is embraced by the residential units, the mosque forming the major open space of the city.

when Islam had spread to West Africa, India and even to China, it became a much more complex undertaking and required considerable resources. Annual caravans were organized, starting from the most important cities of the Islamic world and all converging on Mecca. These journeys were major events in the life of the participating groups and individuals, and many literary accounts by medieval travellers such as Ibn Jubayr, Ibn Battuta or Nasiri Khosraw inform us about the perils and joys of the pilgrimage. They also illustrate how the pilgrimage was often combined with other activities or with extended travelling through other parts of the Islamic world. Many pilgrims brought rare and precious objects from their countries to Mecca and vice versa, to sell or to exchange them, thus combining the pilgrimage with commercial activities and covering part of their expenses.

For centuries the main transportation mode of the pilgrimage was by camel, especially as the access to the holy cities led through vast desert areas. Jedda was the main arrival point for pilgrims crossing the Red Sea or arriving by boat from the Indian Gulf. In the 19th and early 20th century, new technologies and transportation modes, such as railways and steamboats, were developed, which eased the journey and led to a first increase

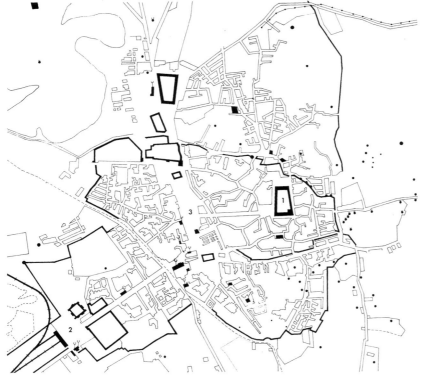

192 Plan of Medina around 1910: the Prophet's Mosque (1) is still surrounded by the walled city. To the north and the east of the walled city are the Ottoman suburbs of Bab al-Majidi and Zuqaq at-Tayyar. On the south-eastern corner is the new Hejjaz railway station (2), the new main entry point to the city, from where an avenue continues towards al-Manakha Square (3), the open arrival place for caravans in front of the main gate of the walled city.

in the numbers of pilgrims. In the early 20th century the Ottomans built the Hejaz Railway to connect Damascus with the city of the Prophet. But the decisive turning point came during the fifties and sixties of this century with the advent of motor cars and airplanes which allowed for easy mass movement. Combined with the rapid demographic growth of the Islamic world in the past decades, this initiated a tremendous quantitative and qualitative change in pilgrimage. Considering that the pilgrims have numbered over 2 million in recent years, and taking into account the fact that certain ritual acts and movements in the plain of Arafat, in Muna and around the Ka'aba have to be performed within the fixed period of a couple of days, it is clear that the increased mobility has produced towering logistical problems in terms of crowding, mass movement, transportation and housing. This was reflected in the development of the urban structures and religious buildings and planners were thus confronted with three major issues:

193

a) The temporary expansion of urban functions, due to the fact that each city must accommodate a population double or triple its normal size during a few weeks of the year, while for the rest of the time it recedes to its normal provincial scale, keeping an oversized and largely empty urban structure, especially as far as open spaces, road networks and housing are concerned.

b) The environmental impact of mass movements of pilgrims at urban and downtown level, requiring an adequate type of public transportation and the establishment of efficient transitions from vehicular to pedestrian modes of movement and vice versa.

c) The massive extension of the old structures of the two sanctuaries, as opposed to the conservation of the surrounding historic urban fabric and the preservation of a human-scale environment benefiting the religious experience.

According to their different urban topography and the specific religious functions they fulfill, the two cities of Mecca and Medina had to face these problems in somewhat different terms, although the basic issues remained the same in both cases. In the Prophet's city, the problems are more easily manageable, mainly because the whole city is spread over a large plain, whereas Mecca is located in a narrow depression surrounded by steep hills and mountains. In addition, the pilgrimage to the Prophet's Mosque, although usually included in the journey of every Muslim, is not mandatory in ritual terms, as opposed to the circumbulation of the Ka'aba. Pilgrims flock to Medina during the weeks before or after the actual Hajj ritual, which means that the concentration of people staying simultaneously at the same place is lower than in Mecca.

193 Early 19th-century view of one of the alleyways of Medina leading through the Aghawat district to the Prophet's Mosque.

194

195

The development pressures on the holy cities generated by religious mass tourism have radically changed the traditional townscape of both Mecca and Medina during the past 20–30 years. The main factors of change were the increasing demand for vehicular access to the central area and the Holy Mosque, combined with large-scale commercial construction of apartment buildings for seasonal pilgrim accommodation. This was compounded by the necessary massive enlargement of the sanctuaries, which started in the fifties and sixties and culminated in the eighties. During the early seventies there were attempts to control the development of the holy cities by two master plans. However, the plans could not be effectively implemented due to the lack of efficient follow-up and consistent monitoring of building activities. A few years after their publication, they were already outdated and contradicted by sectoral projects such as urban highways, tunnels and housing schemes which were commissioned independently of more comprehensive concepts of urban planning. Development pressures were so strong that hasty day-to-day decisions often overruled desirable long-term strategies – a current phenomenon in rapidly growing cities all over the Third World.

194 City map of Mecca representing conditions around 1970, after the first major extension of the Haram.

195 Reconstruction of the plan of Mecca in the mid-19th century, based on a sketch by Richard F. Burton and combined with the topographic information of the map on the left. The dark hatching indicates the areas demolished in the sixties for the construction of the new extension and the surrounding roads.

The case studies described in the following two sub-sections are intended to illustrate in greater detail the type of problems encountered in both cities during the early eighties. They also include preliminary development schemes which, although not implemented, document alternative – and arguably less disruptive – urban design approaches.

Transportation and Urban Design Strategies for the Inner City of Mecca (1984)

The particular topography of its mountainous site has contributed to the unique character of the city, but it has also imposed heavy constraints on Mecca's urban development: the historic centre at the bottom of the valley was laid out around the courtyard of the sacred Ka'aba which traces its tradition back to the times of Abraham. In ancient times, and in fact up to the middle of this century, the surrounding houses formed the walls, as it were, of the holy mosque and were considered as part of the Haram, the inner precinct of which was defined by a modest arcade, attributed to the Turkish master architect Sinan. The gradual expansion of both the precinct and the city forced the residential districts to climb up the steep and rocky hillside, producing the city's typical bowl-shaped townscape. Most of the traditional houses followed the model of the Arabian tower houses, doing away with the central courtyard but providing enclosed roof terraces for protected open space.

During the last few decades, the development of Mecca was marked by a considerable demographic growth, a dramatic increase of vehicular circulation and an explosive rise in the numbers of pilgrims. As in many other places, authorities and planners have attempted to satisfy the ever-increasing demand for traffic space by constructing new roads. In this case, however, they were faced with almost insoluble problems, due to both topographic obstacles and a mass transportation problem probably unrivaled in any other city. During the seventies, the Saudi government spent enormous efforts on building urban highways, multi-storey car parks in the inner city and tunnels through the mountains for both vehicular and pedestrian use during the Hajj period. This was done with the best of intentions, and the achievements are impressive, at least on the technical level. Yet the impact on the environment also reflects in an almost caricatural way what happens if one function of the urban system – vehicular traffic in this case – is stressed at the expense of other equally important considerations. This process can be compared with the well-known effects of over-exploited natural resources: uncontrolled accessibility may easily destroy the balance of a landscape and jeopardize values which were the very reasons for attracting vis-

196

197

196/197 Views showing the problematic interference between pedestrian and vehicular circulation around the first Haram extension, off the peak of the pilgrimage season (1982).

itors. In a similar way, the townscape of Mecca and the traditional character of the holy site is in danger of being compromised by short-sighted traffic planning measures which do not adapt their tools to a more comprehensive image of the city and the functions they are to serve.

During the sixties, large portions of the historic city centre had to be sacrificed to the first and major mosque extension. A large vehicular road was built around the Haram, which separated the sacred area from the surrounding urban city fabric and immediately became congested with cars. Further demolitions followed to increase the circulation space for pilgrims during the Hajj season and to ease vehicular traffic during the rest of the year. Eventually, a number of radial tunnels converging on the Haram area were built during the early eighties for the same dual purpose. Not so surprisingly, this improvement of accessibility again increased the pressures around the mosque, resulting in additional congestion and calling for further road enlargement, car parks and underground structures. New high-rise developments on the fringe of the inner nucleus had already been started and drastically changed the character of the city, obstructing the natural topography and disturbing the self-contained atmosphere inside the Haram courtyard by the visual impact of the new skyline.

The original master plan for Mecca, established in 1971, had foreseen a system of ring roads, in order to bypass the Haram and to create a low traffic zone around the Holy Mosque. Most of this system was completed during the early eighties and, if correctly used, should have provided relief to the central area. It would have been the appropriate tool for reestablishing the dignity of the Haram, by enveloping it with a predominantly pedestrian area. Instead, the newly built radial tunnels leading to the Haram undermined the very raison d'être of the ring road concept, since they pumped more and more vehicular traffic into a sensitive zone which should have been reserved for pedestrians and could never absorb such amounts of traffic anyway. A further number of car parks were envisaged near the Haram, to replace residential buildings or to be dug into the mountains. Besides its undesirable environmental consequences, this policy would have been unviable even from a strictly transport-oriented point of view, for it would never be able to cope with the demand generated by increased accessibility. And even if further disruption of the urban structure were accepted as a sacrifice to accessibility, it could be anticipated that the incoming and outgoing radial traffic streams, combined with the circulation generated by large car parks around the Haram, would result in a collapse of traffic during peak hours due to the system being overcharged.

During the mid-eighties, the growing planning problems of Mecca, as well as the prospects of possible alternative solutions were of major concern

198 Aerial view of the city centre of Mecca (around 1982), after partial clearance of the historic districts, destroyed to ease traffic around the Haram. On the hill to the south of the Holy Mosque is the Ottoman Jiyad Fort (the site of the project described below) and to the west the new Royal Palace. (Courtesy Hajj Research Centre, Jedda)

to the Hajj Research Centre in Jedda, a newly created academic institution in charge of analyzing all aspects of planning pertaining to the Hajj and the two holy cities and advising the authorities in this respect. During the winter of 1983/84, discussions were held between the Hajj Research Centre, representatives of the Transportation Division of Westinghouse Corporation and the author, to explore the possibilities of a pilot project which would demonstrate the potential of alternative transportation solutions for the inner city around the Haram, combined with an attempt to repair the destroyed urban form in a key area opposite one of the main entrances to the Holy Mosque. An urban design scheme for this site should at the same time illustrate the overall functional, aesthetic and economic advantages of an integrated approach combining public transportation efficiency with environmental improvement.

The premise for these studies was that, with the new ring road system now in place, the main problem was no longer how to increase the existing traffic capacity but rather how to make optimum use of the existing infrastructure and how to repair the townscape around the Haram, while offering visitors and pilgrims adequate accessibility to the Holy Mosque. Thus the proposed option was to stress the original master-plan concept with the recently built outer ring roads and ban private vehicular traffic from the Haram area. In addition, it was suggested that more efficient public transportation systems be promoted, namely by reserving the existing radial tunnels for a special shuttle train system. The strategy also implied the establishment of a "screen" of car parks outside the inner city, where incoming vehicular traffic streams could be intercepted and passengers could conveniently change to shuttle trains leading them to the Haram area. Large empty plots located around two kilometres from the Haram were still available at that time and easy to connect with the existing highway and ring-road system. Land prices there were much cheaper and construction much simpler than in the highly developed central area. Also, there was the opportunity to provide well-located accommodation for pilgrims, in conjunction with the planned shuttle terminals and car parks.

It was anticipated that the low construction costs of these peripheral car parks, together with the reduced need for further road construction and parking garages in the inner city, could result in a substantial saving of public funds, which in turn could be used to finance efficient, safe and comfortable public transportation. The "People Mover" system, successfully applied in large American airports for convenient short-distance transportation was suggested for this purpose. As a quiet and non-polluting train, it had the advantage of being fully compatible with a pedestrian Haram area and of needing only minimum space provisions for the stations at both ends.

199

A feasibility study carried out jointly by the Hajj Research Centre and Westinghouse Corporation showed that two recently constructed large pedestrian tunnels would offer an ideal opportunity to incorporate this new public transport system. The tunnels would make the system independent from the existing road network and therefore ensure maximum operational efficiency. Above the train, a pedestrian deck could be constructed for additional pedestrian movement during the peaks of the Hajj season. The system involved using an enclosed railtrack to save space at the inner-city stations and establish clear divisions between pedestrian and mechanical movement. On the periphery of the city, the stations were to be developed as interchange nodes combined with large parking lots, providing quick and easy transition to the public transport system.

The scheme acknowledged that the need for public transportation in Mecca varies according to specific days and seasons. The following situations were distinguished:

– Normal situation, applicable to usual workdays and involving mainly residents and business traffic.
– Holiday situation, relating to the increased influx of visitors from Jedda and Taif during holidays, Fridays and Ramadan.

199 Map showing the branches of the proposed public-transport system leading from peripheral transfer and car parking stations to the Haram, on the background of the planned or existing road network. The southern branch is the Kodai line described below, while the eastern branch links up with Muna and the plain of Arafat.

— Seasonal situation, resulting from an increase in the number of foreign visitors before and after the Hajj days, or from performing Umra during certain favourable seasons.

— Hajj situation, concerning the peak days during the main pilgrimage season, when transportation from Arafat to Muna and to the Haram has to occur during a fixed period of time.

The purpose of the suggested public-transport system was to deal with the first three of the above cases. The fourth case involves such concentrations of people that no mechanical system can fully cope with the required turnover. There, pedestrian movement would have to prevail, but the public transport system could be useful for elderly or handicapped people, carrying them close to the Haram.

The existing pedestrian tunnels would have allowed the accommodation of a public transport system with at least two branches – from the south through the Kodai tunnel and from the east, i. e. from Arafat, through the Muna tunnel. Both branches would converge on the pedestrian area around the Haram. To test the feasibility of the system, a pilot project was worked out on the Kodai tunnel route, leading from the Jabal al-Thour and the al-Misfala areas to the King's Gate of the Haram. This line was intended to serve the large parking area for the land pilgrims near Jabal al-Thour and the car park in al-Misfala, both in the south of Mecca. For periods other than the Hajj it was thought that these parking lots could also be used to intercept vehicular traffic from Jedda, benefiting from the outer ring road.

While the city of Jedda, located at a distance of 70 kilometres on the Red Sea, has always been the gateway to Mecca, modern development has transformed them into twin cities. Their ring roads were connected by an effective expressway which also establishes a direct connection between Mecca and the new Hajj Terminal at Jedda airport, now the main arrival place for pilgrims.

To maximize the use of the proposed system, the possibility of constructing temporary pilgrim villages near the southern stations of the shuttle train was also considered. The strategic location of such villages would help reduce the congestion in the streets near the Haram during the peak season (when large numbers of people sleep on the street) and would allow them quick access to the Holy Mosque.

Although the Kodai line, as proposed, could have been realized on its own, it could also be seen as a first step towards an integrated regular public-transportation network for the inner city of Mecca. In order to illustrate the advantages of the proposed transportation system and show how the sensitive problem of new stations close to the Holy Mosque could be solved,

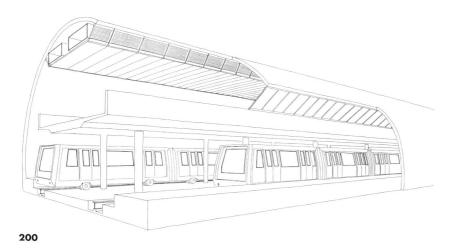

200

201

a more detailed study on the Kodai tunnel and the station opposite the King's Gate of the Haram was prepared. The Kodai tunnel has a length of 1725 metres and a diameter of 16 metres. The proposed People Mover system would serve the large existing southern car parks, the newly developed residential district of Jabal al-Thour and possibly a future pilgrim village. Due to the short length of the tunnel, a capacity of up to 16 000 people per hour could be achieved by shuttle trains with four cars each. More cars could always be added to increase the capacity, if and when required. According to the studies done by the Hajj Research Centre, this capacity would be more than sufficient to serve the visitors arriving by car or by bus from Jedda (10–30 000 people per day during religious holidays).

200 Schematic drawing showing how the People Mover system fits into the existing tunnel profiles.

201 View of the northern outlet of the Kodai tunnel, below the Jiyad Fort and facing the King's Gate of the Haram, after cutting into the hill.

202

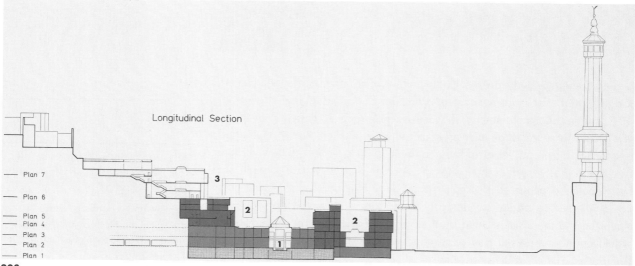

Longitudinal Section

— Plan 7

— Plan 6

— Plan 5
— Plan 4
— Plan 3
— Plan 2
— Plan 1

203

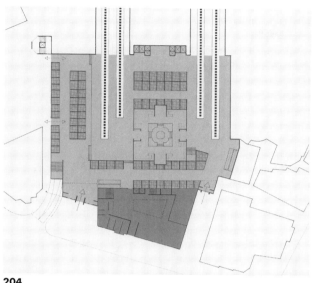

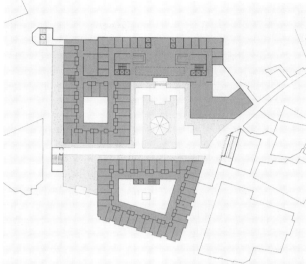

204

205

The area at the northern exit of the tunnel, opposite the King's Gate of the Holy Mosque, posed a critical design problem: a whole section of the former residential district on the hillside had been demolished, and the mountain slope was cut vertically at a height of approximately 20 metres, in order to build the recessed tunnel portals. This intervention caused a major townscape disruption in a sensitive location, opposite one of the main entries of the Haram and beneath the historic Turkish fort that sits above the tunnel. Accordingly, the pilot project for the train station opposite the Kings's Gate was conceived in such a way that it would reshape the disrupted slope by means of an integrated architectural intervention. The new infill structures were arranged as a series of gradually ascending buildings and terraces, crowned by the Jiyad Fort. The whole complex was planned to wrap the main station of the People Mover system into a larger complex with hotels, commercial and cultural facilities – complementary functions much needed in the vicinity of the Haram.

The lowest building of the proposed complex, facing the Haram and its pedestrian area, was a four-storey hotel, keeping the same height as the existing public library adjacent to it. Thus the new building would not overshadow the Holy Mosque, and the fort, an outstanding landmark of Mecca, would remain visible from the pedestrian plaza (the former Suq al-Seghir). The Haram station of the shuttle with its two train tracks was to be located immediately behind this building, accessible through a public hall with a central light dome. Large pedestrian areas were to be incorporated into the station, including ablution and toilet facilities for visitors to the

202/203 Perspective view and cross-section through the infill complex proposed above the outlet of the Kodai tunnel, including the terminal hall and commercial facilities on the lower floors (1), as well as hotels (2) and a conference centre (3) on the upper floor.

204/205 Ground-floor plan with arrival hall (plan 2) and typical hotel floor (plan 4), as marked in the section.

mosque, as well as shops. Elevators at the southern end of the station and the shopping areas would provide vertical connections through the whole complex and up to the platform under the fort.

The second main level of the whole complex, above the train station and behind the front building of the hotel, was to include a garden terrace surrounded by the wings of the upper hotel building, the roof of which formed the base for the cultural centre. The focal point of the garden was the transparent dome of the station below. This level also provided pedestrian connections with the alleys of the adjacent residential district which were disrupted by the tunnel construction.

A new, generously dimensioned cultural centre was proposed for the highest portion of the infill, beneath the Jiyad Fort. It could contain two conference halls, as well as exhibition rooms for permanent or temporary displays on the history of Mecca and the Hajj, or on other cultural subjects. The central foyer with its stairs and galleries matching the slope of the mountain would act as a meeting place and offer further opportunities for occasional exhibitions. Through the foyer, the public had access to the roof terrace offering a splendid view of the city and the Haram.

This project was eventually discontinued due to lack of support from the authorities. The development of the whole Haram surroundings has been left to a semi-private development corporation which opted for a much denser (and more profitable) scheme with high-rise apartment and hotel buildings.

Planning and Urban Design Concepts for the Central Area of Medina-al-Munawara and the Extension of the Prophet's Mosque

Many of the development pressures described in the case of Mecca also apply to the city of Medina. While the number of the resident population rose from around 50 000 in 1950 to 350 000 in 1980 (hardly more than half the size of Mecca), the increase in vehicular traffic has exerted considerable pressures on the urban fabric. Since the plain of Medina allowed for a relatively loose urban structure, the urban development encountered less physical resistance than in the case of Mecca.

The former walled city of Medina was surrounded by suburbs dating from the 19th/20th century, originally constructed and occupied by the Turkish administration, similar to the pattern used in Baghdad, Aleppo and other provincial cities of the late Ottoman period. The largest of these historic suburbs – Zuqaq al-Tayar – was separated from the walled city by a large open space called al-Manakha. Dominated by an Ottoman fort, it served as the arrival square and assembly point for the incoming or depart-

206 The progressive clearance of the historic fabric of Medina in the context of successive urban interventions around the Prophet's Mosque.
In the left column, at the top, the conditions around 1910, with the newly constructed avenue leading to the gate of Bab al-Salam; at the centre, conditions around 1960, after the construction of the new Saudi mosque and various provisions for vehicular traffic, including new access to Bab al-Salam from the south; at the bottom, conditions around 1970, after clearance of part of the historic fabric west of the Haram.
In the right column, at the top, the conditions around 1978, after further clearance due to the construction of temporary prayer sheds; at the centre, conditions around 1983, after a fire which destroyed the left portion of the Aghawat district; at the bottom, conditions around 1990, after total destruction of the Aghawat district.

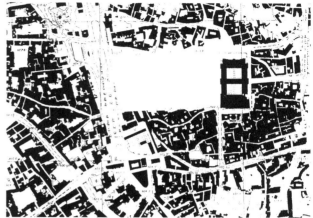

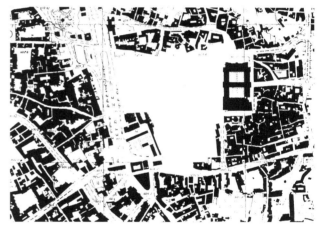
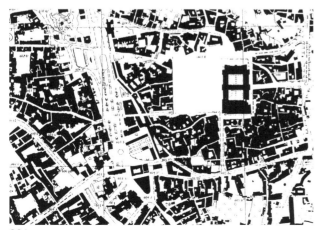
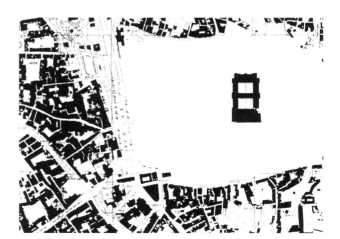

ing caravans, as an open market and as the forecourt to the western city gate which, through a narrow suq, gave access to Bab as-Salaam, the main entrance to the Prophet's Mosque (see page 220).

The mosque occupies the place of the Prophet's former house, the courtyard of which had served as the first social and religious centre of the early Muslim community. Later, the building became the heart of the small city which grew around it. Although the main reference points of the initial house and the first Umayyad mosque are known, no physical structures from the early times have survived, except the tomb of the Prophet, which marks the place of one of the rooms of his former house. The mosque was rebuilt several times during the Mamluk and the late-Ottoman periods, but the green dome above the Prophet's tomb has remained the landmark of the historic city and the symbol of the second holy city of Islam.

We are fairly well informed about the traditional city structure of Medina thanks to the maps drawn by L. Burckhardt and R. F. Burton during the early 19th century, and it seems safe to assume that the conditions shown at that time reflect a much earlier stage. Later pictures and maps show that only little change occurred until the early 20th century, in spite of the renewal of the mosque under Sultan Abdulmajid in the second half of the 19th century. It was only during the last years of the Ottoman rule, shortly before World War I, that a straight avenue with lateral arcades was cut out from the old city as a direct access to the main entry of the Haram.

In the early fifties of this century, most of the late-Ottoman mosque, except the hall close to the qibla wall, which contains the references to the original Prophet's mosque, was replaced and enlarged by a new Saudi structure. This was also the time when parts of the walled city started to be demolished, in order to provide wider open spaces around the enlarged mosque. The erosion process was accelerated by further cuts into the historic fabric, made in order to achieve better vehicular access and to build car parks near the mosque. It was also fuelled by general neglect of the old city and by a partial burning and subsequent demolition of the historic districts adjacent to the mosque. This process reached a first climax around 1980, when most of the old city core had disappeared in order to allow for a temporary mosque extension west of the existing building and large car parks south of it.

Clearly, the enlargement of the mosque by itself would not have justified the disappearence of three quarters of the old city *intra muros,* especially as an extension to the south of the original qibla wall had to be ruled out for religious reasons. This is why the remaining part of the al-Aghawat district was initially kept on stand-by, to be demolished at a later stage. The Aghawat quarter contained some of the oldest historic sites of the Holy City

208

207 Aerial view of the central district of Medina in 1982, showing the remaining part of the historic district of al-Aghawat, south and east of the Prophet's Mosque, the conservation of which was attempted in the early eighties. To the west of the mosque, the temporary prayer sheds (Courtesy Hajj Research Centre, Jedda).

208 Interior view of the Saudi extension of the Prophet's Mosque, constructed in 1952 (National Geographic Magazine).

and was originally built to accommodate the "servants of the Haram". It featured a number of interesting houses from the 18th/19th century, built with volcanic stone and bricks. The architectural typology of these houses was reminiscent of Egyptian houses of the Mamluk typology, with their iwans and qa'as. Being close to the mosque and having been mostly abandoned by the old owners, the houses were rented to pilgrims from poorer Islamic countries who could not afford expensive accommodation and yet wanted to live near the Haram.

In the early eighties, the need for a more comprehensive development vision of the city centre was felt, and a master plan was commissioned to the Saudi firm of Moussali, Shaker, Mandily. It was to include the plan for a "Cultural Area" around the Haram, covering the whole district of the former walled city. This action area plan, established under the direction of the author, was intended to become the keystone of the master plan, since the overall development of the city had to obey a certain number of constraints resulting from the planning of the Haram area.

The survey of existing conditions is exemplified by a number of maps showing the progressive destruction of the historic fabric between 1950 and 1982 (see pages 233 and 234) and by a number of contemporary pictures of the site. The situation could be summarized as follows:

- The Prophet's Mosque was almost totally isolated from its historic urban context, and its provisional extension, covered by prefabricated aluminium roofs, appeared rather inapproporiate.

- Large empty surfaces were created around the precinct of the Holy Mosque and used as parking lots.

- Intense vehicular traffic in the immediate surroundings of the Haram conflicted with the pedestrian flows and created congestion all over the central area, especially during prayer times.

- The remaining parts of the old city were rapidly decaying due to lack of maintenance and suitable rehabilitation policies.

- Land speculation in the central area was getting out of control, generating high redevelopment pressures and corresponding townscape problems, with more and more high-rise buildings being erected in the immediate vicinity of the Haram.

- Green areas within the city had disappeared at a rapid rate, with the effect that hardly any trees were left in the inner city, which was traditionally known for its beautiful palm gardens.

The general planning and urban design scheme for the central area, conceived as part of the 1982 master plan, was rooted in the traditional image

209   **210**

of Medina, as determined by a sanctuary embedded in a cluster of surrounding houses. Indeed, the large courtyard of the Prophet's Mosque had always served as the centre of the whole urban structure, which could be considered as an extension, as it were, of the Haram. Whilst the present conditions had radically changed, it did not seem unreasonable to adopt this powerful image as a basis for a contemporary urban design interpretation.

During the planning process, it was realized that the question of how to utilize and complement the existing circulation network would be decisive for the future of the central area: the boundaries of the present central area of Medina had recently been redefined by the construction of the first ring road, which separated the urban nucleus from the outer districts. The enclosed area corresponded, by and large, to the previous historic city *intra muros*. If the ring road was to be used mainly as a distributor of vehicular traffic into the Haram area, it would increase congestion and promote further destruction of the environment. If, on the other hand, it could serve to intercept the radial traffic flows that tended to converge on the Prophet's Mosque, it would provide a means for protecting the Haram from the pressures of traffic. It would thus open new opportunities for the appropriate development of the most sensitive parts of the central area, preserving the integrity of the urban nucleus.

Accordingly, the master plan suggested surrounding the Haram area with a specially treated pedestrian zone, which would cover large parts of the central district. This protective envelope would in turn be surrounded by a zone with limited vehicular access, covering the rest of the central area inside the first ring road and forming a buffer zone around the pedestrian urban nucleus. Only residents, public transport, taxis and service vehicles

209 The Prophet's Mosque and Bab al-Salam as approached from southeast (1984).

210 The northwestern corner of the Prophet's Mosque and the western square with the temporary prayer sheds during the pilgrimage season (1983, courtesy Hajj Research Centre, Jedda).

would be allowed to circulate within this low-traffic zone, which was to include special drop-off points on the edge around the Haram. Through-traffic would be discouraged by a specially designed circulation system consisting of self-contained loops and cul-de-sacs. Multi-storey car park facilities, strategically located along the first ring road, would enable non-residents to leave their cars and proceed to the inner city on foot or by public transport.

Through the combined effects of all these devices, the first ring road would function like a new city wall: vehicular traffic would be filtered and adequate accessibility would be offered to the Haram zone and to the residential quarters in the corners of the central area. Walking distances from the main drop-off points to the Prophet's Mosque would not exceed 200–300 metres. The pedestrian routes were arranged in such a way that they passed through the ancillary buildings of the mosque, or they were designed as pleasant and attractive walkways with shading structures and attached gardens and commercial facilities. Accessibility was to be improved by the use of public transport and minibuses servicing the pedestrian area along its edges. Special provisions were made for giving dignitaries and handicapped people direct access, as well as for emergency cases.

The above planning concept had an important repercussion on the broader context of the master plan context, since it was instrumental in restructuring the whole circulation network. Thus it was recommended that the predominant radial traffic flows converging on the Holy Mosque be diverted, since they affected the environmental quality of the Haram area. At any rate, they were inefficient even in their own terms, because of the congestion they caused in the city centre. At that time, a second ring road had been initiated around the urban agglomeration as a whole, but it was too far away to take pressure off the inner ring road. The master plan therefore recommended reinforcing the circular patterns in the most critical zone by establishing a new intermediate ring road system which would intercept and distribute the radial traffic flows before they reached the inner ring road. For this purpose it was sufficient to interconnect a number of existing roads by short new linkages. Through-traffic could thus become more efficient, bypassing the central area and protecting the distributor function of the inner ring road.

Before describing in greater detail the urban design proposal which hinges on the above re-organization of vehicular traffic, it is necessary to provide basic data concerning the very special parameters the project had to take into account. In Medina the pilgrimage season has a lower peak than in Mecca, since pilgrims flock in before and after the specific days of the Hajj and are therefore distributed over a longer period. It is mainly foreign pilgrims who visit Medina, in combination with their journey to Mecca,

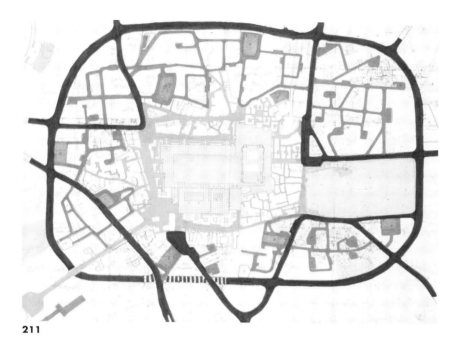

211

while residents of Saudi Arabia usually prefer other seasons. As a result, the number of pilgrims staying simultaneously in the city during the Hajj season is much smaller than in Mecca.

Statistical data to determine the maximum number of pilgrims staying in Medina on the same day was not available. However, a fairly accurate indication was possible by interpreting aerial views of the Haram area during the peak period, i.e. during the noon prayers on the first Friday after the Hajj. From an aerial photograph shot in the year 1981, the maximum number of pilgrims assembled simultaneously within and around the mosque was computed at approximately 105 000 persons (assuming a gross area of one square metre per person). This would correspond to about five to six percent of the total number of pilgrims participating in the Hajj during the same year.

The question that arose with regard to the needs of future expansion was whether the quantitative mechanics of development should be allowed to determine the character of the city forever, or whether it was possible to assume certain limits based on a reasonable "carrying capacity" of the site and the city, as related to the desired environmental quality. The master plan team finally adopted the decision to assume a limit of around 200 000 simultaneous visitors as a basis for the new design of the Haram area, with a certain flexibility provided in the open spaces around the future mosque buildings.

211 Proposal for a pedestrianised zone (in dark) around the Prophet's Mosque and its western extensions, developed by the author on behalf of the Hajj Research Centre in Jedda (1982). The plan suggested the conservation and rehabilitation of the remaining part of al-Aghawat (as well as the historic arteries of Bab al-Majidi and Zuqaq at-Tayyar), an array of car parks on the inner ring road and a scheme of vehicular loops for drop-off and public transportation reaching the corners of the pedestrian area.

212

213

212-214 Visual scenarios for the rehabilitation of low-traffic and pedestrian areas in the historic areas inside the first ring road. On this page, above, the main west-east spine of Zuqaq at-Tayyar leading to al-Manakha Square (top), and a communal courtyard (howsh) inside the old residential fabric of Zuqaq at-Tayyar. On the opposite page, the spine of Bab al-Majidi, north of the Haram extension. (Drawings by Werner Muller, Baltimore)

214

The ground floor space of the existing mosque and its present extension amounted to approximately 78 000 square metres, which allowed for a maximum of 80 000 people in praying position. An easy possibility of extending the space would have existed to the south of the current sheds in the empty Shuna area, now occupied by open-air car parks. This would, however, have implied that the Imam's position be shifted from its present place to the southern edge of the Shuna site, at least during Hajj time. As this was not acceptable to the religious authorities, the present qibla wall had to be maintained as the southern limit of the future mosque extension. Other such possibilities existed to the north and northeast of the present Haram complex and concerned the plots between Sahah Street and Suheimi Street, as well as the commercial premises north of King Abdul Aziz Street, none of which represented any historical or architectural values. Compensation for demolished shops, hotels and restaurants in this area could be provided in the form of development rights in the Shuna district, south of the Prophet's Mosque.

Considering the size of the extension needed, it became clear that one of the major problems in the urban design of the new Haram area was one of scale, i. e. the problem of how to relate the enormous volume of the prayer spaces required to the surrounding urban texture and to the standards of human perception. For a better understanding of the actual dimensions involved, the site map of the Haram was superimposed with plans of the most monumental urban spaces of both the Islamic and the Western world. These overlays, done at the same scale, made it evident that treating the new mosque extension as one single monumental block would dwarf the original mosque and jeopardize any attempt at an integration with the urban environment. The thing to be avoided – so it seemed – was creating a monstrous isolated building with vast empty spaces around it, an ill-suited approach for what can rightly be called the most significant mosque of the Islamic world.

Therefore, the urban design scheme adopted the idea of articulating the huge mass into a number of interconnected units forming a complex architectural fabric which related to the scale of the existing building. The predominance of the old Prophet's Mosque was emphasized by the fact that its two axes of symmetry would be used as the "backbones" governing the composition of the added architectural units and that the elevations of the old building were exposed by a series of courtyards (see page 245).

Since one of the objectives of the project was to re-establish a coherent urban form in the central area and to link the Haram extension with the surrounding structures, great importance was attached to the development of pedestrian interconnections. Accordingly, the historic streets of Zuqaq at-Tayyar and Bab al-Majidi were maintained and continued as major spines leading into the Haram precinct. In the areas which had been subject to recent wholesale demolition a new urban fabric had to be created. The redevelopment of the Shuna area (southwest of the mosque) played a major role in this endeavour: its layout was structured by a new pedestrian mall leading towards the main Haram entrance of Bab as-Salam and focusing on the Prophet's dome. In order to enhance the vista by a surprise effect, a bent transition from Ghamama Square into this axis was proposed. At the end of the street, on the corner opposite Bab as-Salam, an Islamic conference centre was suggested. The irregular square in front of it contrasts with the rectangular forms of the mosque extension and mediates between the new diagonal mall and the old Bab as-Salam Street which, being aligned with

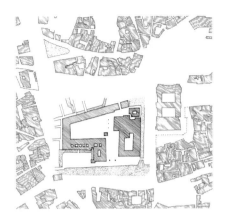

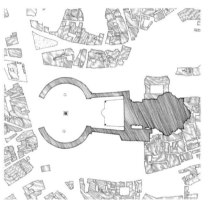

215

215 Diagrams comparing the Piazza San Marco (above) and the Peter's Dome in Rome (below) with the Haram Square in Medina, at same scale.

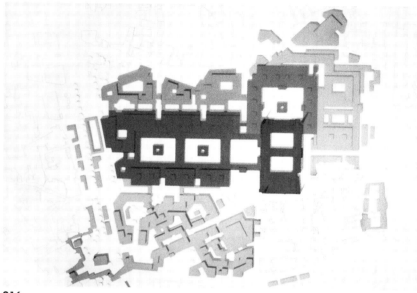

216

the qibla wall, would continue to serve ceremonial purposes. On the southern side of the diagonal mall, a system of secondary commercial streets with
small interjected courtyards would connect the new infill with the remains of
the historic Aghawat district, which would be conserved and integrated as
an essential component of this scheme. On the other side of the mall, intermediate links with Bab as-Salam Street were proposed, featuring a number
of larger landscaped courtyards.

In the southern part of the Shuna area, accessible through Darb al-
Janaiz Street, a taxi and bus station was proposed, from where the visitors
could reach the Haram area. Other drop-offs were planned at the end of
Anbariya Street, with special entrances into the holy precinct through the
pedestrianized zone of al-Ghamama. From there, pilgrims could access
the former al-Manakaha Street, now pedestrianized and planted with
groups of palm trees. Or they could reach the Prophet's Mosque by choosing between the formal mall and smaller, more informal approaches, one of
them leading through the old southwestern city gate, Bab al-Masri. In this
area, covered passages, courtyards and arcades would provide opportunities for social intercourse, shopping, eating and relaxing in the immediate
vicinity of the Haram.

Similar public-transportation access points, interconnected with pedestrian paths, were foreseen with regard to the northern street loops on the
opposite side of the Haram complex. The drop-offs were to be located close
to the northwestern and the eastern boundaries of the new Haram complex,

216 Final proposal for a phased Haram
extension developed by the author on
behalf of the Hajj Research Centre (1983),
based on the planning scheme on page
239. The aim of this urban design scheme
was to articulate building masses and
open spaces in ways which would relate
them to the old Prophet's Mosque and
reweave the fringe of the destroyed urban
fabric. The dark tone indicates the proposed extent of the first phase, leaving
options for two further extensions at a later
stage.

217

one near the little garden of Saqifat Bani Saada, and the other near the cemetery (al-Bakkiya). From there, shaded arcades would lead to the main entrances of the Haram complex. The former Sahah Street was to be kept as a major pedestrian axis, serving the large northern courtyard of the Haram extension. In keeping with the other main approaches, the intention was to stress the rhythmical sequence of these pedestrian paths by a series of gateways, porches and first-floor building connections bridging across the walkways.

The integration of the mosque extension with associated functions and surrounding buildings was another prime objective of this urban design scheme. In most traditional Muslim cities, commercial activities and social facilities were closely related to the prayer hall, and associated functions such as education and jurisdiction took place within the mosque. Accordingly, an attempt was made to surround the new extension with new suqs dealing in books, perfumes, prayer carpets etc. Ablution facilities were to be dispersed in small units all along the northern edge of the extension, in

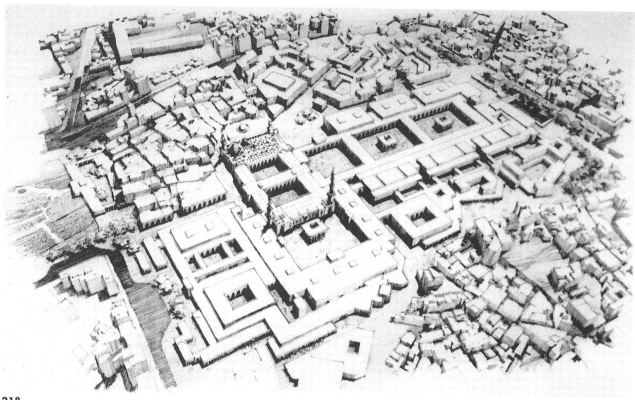

218

order to avoid congestion. In the northwestern corner of the extension, a traditional Qur'anic university, using this part of the prayer hall as a public lecturing place, was suggested. The upper floor and the buildings across Sahah Street could contain supporting administrative and educational facilities and possibly even accommodation for students and teachers, reviving the madrasa concept within the Haram and contributing to a lively use of the large prayer halls throughout the year.

The building volumes of the new infill proposed between Sahah and Suheimi Streets were treated in such a way as to establish an architectural transition between the formal Haram structure and the northern part of the urban fabric. They were to have a flexible ground floor plan, allowing the available open space to be used for prayer whenever needed (particularly during the peak season), while during other periods it would be allocated to informal commercial use. This multi-functional approach would sustain the Haram's integration in the urban fabric, while preventing the central area from becoming a "dead place" during the low season.

217/218 Bird's-eye renderings of the proposed extension (1983) and the surrounding urban fabric from southwest (left page) and from northeast. The Aghawat district, earmarked for conservation, is to the southeast of the Prophet's Mosque. (Drawings by Werner Muller, Baltimore)

At this preliminary urban design stage, the scheme presented had no ambition of committing the proposal to precise architectural features. Its main intention was to clarify the major conceptual principles with regard to issues such as distribution of volumes, relations between solids and voids, and interaction of the Haram extension with the surrounding urban fabric. It seemed appropriate, however, to visualize the extension in a rhythm compatible with that of the present mosque building. This implied, for instance, providing for reasonable maximum distances between structural columns (up to eight metres), in order to prepare for suitable proportions of arches and arcades. Shading the courtyards during the summer season was also seen as a critical issue. Therefore, the inclusion of pavilions with shaded fountains in some of the larger courtyards was envisaged. Their structures would also allow canvas awnings to be attached, which could span the space between the edges of the pavilions and the surrounding arcades.

The total prayer surface within the boundaries of the new Haram extension amounts to approximately 160 000 square metres. By including the flexible ground-floor space of the intermediate buildings and the surrounding pedestrian streets (available for temporary prayer use during peak seasons), this surface could be increased to about 240 000 square metres. The scheme could thus easily accommodate a maximum prayer capacity of at least 240 000 persons, which would meet the needs for the foreseeable future.

Besides obvious aesthetic considerations, one of the main reasons for subdividing the Haram extension into a number of interrelated individual buildings was to grant optimum flexibility for future design and implementation. Detailing and implementing the project in reasonable increments without incurring the risk of "fragmentary" intermediate stages was seen as an important design task. The suggested phasing and the approximate capacity of the corresponding buildings are represented in a diagram which shows that the building could have a "complete" character at each stage of its future development. The benefits of the proposed incremental approach are specially evident if one considers the necessary demolition and replacement of existing buildings and the disruption this could cause in the central area.

Together with the above urban design scheme for the Haram extension, an effort was made to convince the authorities of the need for a sensitive conservation and rehabilitation of the remaining architectural heritage of the Prophet's city. Here, the main problem was to overcome the prevailing opinion that neglected historic areas must by necessity remain "backward" and that they should be abandoned altogether in favour of modern re-development. Since the proposed master plan for the central area implied the

219

219 Visual scenario of the rehabilitation of one of the main alleyways in the historic al-Aghawat district, east of the Haram (1982), to be conserved under the proposed extension scheme.

220 Proposed conservation area in the Aghawat district, destroyed in 1983/84.

221 View of the model of the new mosque extension, as built in 1988 - 1995, seen from southwest.

222 Site plan with the massive block of the mosque extension floating on the deck of a vast and exposed open plaza, which was "Islamicized" by oversize ornamental patterns. The project functions only in terms of mass accommodation during the critical days of the Hajj, but makes no attempt to deal with the urban context during the rest of the year.

220

conservation of the few surviving parts of the old city and their integration into the new scheme, it was important to sketch out a number of simulations illustrating the possible effects of restoring the buildings and upgrading the area, in combination with corresponding transportation and environmental improvement measures. The very function of the city as a "guesthouse" of the Islamic World, the desire of many Islamic communities to have a permanent "home" in the Holy City, near the Prophet's Mosque, and eventually their willingness to participate in a joint venture would have offered opportunities for a unique rehabilitation project, without jeopardizing the necessary extension of the Haram complex.

Postscript

During the official submission and approval period of the 1982 master plan, the government authorities commissioned an independent project for the Haram extension by a major Saudi contractor, which ignored most of the conceptual guidelines put forward by the master plan and the central area action plan. The new project, executed during the late eighties, illustrates the consequences of a radically different approach, which stresses architectural monumentality while ignoring human scale and integrated urban form considerations (see next page).

221

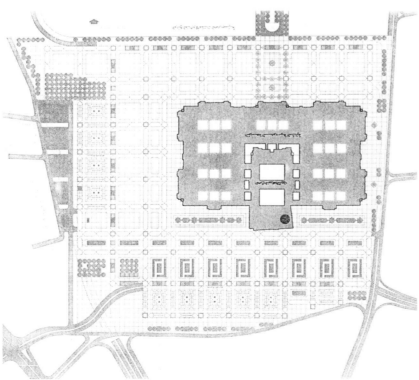

222

Case Study II:
Baghdad – an Arab Metropolis between Conservation and Redevelopment

Historic Background and Project Context

Founded during the early Abbasid period (756 AD) with the intention of re-placing the Umayyad capital of Damascus, Baghdad was for two centuries the sole seat of the caliphate and the main centre of the Islamic empire. It was to lose its exclusive position with the rise of the Fatimid, Ayyubid and Seljuk dynasties, which introduced Cairo and Isfahan as competing centres of power. Yet until the early 13th century, Baghdad remained an important cultural centre and survived the fatal blow of the Mongol invasion, although this event led to the destruction of large parts of the city in 1258 AD. Eventually, after a long period of political struggle between rival tribal powers, the city found political stability again under Ottoman rule (1683 to 1917 AD), but was henceforth reduced to the status of a provincial centre. After the mid-twentieth century, with the end of the British colonial regime and the recent resurgence of Iraq as an independent state, it re-affirmed itself as a major capital of the modern Arab world with high political ambitions.

The first settlement of Baghdad was the famous "Round City" of al-Mansur on the western bank of the Tigris (756 AD), of which detailed written accounts, but no physical evidence, have survived. As with other Islamic capitals, the city outgrew its original shape of a planned palatial and military settlement, giving birth to other, more spontaneously established urban districts. Its suburbs reached out to the eastern bank of the Tigris, generating the district of Rusafa, which over a period of time shifted over one kilometre southwards from its original position. When the Abbasids came back to Baghdad after a short intermezzo in Samarra (836–892 AD), it was Rusafa that they selected for their new residence, abandoning the previous northern settlements and confirming the shift of the urban system which had occurred.

During the Seljuk rule (1052–1152 AD), Rusafa was surrounded by new city walls, and this fortification was to determine the site and the size of the city until the beginning of the modern age. The late Abbasid reign (1152–1258 AD) was a privileged period – almost a reflection of the earlier golden age of Baghdad. A number of historic buildings such as the Mustansiriya Madrasa and the so-called Abbasid Palace, though heavily restored, have survived from this period, but the then Royal Palace located

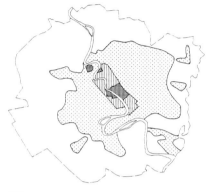

Phase-1: Traditional city
Phase-2: Urban change up to 1950
Phase-3: Modern metropolis from 1950
223

223 The major phases of urban development in Baghdad.

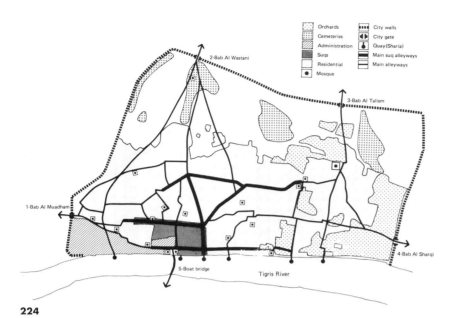

Orchards		City walls	
Cemeteries		City gate	
Administration		Quay (Sharia)	
Suqs		Main suq alleyways	
Residential		Main alleyways	
Mosque			

2-Bab Al Wastani

3-Bab Al Talism

1-Bab Al Muadham

4-Bab Al Sharqi

5-Boat bridge

Tigris River

224

north of the present Khulafa Street was lost, probably due to the Mongol invasion. The beginning of the modern era dates from 1869, when the Ottoman administration under Midhat Pasha started modernizing the city, tearing down the old city walls and constructing the first residential extensions *extra muros*.

Among the dominant features of the old city, as seen in the plan by Felix Jones from 1854, were the enclosed citadel and the "Sarai" (the Turkish governor's palace), both at the northern end of the city, as well as the "Meidan" near the citadel, which was the forecourt and main entrance to the city. The Meidan led into a market which, running parallel to the river, connected the square with the central suq complex near the Mustansiriya Madrasa. This was the focal point of the urban system, where other spines coming from the shrine of al-Gailani and from the eastern gates of Bab al-Thalassa and Bab al-Wastani converged. The central suqs were accessible from the Tigris, which functioned as the main transportation axis of the city. Attached to the Mustansiriya was a customs station, from where a pontoon bridge provided a direct connection with the al-Karkh quarter on the other side of the river.

The bulk of the historic urban fabric was formed by the residential districts (mahallas) of the walled city, which covered an area of approximately 3 by 2 kilometres. It can be assumed that their basic layout did not change much between the Seljuk period and the end of the 19th century. Yet most of the surviving residential structures are no older than 60–100 years, since

224 Diagrammatic scheme of the historic urban system of the Rusafa district, within the former city walls.

225 Felix Jones' plan of Rusafa from 1854, superimposed with the road network of the modern urban system carved into the historic fabric.

the houses were built from brick and timber and had to be reconstructed periodically, due to frequent flood damage, fire and termite infestation.

The establishment of Rusafa's modern urban system started in 1914, when al-Rashid Street, an avenue for horse carriages and vehicular traffic with attached pedestrian colonnades, was cut through the historic fabric. In 1936, this operation was followed by Kifa Street, a second parallel axis at a greater distance from the river, built by German engineers. Thanks to the moderate height of their street fronts (two upper floors) and the careful re-weaving of the open meshes, these colonial-style street arcades, while clearly introducing new development parameters, caused limited harm to the then existing urban fabric.

The same could not be said of the new urban corridor of Jumhuriya Street (now Khulafa Street), carved out in 1956 and bordered by free-stand-

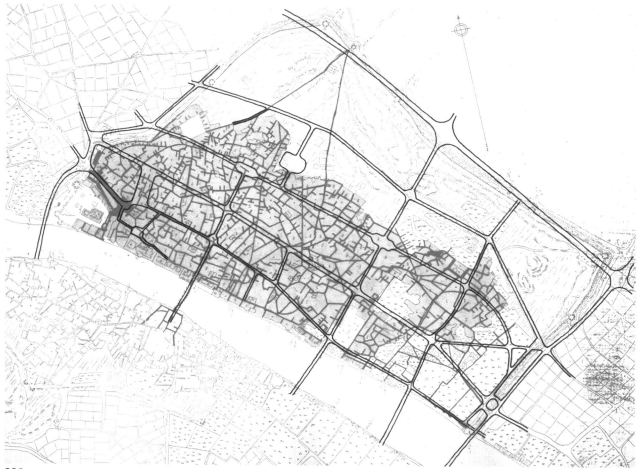

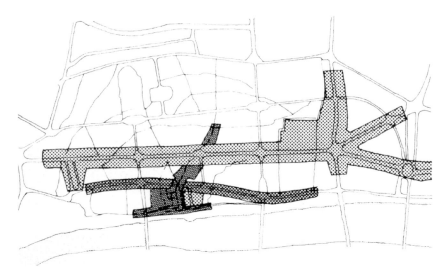

226

ing blocks with heights of up to 32 metres. This new axis, again parallel to the Tigris, linked the northern and southern ends of the rapidly growing metropolis and formed a new linear central area which was intended to become representative of modern Iraq. It was complemented by a system of perpendicular roads and two new bridges across the Tigris. In this case, the problem of mending the disrupted urban form was not really solved: large areas on both sides of the new road were given over to wholesale redevelopment, many old residential districts were destroyed and the fringes of the traditional urban fabric left to neglect and decay.

As a result of this orthogonal grid of modern vehicular roads, Rusafa's once continuous urban fabric was dissected into isolated fragments. Implicitly, it was assumed that the historic districts were condemned to disappear, and they were therefore used as a quarry for the progressive establishment of the modern city centre. While the need for new vehicular corridors was ineluctable, no attempt was made to reconcile the two conflicting urban systems and adapt urban interventions to the existing context. Developing the modern city centre thus became synonymous with sacrificing the historic quarters – an ideology which lead to the creeping destruction of the old city: physically, by the fragmentation of the historic fabric and the isolation of its components; socially, by the exodus of the old bourgeoisie into new residential suburbs.

The vacuum was more than compensated by the influx of a rural population in search of opportunities and employment. The old city became a welcome refuge and intermediate station for immigrants, who rented the old houses, often at the rate of one family per room. The resulting densification,

226 The three successive central areas of Rusafa: in dark grey the old suqs on the riverfront and the spine towards Gaylani; in medium grey the "colonial" shopping street of al-Rashid Street; and, in light grey, the new central business district and government administration developing around Khulafa Street.

coupled with the fact that absent landlords were not interested in maintaining their houses (investments being discouraged by strict rent control),
accelerated the physical decay. In addition, a new type of rampant semi-
industrial production geared to immigrant workers occupied all available
niches inside and outside the historic city, often transforming old houses into
workshops. Along Sheikh Omar Street, the belt of previous unbuilt areas
intra muros was progressively filled by industrial activities and services,
such as mechanical workshops, garages, car repair shops and factories, all
of them taking advantage of easy vehicular accessibility.

Eventually, three separate and partly conflicting urban systems emerged
in Rusafa. Firstly, there was a neglected historic district suffering from insuf-
ficient infrastructure, amenities and social facilities and inhabited by a
crowded, predominantly poor population (largely immigrants and seasonal
workers). It included busy local markets and emerging modern manufacturing facilities (leather, clothes, plastic and household goods) occupying
decaying old suq structures and expanding into the former residential dis-

227 Typical section of Rashid Street.

228 Typical section of Kifa Street.

229 Khulafa Street after destruction of
the adjacent historic fabric, with the new
government centre in the background.

230 Current conditions along the Sheikh
Omar beltway (1984).

tricts. Secondly, there was a modern service centre reflecting the size of the metropolis and catering to the needs of the upper middle class and the new leadership. It featured Western-type shops, banks, government administration, offices, hotels, restaurants and cinemas and constituted an erratic block in the old city, in both functional and architectural terms. Thirdly, there was an industrial zone in the former open belt of the old city, engaging in heavy modern production processes yet still following certain pre-industrial habits which, at this scale, caused enormous congestion, pollution and unacceptable encroachment on public space.

Balancing these contradicting elements and resolving internal conflicts and establishing compatibility (if not synergies) between different types of development would have exceeded the capabilities of almost any city administration. It would have required enlightened leadership, innovative planning tools, creative urban design capabilities, flexible implementation processes, continuous and efficient institutional support and, above all, a high degree of civic commitment and community participation. The combination of such favourable factors did not exist in Baghdad, since the government, eager to develop the "modern" image of the capital (and at that time having seemingly unlimited financial resources at its disposal) opted for the easiest solution – massive redevelopment. In 1980, President Saddam Hussein decided to cut the Gordian knot, as it were, by launching an ambitious large-scale urban renewal programme which was intended to totally reshape the appearance of Baghdad within three years by implementing a number of monumental projects on both sides of the Tigris. In the Rusafa area, two major interventions were planned: one project involved completing the transformation of Khulafa Street into a prestigious main axis of modern Baghdad, and the other tackling the redevelopment of the Bab al-Sheikh area along a new perpendicular road connecting the railway station with the Tigris riverbanks.

The first project on Khulafa Street, as developed by The Architects' Collaborative (TAC) in Cambridge (USA), did not limit itself to the infill of new buildings along the existing urban corridor; it extended laterally into the old city, with large 12-floor mega-structures celebrating the major traffic nodes and opening large squares around important intersections. In addition, a large-scale river bank scheme was proposed, following the model of a typical American waterfront redevelopment rather than interpreting the much finer grain of the historic Baghdad riverfront with its sequence of private terraces overlooking the Tigris. Needless to say, the abstract monumental character of the Khulafa Street project completely ignored the existence of historic urban structures. Rather, it exacerbated the existing rupture between "old" and "modern", by highlighting the main vehicular corridors and celebrating traffic nodes as dominant urban spaces. Lip service was paid to the

231 Urban redevelopment scheme for Khulafa Street and the surrounding zones, as proposed by TAC in 1980, but only partly executed.

232 Typical sections of the redevelopment scheme for Bab al-Sheikh proposed by Arup and Partners in 1982, and partly executed before the war between Iraq and Iran.

cause of conservation by identifying single monuments to be restored, but the layout and scale of the proposed new buildings ruled out any real dialogue with the historic urban fabric.

The second major redevelopment project in Rusafa (there were others in Kharkh on the opposite side of the Tigris and on the Abu Nawas riverfront section) concerned the Bab al-Sheikh spine, perpendicular to the river and to Khulafa Street. This project was subdivided into different sub-sectors handed over to Ove Arup and Partners (London), Richard England (Malta), Ricardo Bofill (Barcelona) and John Warren/APP (UK). Architecturally, it represented a much more interesting approach to redevelopment, since most of the individual projects, while obviously accepting the imposed demolitions, attempted to establish a transition of urban scale between the old city and the new street fronts. All of them endeavoured to create new housing

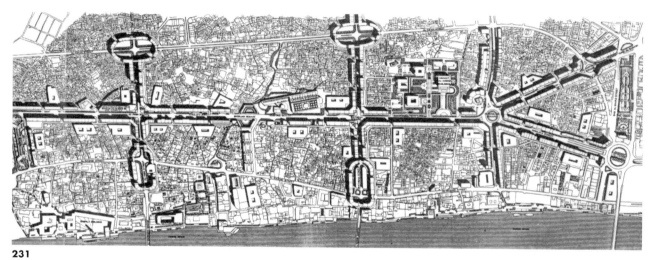

231

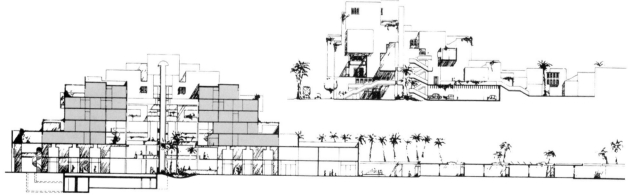

232

typologies relating to traditional models and adapted to local habits and climatic factors by introducing protected private open spaces in the form of enclosed terraces or private courtyards. John Warren's project for al-Gaylani, at the corner between Kifa Street and the new Bab al-Sheikh Avenue, had the merit of proposing the conservation of a number of historic houses in this zone, together with an adapted infill scheme around the Gaylani shrine (an important place of pilgrimage). This area had previously been cleared to expose the shrine and to create parking space. The new infill project repaired the broken urban fabric by providing new town houses with traditional courtyards above an underground car park.

During the preparations for the Khulafa Street project and the Bab al-Sheikh project, the Municipality of Baghdad, benefiting from the advice of the distinguished Iraqi architect Rifat Chadirji, became aware of the fact that major slices of the "old city cake" were being given away for redevelopment without any overarching concept which could establish a relation between the proposed new structures and the surrounding urban fabric, whether old or new. Finally, the municipality decided first to trim down the Khulafa Street project to the central street spine and those components already under execution (government centre) and, second, to initiate a comprehensive planning approach covering the whole of the central area within the old city, in order to establish a modicum of coherence between individual interventions. This desire to coordinate between conservation and redevelopment tasks was the starting point for the Rusafa project. By the end of 1982, a consortium of consultants was appointed by the municipality, including Ihsan Fethi, Sohiko Yamada, Giorgio Lombardi and Stefano Bianca, who also acted as the group's coordinator.

The work of this group, which will be briefly described in the following paragraphs, was completed in December 1983. The final report, a "structure plan" for the whole study area, as well as more detailed conservation and urban design schemes for the most significant elements of the urban system, were presented to the authorities in Spring 1984. The well-known political events, which resulted in practically all major projects coming to a standstill after 1984, did not allow for the project to be followed up by subsequent phases of detailing and implementation. However, its approach may be of interest well beyond the case of Baghdad, as it represents an example of an integrated planning framework, where the conservation of selected historic districts was tackled in the context of broader development policies and in conjunction with related urban renewal schemes. Obviously, the project came in at the last hour, and already committed interventions could not be fundamentally changed or abandoned, but the task of considering and, where possible, repairing the broken urban form was taken seriously.

233

The Rusafa Planning Study

When discussing the objectives of the comprehensive planning scheme for Rusafa, it became clear that "freezing" the historic centre in its present condition (let alone re-establishing its former shape) was not a viable solution. Rusafa's relatively large historic fabric, the size of its resident population (approximately 200 000) and its importance as a central business district would not have allowed for such an approach. Yet it appeared equally wrong to propose a total redevelopment, even if this was to include the preservation of a few isolated historic buildings. The main task therefore was to establish the right linkages between the existing components of the urban system, to consolidate the remains of the historic fabric and to prevent the "strong" elements from overpowering weaker, but precious urban features. For this purpose, conservation and redevelopment had to be conceived as complementary and interactive approaches within a well-balanced overall strategy for the city centre of Baghdad – keeping in mind that dramatic shifts of the present resident population should be avoided, and that living and working conditions in the area should be improved.

233 Map showing the existing conditions of the historic fabric at the beginning of the Rusafa study. The new government centre on Khulafa Street (1) was practically completed and the clearing for the urban redevelopment of the Bab al-Sheikh scheme on the north-south spine crossing the Tigris (2) was already accomplished. The other proposed demolitions for TAC's Khulafa Street redevelopment were suspended during the Rusafa planning works.

In accordance with these goals and the given constraints, the following basic principles of the new master plan were defined:

a) *To establish compatibility between the activities of the Central Business District (CBD) and the physical environment of the historic urban fabric:*
This involved a general reorganization of land uses in order to make them consistent with the specific character and the restricted capacity of distinct types of "architectural containers", especially in the case of the old city morphology, which imposed limitations on certain functions. Implicitly, the objective entailed a subdivision of the CBD into two differently structured zones: on the one hand, a more "traditional" and mainly pedestrian centre in the core of the surviving historic city, attuned to cultural functions, recreation and small-scale retail activities; on the other hand, a more "modern" city centre in the new redevelopment sectors containing offices, administration, large-scale shops and modern facilities and amenities. Both should be seen as being complementary to each other. Since a large-sized modern CBD had already been planned and partly realized by previous and current development, special attention was now to be given to enhancing the remains of the historic city, to rehabilitating certain traditional housing districts and to reviving the suqs as an attractive pedestrian centre within the CBD. This also meant reorienting the further growth of the modern CBD, setting limits to its expansion in sensitive areas and introducing appropriate linkages between old and new urban structures.

b) *To reduce pressures of vehicular traffic in the central area to levels which could be accommodated without wholesale redevelopment of the historic fabric, while optimizing accessibility through appropriate modes of transport:*
This called for review and better management of the existing road network, giving high priority to efficient public transport systems and limiting private car access to certain areas, in conjunction with the creation of car parks at the fringe of the modern CBD. In this context it became necessary to review the function of the various bridges across the Tigris which pump vehicular traffic directly into the heart of the Rusafa district.

c) *To rehabilitate the old residential quarters, to improve their physical structures and enhance their amenities and environmental qualities:*
This involved a number of basic measures such as careful improvement of accessibility, protection from through-traffic, relocation of harmful industrial activities, as well as the introduction or improvement of necessary social facilities, playgrounds and community services. The bound-

aries of traditional residential areas within an increasingly commercialized downtown area were to be protected by special legal measures, land use prescriptions and appropriate criteria for restoration and substitution of existing buildings.

d) *To reorganize industrial activities on the northeastern edge of Rusafa with regard to the needs of the old city and the whole urban system:*
This implied a two-step intervention: first, the progressive transfer of emerging (and no longer appropriate) heavy industries from Sheikh Omar to the outskirts of Baghdad and second, a relocation of certain manufacturing and wholesale activities from the old city to the vacated Sheikh Omar area, in order to free the historic fabric from expanding semi-industrial activities, while minimizing disruption to the old city's socio-economic system that relies on close links between the working and the resident populations.

234

e) *To develop and enhance a number of major pedestrian spines throughout the Rusafa area, in order to improve the coherence between the historic and the modern sectors:*
This involved the rehabilitation of the historic suqs, the reinforcement of pedestrian linkages between the river and the gates, the environmental improvement of the riverfront and the conversion of certain roads in the heart of the historic CBD to low-traffic or pedestrian areas. All the existing points of conflict between the traditional pedestrian network and the vehicular system were to be treated with great care, so as to re-establish the continuity of the pedestrian system as much as possible and to create optimum environmental conditions at significant intersections and focal areas.

235

The implementation of the above objectives obviously entailed critical choices with regard to the conservation or appropriate redevelopment of specific areas of Rusafa. These choices were based on a thorough review of socio-economic conditions in the various sub-districts and on the assessment of existing land uses and perceived needs in terms of amenities and facilities. Present traffic conditions and desirable future transportation policies were also examined in order to anchor future transportation plans in a comprehensive development strategy. (Baghdad was in the process of planning a new metro system passing through Rusafa.) In potential conservation areas, a plot-by-plot survey analyzing building use, historical value, architectural typology, physical conditions and ownership was carried out as a basis for both general decision-making about sustainable conservation districts and future in-depth rehabilitation projects. A morphological compatibility schedule was established to determine what type of activities were

234 View of the unresolved fringe situation around the newly built government centre (1983).

235 High blocks along Khulafa Street interfering with the continuity of the perpendicular residential alleyways of the historic fabric.

compatible (or incompatible) with which type of urban fabric, in order to relate future land-use decisions to the constraints of urban form, enabling the complementarity between historic structures and modern development to come into play.

All of this information and all these studies were brought to bear in the new "structure plan" – a framework for action backed up by more detailed planning and urban design proposals for specific areas such as the riverfront, Rashid Street, the historic suqs, traditional residential districts to be upgraded and the adapted redevelopment of peripheral areas around the historic core. In the following, a brief summary is provided of the main strategies and actions implied in the "structure plan".

It soon became evident that the key to the viability of Rusafa as a historic area combining a Central Business District with integrated "pockets" of traditional residential quarters did not lie in the grand new scheme of Khulafa Street (as proposed by TAC), but rather in a judicious redevelopment of the Sheikh Omar District, the belt along the former city walls, now clogged with developing industrial activities. The proposal thus envisaged the transfer of all heavy industrial activities to a new industrial zone on the periphery of Baghdad, allowing for the widening of the street and redevelopment of the adjacent strip. Continued at each end by Port Said Street and Muadhan Street, the widened Sheikh Omar road would form a high-capacity highway around the historic area so as to divert and absorb existing traffic pressures. Along this belt, a number of interchange nodes with multi-storey car parks, bus stations, taxi ranks and commercial facilities would be located, to encourage the desirable shift from private vehicular traffic to public transportation and to pedestrian movement. By including large pedestrian plazas, these nodes would have the function of "vestibules" to the inner city, providing organic connections with the pedestrian spines of the old city and linking Sheikh Omar Street with the riverfront.

The northern part of the new Sheikh Omar area would be redeveloped as a mixed-use zone with a fair amount of public housing, but also offering opportunities for relocating from the old city small-scale commercial and industrial activities no longer compatible with the historic fabric. The nodes and the street front developments of Sheikh Omar would provide additional space for the expansion of the modern business district, while towards the old city a graded soft edge would be established to improve the transition between different types of urban form.

The implementation of this new bypass of the old city constituted the key for redistributing the traffic loads on the existing bridges: Jumhuriya Bridge and Muadhan Bridge, as direct extensions of the Sheikh Omar belt across the Tigris, would function as the major river crossings, while the intermed-

236/237 Volumetric plan for the proposed redevelopment of the belt area around the historic fabric, along Sheikh Omar Street, and detail of one of the major transition nodes.

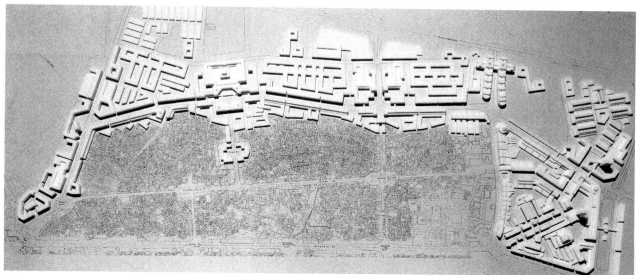

236

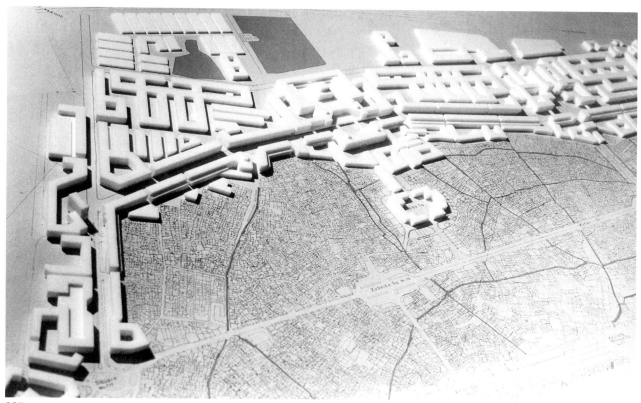

237

iate two bridges (Ahrar and Shuhada) would be downgraded to provide exclusive traffic access to the old suqs, thus strengthening the potential for undisturbed pedestrian connections along the riverfront. Accordingly, the prolongations of the intermediate bridges toward Sheikh Omar were not to be used as major through-traffic routes, but were to be reserved for public transport, thereby improving the accessibility of the Central Business District and the historic areas. Within this framework, relief would also be provided to the areas on Rashid Street and to Kifa Street.

Rashid Street would be reserved for buses, taxis and for servicing the suqs. Public accessibility would be enhanced by a comfortable shuttle bus operating along the whole length of the street and connected to the bus terminal in Maidan Square. The suqs would remain fully pedestrian and would benefit from the rehabilitation of an enhanced riverfront development, which would restore the historic significance and the environmental potential of the site.

On Kifa Street, through-traffic would be discouraged by appropriate traffic control measures and corresponding physical interventions ("gates", widening of pavements, one-way sections, etc.), in order to maintain it as a low-traffic district spine serving the surrounding residential community. The downgrading of Kifa Street was a basic requirement for the future rehabilitation of the main historic urban fabric located between Khulafa Street and the Sheikh Omar belt. Being defined as the prime conservation area of Rusafa, this zone needed to be protected from further large-scale redevelopment and encroachment by massive new buildings.

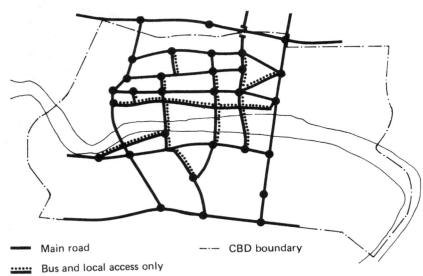

—— Main road   —·— CBD boundary

⋯⋯ Bus and local access only

238

238 Proposed traffic scheme for the inner city, on both sides of the Tigris River.

239

Meanwhile, Khulafa Street would remain the major transit connection through the study area and the most important spine of Baghdad's central business district. Between Muadhan Square and Khulani Square, it would be restricted to the present linear corridor and no lateral branching out of the planned development into the historic area would be allowed. Compensation for these lost extensions of the CBD would be provided in two triangular areas at the southeastern end of Khulafa Street (Bab al-Sheikh and Bab al-Sharqi). There, the historic fabric had already suffered greater damage than in other areas of Rusafa and further need for demolition was anticipated with the planned construction of two new metro stations. For these reasons, it was decided to sacrifice the residential districts of Bab al-Sheikh and Bab al-Sharqi, on condition that all of the more coherent portions of the historic fabric between Kifa Street and Sheikh Omar be conserved and rehabilitated. Meanwhile, the transformation and redevelopment of Bab al-Sheikh and Bab al-Sharqi should allow for a reasonable future growth of the Central Business District in a strategic area destined to become the very heart of the modern city. Moreover, the large urban space around Umma Park, adjacent to Bab al-Sharqi, was in need of a new development concept which would take into account its scale and its strategic location as a pivot for the modern business district (see page 269).

239 Example of a rehabilitation plan for one of the "islands" of the historic city located between Khulafa Street and Kifa Street. To the right, a section of the rehabilitated traditional suq spine (see next page). The conservation and rehabilitation plan for the historic fabric was based on detailed assessment of each "island". It indicates plot-by-plot proposed intervention measures, such as conservation of traditional houses, substitution by typologically related new units, re-use of open spaces for residential car parks (P) and re-use of ruined or vacant plots for communal facilities (CC), including primary schools (PS), secondary schools (SS), high schools (HS), or neighbourhood centres (NC) with youth clubs and health facilities.

Urban Design Sketch Proposals

On the premise of the above "structure plan", more detailed urban design guidelines and project proposals were developed by the team, recognizing that two complementary lines of intervention had to be pursued in parallel: on the one hand, it was necessary to provide flexible, but comprehensive guidelines for steering and controlling the ongoing transformation of individual properties in the historic districts, thereby ensuring that their necessary evolution would not destroy the essential qualities of the traditional urban morphology; on the other hand, there was also the need to stimulate the revitalization of the old city by selective rehabilitation and adapted redevelopment projects, tailored to meet the needs of a number of critical focal areas. While the first approach could be labelled as "passive control", intended to mould and monitor the development initiated by the private sector, the second approach implies more "active" direct interventions by the municipality, which could stimulate matching follow-up development in the surrounding areas.

Proposed Land Use Scheme

- Suq shops
- Storages
- Workshops and handicrafts
- Mixed-use of shops, restaurants, hotels and offices
- Public facilities
- Mixed-use of commercial and residential

0   50   100   200m

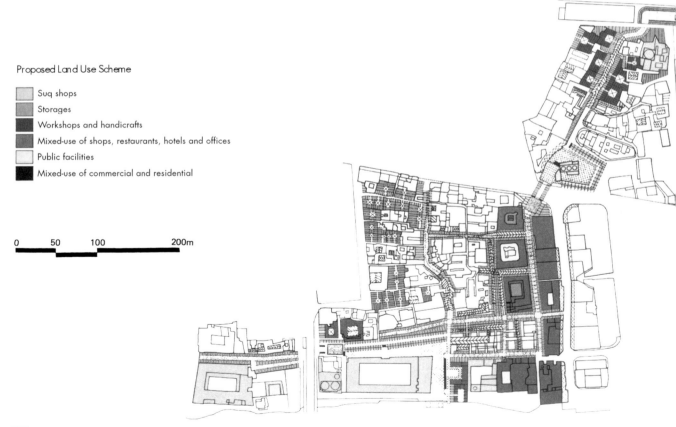

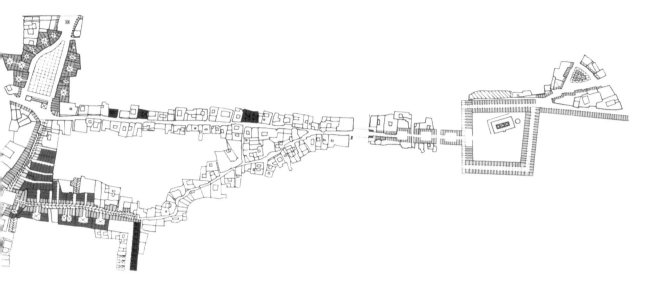

241

240 Proposed scheme for the rehabilitation of the main traditional suq spine leading from the Tigris riverbank to Gaylani.

241 Schematic urban design sketch for the depressed square around the Mirjan mosque, articulating the intersection of the traditional suq with the axis of Rashid Street, screened by an arcade.

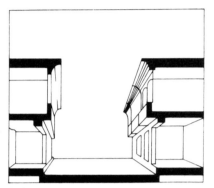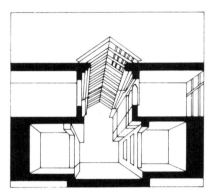

242

To control the transformation of the historic tissue in the designated conservation area, a manual proposing specific design criteria for dealing with the various types of buildings occurring within the historic fabric was developed. It covered a broad range of interventions from restoration to rehabilitation, including substitution of ruins with new adapted structures. Being based on the original plot-by-plot typological survey of the old city, the manual provided a matrix defining the appropriate type of intervention for each building, taking its architectural character, historic value and physical condition into consideration. It was intended to guide the staff of the municipality both in their response to private building applications and in their own urban interventions, thus facilitating a consistent step-by-step rehabilitation of the historic districts.

The manual was complemented by a more active rehabilitation scheme for each residential district of the historic fabric, indicating recommended land uses, improved service accesses, small neighbourhood car parks and new community facilities to be introduced in order to improve the viability and the living standards of the surviving traditional housing clusters. The plan made productive use of existing opportunities in terms of irretrievably ruined plots, vacant areas and already demolished buildings.

A similar scheme was prepared for the rehabilitation of the old central markets and the traditional suq spines, combining restoration of existing suqs with infill proposals for new market structures that were to interpret traditional typological principles while providing improved vehicular servicing opportunities. The main element of this new urban design scheme was the linear suq string stretching from the central markets near the Madrasa Mustansiriya to the Gaylani shrine, which would include a number of nodes and enclosed courts at every important articulation of its spatial sequence. Particular attention was given to the intersection between the old suq and the new "corridors" of the more recent Central Business District such as

242 Typology of various suq sections to be reconstructed, from open shopping street to covered alleyways.

243/244 Sketches for the proposed Tigris-riverfront redevelopment, including low-height public facilities reminiscent of the previously existing river balcony structures.

243

244

Rashid Street and Khulafa Street. At the main crossing with Khulafa Street, a special urban design scheme involving a new two-level pedestrian square (with access to the future metro station) was developed.

In parallel to the rehabilitation proposal for the traditional suqs, a new pedestrian walkway along the Tigris riverfront was proposed, together with a series of infill structures which would highlight certain focal points, where perpendicular lanes of the suq network provide good access to the riverfront. For these focal points, steps descending to the river, small boat-taxi stations and projecting structures with terraces, colonnades, shaded seating spaces and public coffee houses were designed. The proposed new structures would frame the views onto the river and provide attractive meeting places for visitors to the central area. Some of their architectural features, mainly the pillared balconies overlooking the river, would evoke the lost traditional aspect of the riverfront, without attempting to replicate pre-existing historic structures.

In close association with the above conservation and rehabilitation proposals, two major redevelopment schemes for the peripheral areas around the core of the remaining historic fabric were prepared. They were intended to materialize in schematic three-dimensional form the development principles contained in the "structure plan", providing the necessary window of growth to the modern CBD without jeopardizing the survival of the designated conservation area.

The urban design scheme for the proposed Sheikh Omar development was seen as an essential prerequisite for the conservation of the historic centre, as was pointed out during the discussion of the "structure plan". It suggests a continuous and coherent urban form with up to five storeys along the Sheikh Omar belt and up to eight or ten storeys around the main interchange nodes. The volumes step down to two to three storeys on the fringe of the old city, in the mixed-use areas in the northern sector of Rusafa. The concentration of volumes and of activities around the nodes is meant to break the monotony of the street-front development and to highlight the new entry zones into the central area. Typical sections of the schematic volumetric layout have been made to demonstrate the feasibility of the project and to serve as a basis for future detailed development of smaller sub-units of this overall scheme.

The redevelopment scheme for the Bab al-Sheikh and Bab al-Sharqi areas uses the opportunity to review the given road system and to rearrange it in the light of an integrated urban design solution for this important new sector of the CBD. Some of the existing roads were in fact redundant and created unnecessary congestion at the junctions of Khulani and Tayaran Square. The deviation and partial pedestrianization of the eastern branch of the Khulafa Street fork would not only ease the traffic problem at Tayaran Square; it would also enable a more coherent urban form to be created facing the square and its longitudinal southwestern extension of Umma Park. The urban form of the new development could then be conceived around a series of pedestrian plazas, rather than being dominated by conventional linear blocks following the existing street alignment. The deviated northeastern branch of Khulafa Street has been brought into

245 Volumetric master plan for the redevelopment of the Bab al-Sheikh and Bab al-Sharqi areas as parts of a modern CBD extension. In the centre, at the bottom, Khulani Square, where Khulafa Street and Bab al-Sheikh Street cross each other. To the left, at the top, the intersection between Bab al-Sheikh Street and the Sheikh Omar beltway. To the right, at the bottom, the elongated Umma Park, leading up to Tayaran Square.

246 Typical sections showing development principles for new town-house units to be included in the redevelopment of the Bab al-Sheikh and Bab al-Sharqi areas.

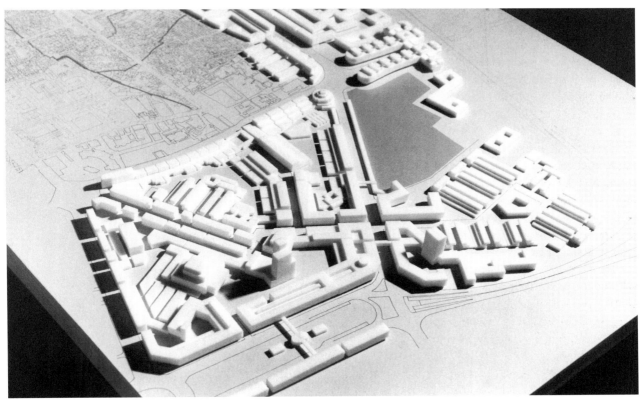

245

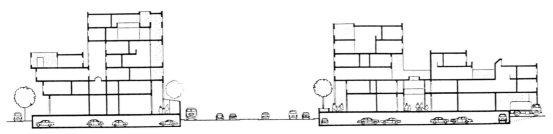

TYPICAL CROSS SECTION THROUGH SHEIKH OMAR DEVELOPMENT

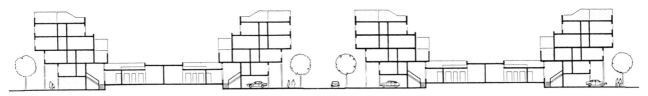

TYPICAL CROSS SECTION

246

the Sheikh Omar belt and continued into a feeder road for a new inner-city housing development in the pocket of vacant land between Port Said Street and the Sheikh Omar cemetery. The urban form of this self-contained housing scheme is based on terraced housing units, providing a further variation of the architectural vocabulary used in Arup's redevelopment of Bab al-Sheikh Street.

Postscript

The tragedy of Iraq's sequence of wars with Iran and Kuwait, initiated by an over-ambitious and misguided political leadership, brought to a grinding halt all development and conservation projects initiated in the early eighties. At the time of completion of the manuscript for this book, the author was unable to recieve any information on the current status of the Rusafa projects, but it must be assumed that no significant activities have taken place during the past ten to fifteen years, in which time the city has probably suffered losses as a result of intensive bombing by American war planes.

Case Study III:
Fez – Protecting the Integrity
of the Historic Fabric

Historic Background and Project Context

Fez was founded around the year 800 AD by Prince Idris, a descendant of the Umayyad dynasty from Damascus who had escaped persecution by the Abbasids. Old chronicles speak of a first settlement on the eastern bank of the river, founded by Idris I in 789 AD, and a second settlement on the opposite side, founded almost 20 years later by his son Idris II. During the 9th century, the new city attracted immigrants from Kairouan (Tunisia) and Andalusia, and eventually developed into a flourishing centre of Moorish art and culture. Its rise was sustained by a series of consecutive Berber dynasties which, emerging from the desert, took pride in the city. The Almoravids conquered Fez in the late 11th century and unified the twin city by building a new single city wall. They were followed, less than a century later, by the Almohades, who also kept Marrakesh as their capital. It was not until 1276 AD, with the advent of the Marinids, that Fez became the capital of Morocco for almost three centuries. The Marinids founded the new palace city of Fez Jdid and became the patrons of a series of outstanding mosques and madrasas, bringing the urban culture of Fez to its summit and enhancing the city's position as major commercial centre at the junction of important trade routes linking the Mediterranean with black Africa. After the fall of Granada (1492), Fez absorbed another wave of refugees and became the legitimate heir and custodian of Andalusian traditions. Although during the later centuries, due to tribal vicissitudes, the city lost much of its political predominance, it remained the cultural, economic and spiritual centre of Morocco until the beginning of the French Protectorate in 1912.

In terms of cultural continuity, the western edge of North Africa (called the Maghreb) benefited from its peripheral location, since it was shielded from major geopolitical conflicts which hit the Fertile Crescent and Egypt, such as the Crusades and the two waves of Mongol invasions. Thus, although exposed to regional power struggles, Fez was able to build up a strong local tradition, undisrupted by the external shocks that befell other cities such as Baghdad, Damascus or Cairo. The relatively good physical preservation of the old city is also due to the fact that Western influences became active at a later stage than in most other Islamic cities. In Morocco, the colonial age started around the time of the First World War, and its

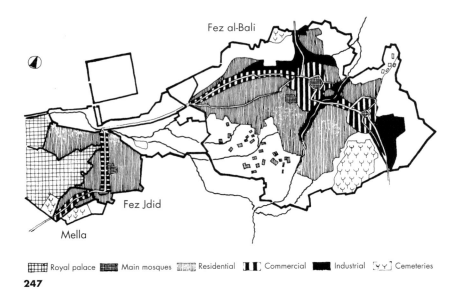

Fez al-Bali

Fez Jdid

Mella

⊞⊞ Royal palace ▦▦ Main mosques ▥▥ Residential ▐▐ Commercial ▬▬ Industrial ⌄⌄ Cemeteries

247

impact on Fez was mitigated by the fact that most of the modern development pressures were focused on the coastal cities. While Fez remained the acknowledged "spiritual capital", economic and political primacy shifted to Casablanca and Rabat. Moreover, the topographic situation of Fez went a long way in preserving its historic urban fabric. The old city had developed in a natural bowl, and this location, chosen for its ideal irrigation potential (in spite of obvious strategic disadvantages), required the new colonial city to be built at some distance, on the plateau above the old city.

The national authorities, as well as Unesco, soon became aware of the fact that the old city of Fez constituted a unique cultural heritage. The urban dimension of this heritage made conservation highly complex and challenging. It was clearly inconceivable to transform the whole city into a museum, as may have been done in the case of a single architectural monument. A historic nucleus must be kept alive if it is to sustain the essential qualities for which it is being preserved. This, however, is a delicate task and requires planners and decision-makers to achieve a subtle balance between contradicting forces: too strong a dose of modern development, especially if administered without the necessary precautions, may be detrimental to the specific character of the old city, causing considerable social and physical losses; too many restrictions, imposed in order to conserve the physical appearance of bygone ages, may fossilize the urban structure and deprive the city of vital internal stimuli. The choice was further complicated by the fact that the walled city could not be treated as an isolated entity, within its own perimeter. Its future evolution was clearly dependent on the

247 Diagram showing basic land-use structure of Fez around 1900.

functional connections between the historic districts and the modern extensions, which in the meantime had assumed important new roles.

The Unesco project acknowledged this situation by initiating a conservation plan for the historic city of Fez, combined with a master plan for the development of the whole agglomeration. Although institutional shortcomings have affected the implementation of this master plan (completed in 1978), its technical approach was correct inasmuch as it went beyond inventorizing, protecting and conserving individual historic buildings, in order to focus on the complete urban context. Complementarity and, where possible, interaction between old and new parts of the city were taken into account with a view to retaining and strengthening the viability of the historic quarters and the traditional markets. Meanwhile, it was necessary to control the pressures deriving from the modern urban system in order not to exceed the capacity defined by the given physical constraints of the historic fabric. The problem therefore was one of adjusting modern urban facilities to the morphology of the old city, because the inverse procedure, i.e. adapting the old city to modern modes of development, would have entailed the destruction of historic structures.

This is especially true in the case of vehicular traffic, the most dynamic (not to say explosive) of modern urban functions which, in association with speculative development pressures, usually opens the breach for the irreversible erosion and subsequent decay of the traditional urban fabric. The present case study on Fez again confirms that accessibility is the single most critical factor for the rehabilitation of almost every historic city, especially in the closely knit urban structures of the Arab world. To some extent a necessary requirement for survival, vehicular traffic can also turn into a potential force of destruction. The following paragraphs will address this issue in the context of the master plan's search for balanced conservation and development strategies. A subsequent section shall focus on the adapted redevelopment of the covered riverbed of the Oued Boukhrareb as a main access to the heart of the old city – a key project for demonstrating possible ways of managing acute traffic pressures in an historic environment.

Sustaining the Function of the Traditional Centre of Fez

Today the city of Fez represents an agglomeration of several separate but interconnected entities: first, the "medina", composed of Fez al-Bali (the old twin city) and the former Marinid palace of Fez Jdid with the attached Jewish quarter (Mella); second, the French colonial city (Dar Debibagh) laid out by H. Prost (the urbanist associated with General Lyautey) in the early twenties on the plateau of the river Fez, above the bowl of the medina; third, the nucleus of Aïn Qaddous, a sort of dormitory city for low- and middle-income populations, planned in the early fifties according to the principles of the "Charter of Athens" and located on the hillside north of Fez. A number of "illegal" settlements built by rural immigrants, which have developed spontaneously around the eastern periphery of the old city and in the old quarries near Aïn Qaddous, should also be added to these entities.

The particular character of this agglomeration is due to its polynuclear layout, which responds to the existing topographic constraints and separates the various urban entities by large intermediate spaces, such as the royal palace, its vast enclosed gardens and several cemeteries outside the old city walls. Even more unusual, at least in comparison with capital cities such as Damascus, Cairo or Baghdad, is the fact that the old city remained the predominant element of the composite urban structure until well into the eighties, both in terms of the number of inhabitants (around 250 000 in 1980) and in terms of economic activities and employment. The modern colonial city, with its extensive residential quarters (around 120 000 inhabitants in 1980), became the preferred district of the local bourgeoisie, but has remained a small provincial town, accommodating the local administration and relatively modest commercial and industrial activities. The old city, in contrast, has managed to retain and to develop thriving commercial activities within the given historic fabric, but not without considerable changes in the traditional production and distribution system. Many industrial goods are now brought from outside into the suqs to be sold there at cheaper prices, often to customers from the new city or from the region. Meanwhile, most of the traditional crafts survive and continue to manufacture products for local consumption, for rural customers or for a touristic clientele inside and outside Fez. Some of them have however evolved towards semi-industrial types of production (clothes, shoes, plastic materials, etc.) that rely on processing imported materials with relatively simple but bulky machinery. The traditional food markets in the medina, distributing products from the region and from all over Morocco, continue to function and are extending in parallel with the growth of the population. As a result, the economic activity level of the old city has increased and exerts considerable pressure on the historic fabric, especially with regard to semi-industrial production processes.

The physical structure of the traditional city centre (plan on page 144) is marked by the two main religious buildings, the Mulay Idris Mosque (which contains the tomb of the city founder) and the Qairawiyyin University Mosque, for centuries the centre of learning in the Maghreb. The mosques are connected and surrounded by the central suqs, the whole central complex being suspended, as it were, on a slightly curved pedestrian spine, connecting the centre with the western gate of Bab Boujeloud and the east-

248 Plan of the urban agglomeration of Fez in 1976, the main components being the old city (Fez al-Bali), Fez Jdid (the royal city extension founded in the 14th century), the French colonial town (Dar Debibagh) and the satellite city of Ain Qaddous developed since the early fifties.

ern gate of Bab Ftouh. This west-east axis is bordered by a series of residential quarters, which remain undisturbed by intense through-traffic. Each district has its own small sub-centre, and the street network follows the well-known hierarchy composed of central thoroughfares (often accompanied by rows of shops), residential thoroughfares and semi-private cul-de-sacs giving access to the houses. The inner structure of the urban fabric embodies the principles described in chapter 7, building upon a series of contiguous or overlapping cellular structures of varying degrees of complexity. All single elements, whether houses, residential clusters, suqs, khans, mosques or madrasas, rely on the basic pattern of the enclosure, thus contributing to a totally integrated urban structure where individual buildings, without losing their relative autonomy, can merge into a homogeneous fabric of great complexity. Within this cellular system, gates, interior passages and covered corridors are used to adjust the degree of privacy required for each cellular component of the city.

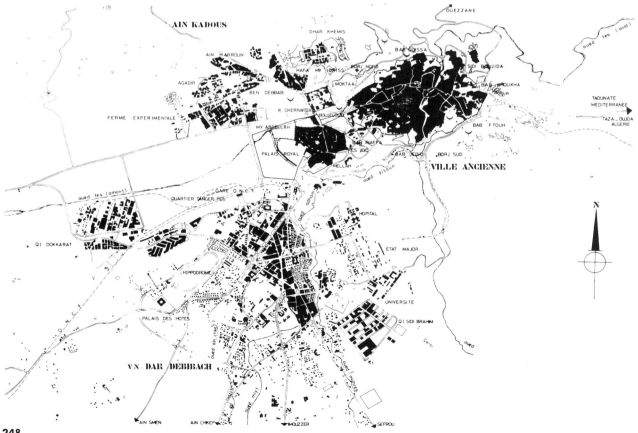

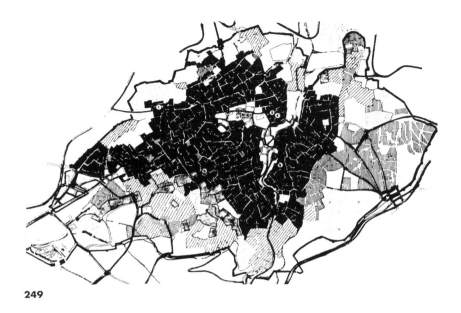

249

As mentioned earlier, the morphological principles determining this type of urban fabric produced an extremely dense and compact architectural texture. However, relief was provided by the many garden courtyards included in the urban fabric and by the orchards and family gardens located in the open areas between the city and its outer walls. These peripheral orchards were fed by the same sophisticated irrigation system that brought water to the mosques, mills, public fountains and domestic courtyards. Regrettably, a large portion of the green belt *intra muros* was progressively built upon since the early twentieth century. During the sixties and seventies, four- to five-storey-high apartment blocks were constructed there almost wall to wall, without providing compensatory open space in the form of interior courtyards. This departure from the traditional morphology, combined with an abusive land-use ratio, created an excessive densification at the periphery, where abundant open space was previously able to compensate for the crowded conditions in the inner city.

The overall trends described above, together with more subtle physical changes at the micro-level of the old residential quarters and the suqs, have to be seen against the background of major socio-economic transformations which have affected the old city since the middle of this century. The departure of the local bourgeoisie towards the new town (or the booming political and economic centres of Rabat and Casablanca) has in a way decapitated the urban community in the old city and deprived it of major socio-economic forces. The parallel immigration of a new, predominantly rural population

249 Diagram showing the development of the residential fabric within the walled city of Fez al-Bali. (Traditional residential districts built until the early nineteenth century are shown in black, neo-traditional housing from the colonial period in large hatching, and apartment blocks after 1950 in narrow hatching.)

more than outweighed this loss in quantitative terms, but was not able to ensure the physical maintenance of the traditional urban system. While in the past the peripheral quarters of the old city always had the function of urbanizing and "civilizing" immigrants from the countryside, the massive influx during the sixties and seventies meant that virtually the complete old city became an intermediate station for a poor population in search of employment, training and education. As with many other historic cities in the Muslim world, old houses left by their owners were subdivided and let or sold room by room to families who often could not afford to maintain the structures. The resulting densification (an estimated 250 000 inhabitants in the old city in 1975, as compared to the traditional benchmark of 100 000 around 1900), together with ever-increasing poverty, exerted tremendous pressure on the physical fabric of the medina. While the major monuments were relatively easy to restore and maintain (most of them had already been restored during the colonial period), many private houses of historic value were *de facto* turned into caravanserais, either for multi-family lodging or for accommodating manufacturing workshops, and fell into a precarious structural state. Both residential districts and markets suffered due to exploding production activities which no longer matched the inbuilt capacity and the traditional land-use patterns of the historic fabric. Provoked by the excessive densities, a number of corollary issues emerged, such as the congestion of the traditional street network, increasing risk of hazards (due to the use of inflammable manufacturing materials) and the collapse of the traditional irrigation and sewage discharge system.

The overriding objective of the 1978 master plan for Fez was to deal with these problems in an integrated manner and to interrelate the different urban entities in such a way as to re-balance the composite urban system. It was hoped that this approach would provide a development framework within which the medina could retain its essential morphological qualities and characteristics and yet remain a viable and living city equipped with the necessary services and amenities. Four major issues were explored in this context, all with particular focus on the historic nucleus.

The first issue was how to preserve the essential physical characteristics of the traditional urban fabric while allowing for the improved accessibility that was needed to ensure the viability of the supporting economic system, absorb excessive congestion and security risks, and retain or attract the middle-income population back to the old city. The answer was a selective type of accessibility which would "irrigate" the medina from the periphery, using a number of small feeder roads penetrating into the old city from the existing ring road. This proposal was designed in such a way as to work without major physical interventions in the historic city centre and to minimize vehicular flows through the residential districts. The idea of introducing a Y-shaped system of new roads cutting through the historic urban fabric (as advanced in the early sixties by M. Ecochard) was discarded in favour of this decentralized system, which implied a soft and progressive shift from vehicular to pedestrian modes of circulation, with a sequence of thresholds or "gates" controlling the degree of accessibility at any given point. These new access points were seen as priority destinations for public transportation, and from the advanced "gates" people could easily reach the central area using the existing pedestrian network.

The second issue was how to reduce the densities in the old city, in terms of both population and production activities, and enable the urban fabric to regain its natural equilibrium. The solution envisaged was a satellite development in the vicinity of the medina, allowing for the relocation of polluting activities without major disruption to the existing functional circuits and social networks. For this purpose, an extension area at Aïn Noqbi, east of the medina and close to Bab Ftouh, was identified, where certain groups of craftsmen, like tanners and dyers, could be transferred and emerging semi-industrial production processes could be accommodated. New low-cost housing districts were also envisaged in the Aïn Noqbi area and on a vacant piece of land near Aïn Qaddous (see last section of this chapter), within walking distance of the medina.

The third issue was how to improve living standards in the old city, especially with regard to infrastructure, sanitation and social facilities, providing a level of comfort equivalent to that of modern cities, but without destroying the traditional character of the medina. Admittedly, the standards could not become identical, but *comparable*, in the sense that the specific residential qualities offered by the old city had to be taken into account as part of a reasonable trade-off. Improving the infrastructure inside the historic urban fabric required innovative engineering, i. e. the invention of custom-made solutions which would adapt to the given local conditions, rather than imposing the constraints of conventional technical solutions. The same qualification applied to architectural design standards, where a structural transposition of modern facilities such as schools or hospitals into the language of the traditional architectural typology was needed. This called for a creative interpretation (and occasional stretching) of the traditional architectural vocabulary to accommodate modern needs rather than imposing conventional modern building types on a historic context. In certain cases the insertion of new buildings could be avoided by clever re-use of existing structures which had become functionally or physically obsolete due to the ongoing socio-economic changes. Occasionally, old buildings would only need a modern annex in order to accommodate extended new functions. At any

250 Aerial view of the city centre of Fez showing the covering of the southern part of the Boukhrareb river, the first phase of an earlier project from 1964, intended to cut two Y-shaped vehicular roads through the historic urban fabric.

251

252

251 View of the R'cif Square from the west.

252 View of the vacant land in the Mokhfiya district, adjacent to the new road above the riverbed.

rate, it was stressed that improved infrastructure and social facilities required an enlightened planning and investment policy by the authorities, in order to support and enhance the neglected historic districts in appropriate ways. The role of the "Awqaf" or "Habous", still the major landowners in the city, could hardly be over-estimated in this respect.

The fourth issue was how to launch a self-sustaining internal process leading to the consistent repair, improvement, rehabilitation and occasional replacement of the existing traditional building stock using appropriate architectural typologies, materials and construction techniques. Qualitative standards and corresponding models were proposed, to ensure that conservation, restoration or substitution of private houses would be done in accordance with consistent typological rules and sound urban-conservation principles. With the exception of certain historic monuments, rehabilitation on the urban scale was only conceivable by motivating private owners to maintain and restore their houses. Clearly, this implied mobilizing the private sector, and therefore a set of corresponding incentives and a clear regulatory framework to be endorsed by the authorities. The need for institutional control mechanisms to prevent excessive profits being skimmed off by private speculators as a result of public investments was also highlighted. The master plan suggested mobilising private interest by catalytic public-sector actions, such as selective improvement of accessibility, reduction of densities, improvement of infrastructure and environmental conditions, and other actions proving the government's determination to sustain the old city. Governmental agencies and private initiative would thus need to work hand in hand for the rehabilitation of the old city. However, a prerequisite of such a partnership is that the various governmental services and administrations, at central and at local level, pursue common policies – an institutional consensus which was difficult to achieve at that time. (Recently, a World Bank-funded rehabilitation project based on selective street improvement seems to have succeeded.)

The more operational application of the above planning principles was pursued by a number of selected strategic projects which addressed various aspects of the overall problem pattern in a concrete manner, relating them to specific locations, conditions and constraints. However, before engaging in a more detailed analysis of two key action areas, it may be apposite to relate a strategic debate that was at the very heart of the whole master-plan exercise, concerning the degree of centrality to be assigned to the old city in the context of the overall agglomeration. Some team members thought that the medina should be kept in a peripheral position with regard to future development and that the city needed a new central business district, which would find its ideal place at the centre of gravity of the whole agglomeration, between the new town, Aïn Qaddous and the former palace city of Fez Jdid. Others felt that establishing a new central area in an "ideal" location was somewhat utopian under the given circumstances. Meanwhile, the Moroccan partners argued that the medina, for historic, symbolic and economic reasons, had to retain its prime centrality within the future agglomeration. Yet, it was also clear that the old city could not supply the necessary sites for the new central facilities needed for a city of 600 000 or 800 000 future inhabitants, unless one was to consider a massive redevelopment.

A compromise between these divergent positions was brought about by the observation that the main pedestrian west-east spine through the medina is continued through Fez Jdid (the former Marinid palace city) and after a short interruption meets the linear centre of the modern city, thus forming a sort of composite arch integrating the various centres of the complete urban agglomeration. The distance between both ends of the arch represents less than one-hour's walk. Although several sections of this configuration, labelled the "croissant structurant", were not as yet fully articulated, the concept provided opportunities for overcoming the segregation between the old and the new city and, by the same token, for eliminating the need for a new artificial centre. Spatial separation and the differing characters of the various urban components did not preclude a certain degree of functional continuity between them. It was therefore decided to support the further development of this virtual linear centre, in order to tie together the individual urban entities and reinforce the unity of the system without destroying the specific character of its components.

Within the old city, the "croissant structurant" would coincide with the main west-east spine stretching from Bab Boujeloud to Bab Ftouh, including the node of the central suqs around the Qairawiyin Mosque. This complete section was to be kept for pedestrian use only, and therefore needed vehicular feeder roads from the north and the south (attached to the existing ring road) to service the main commercial areas. The two dead-end feeder

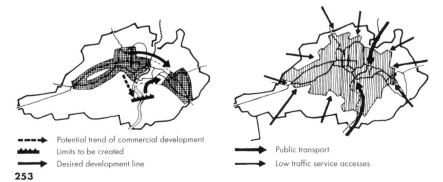

- - - ▶ Potential trend of commercial development
▲▲▲ Limits to be created
➤ Desired development line

➤ Public transport
➤ Low traffic service accesses

253 Containment measures proposed to support the viability of the pedestrian markets of the "croissant structurant".

roads, following the riverbed and embracing but not interrupting the critical section of the "croissant structurant", would constitute the major vehicular links between the modern city centre and the central suqs. To maximize their efficiency under the given space restrictions, they would have to be operated exclusively by public transport, at least the sections leading inward from the ring road. Open-air car parks would be provided at the two junctions of the ring road, while the end points of the two feeder roads were designed to become effective public transportation terminals.

Planning and Urban Design Concepts for the Boukhrareb Area

The above concept was a way of dealing with the road on top of the covered riverbed of the Oued Boukhrareb, constructed in 1967 as part of an intended, but never completed vehicular road scheme cutting through the old city. Due to technical problems and lack of funds, this project, first planned under M. Ecochard in the early sixties, had been stopped halfway, leaving intact the two bridges in the middle of the pedestrian "croissant structurant". The road ended in a highly congested car park, the space for which had been gained by demolishing a number of houses at the turning point of the road. The master-plan team recommended that the authorities abandon the continuation of the road in favour of the above concept and develop a new integrated urban design scheme which would remedy the unsatisfactory existing situation in this area. It was acknowledged that the re-design of the Boukhrareb area was not just a matter of traffic planning or beautification, but of a major infill project which had to reweave the disrupted connections between the two riverbanks of the "twin city", while using this opportunity to introduce lacking facilities close to the central area of the medina.

During the end-phase of the master plan, the team had no opportunity to develop such a project in greater detail. The occasion arose, however, one year later in 1979/1980, when the author of this book was asked to head an urban design studio on Fez at the Architectural School of the Swiss Federal Institute of Technology (ETH) in Zurich. The scope of work of this studio (organized in cooperation with Professor Benedikt Huber) was defined in such a way as to provide a consistent continuation of the master-plan studies, developing in greater depth certain key themes of the plan and fleshing them out in terms of actual urban design projects. The faculty and the participating students were given the opportunity to visit Fez and interact with two representatives of the Moroccan team charged with following up the master plan.

The theme of the Boukhrareb redevelopment was pursued as a collective, field-related academic effort over a period of one year. It exemplified

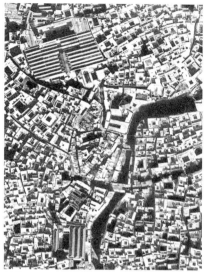

254

255

254 Aerial view of the area before the construction of the Boukhrareb road.

255 View of the Boukhrareb river before the road construction.

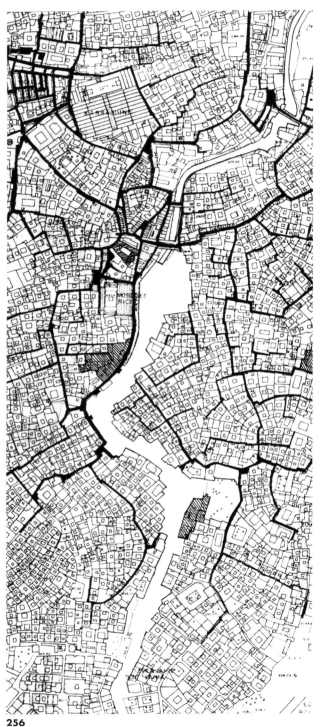

256

257

258

259

the benefits of a focused integrated approach, whereby a wide range of different but interdependent planning aspects could be tackled in a bundled manner, relating them to a specific and clearly defined action area. (The opposite and, to some extent, complementary approach of treating isolated thematic issues at a more general, overall level is often less productive.) The starting point for this exercise was the existing state of the half-completed Boukhrareb intervention, to be revised and redesigned in the light of the recommended master-plan policies. The covered riverbed was seen as an alien intrusion into the organism of the old city, a foreign body as it were, which had to be absorbed and healed up in terms of the morphological rules of the historic urban fabric. The common objectives underlying the student projects were the following:

– To provide maximum accessibility to the traditional centre with minimum physical disruption and waste of space, making use of an efficient public-transport system and excluding private car access beyond the junction with the ring road.

– To define and articulate a precise transition point between mechanical transportation and pedestrian movement, introducing a "filter" for incoming transportation flows, similar to the function of the old city gates.

– To provide corresponding turn-over and storage facilities for merchandise near the new "gate", to smoothen the flow of incoming goods and ease the shift between different transportation modes.

– To take advantage of vacant sites or ruined plots for the purpose of introducing modern facilities which were currently lacking, such as clinics, schools, public services, in order to complement and strengthen the traditional city centre.

– To repair the damaged fringe areas of the historic urban fabric on both sides of the road (and especially in the area of the car park) by using and re-interpreting the traditional architectural typology for adapted new infill structures.

Thus the major theme of this endeavour was to support the traditional city structure by enabling it to regain its physical integrity, while at the same time injecting the needed new functional elements to the extent that they could be made compatible with the traditional city structure. The students were encouraged to work in groups of two or three and given the task of developing both a comprehensive urban-design project and more detailed projects for specific infill structures. On the following pages, the work of two of these small teams is presented in greater detail with the supporting documents and explanatory legends.

256 Map of existing conditions after the construction of the Boukhrareb road and after the demolition of a number of buildings on the fringe, to gain car parking space.

257-259 Pictures showing existing conditions on the terminal square and on the upper and the lower bend of the Boukhrareb access road (1980).

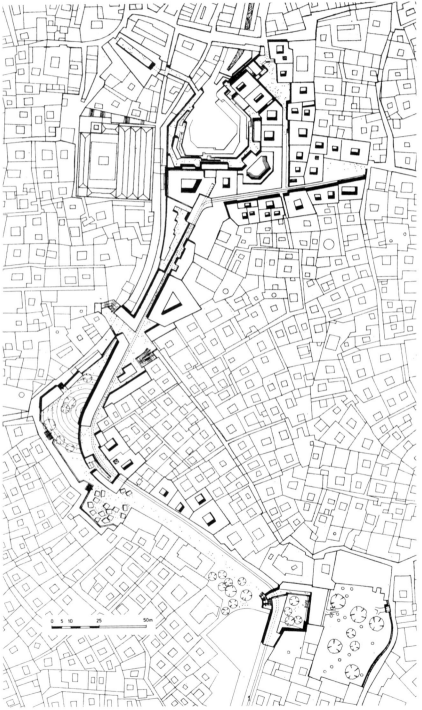

The infill project by Renato Salvi works on the premise of a shuttle train providing transportation for people and merchandise along the covered section of the Boukhrareb river. An interchange station at the southern end links up with the ring road along the walled city.

The terminal at the R'cif Square, on the northern end of the covered river section, is embedded in a multifunctional complex surrounding a public open space in the form of a garden courtyard. Pedestrians can move on two levels around this large courtyard, gaining access to shops on the ground floor and to a number of public facilities and recreational amenities on the upper floor.

The arrival hall is linked via a suq with the bridge across the open section of the river and with the main west-east spine of the "croissant structurant". The shops have ample storage space to the rear, directly serviced by a branch of the train tracks. The markets on the ground floor and the facilities on the upper deck overlooking the garden follow the traditional architectural typology, thus allowing for a genuine reweaving of the damaged urban fabric.

260 Site plan of infill project.

261 Model of the northern terminal complex and garden courtyard, as seen from the east (in the foreground the existing R'cif Mosque).

262 Section through R'cif Mosque and terminal complex, looking south.

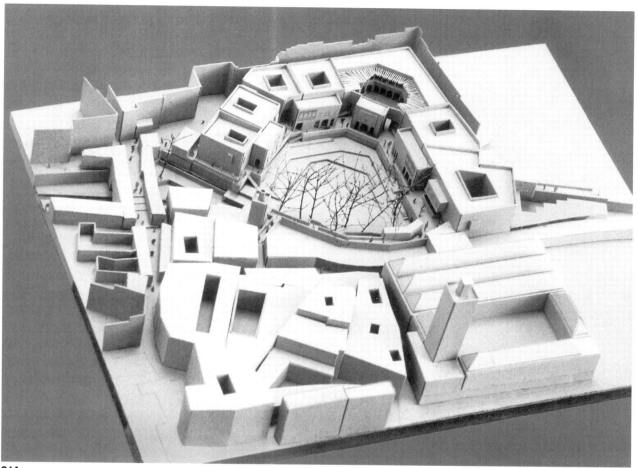

261

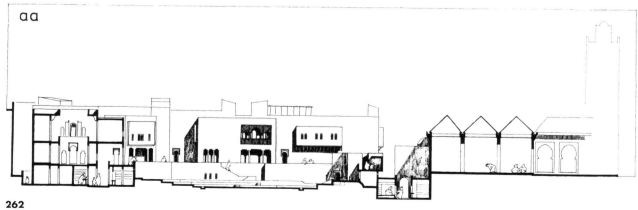

262

A   Arrival hall
B   Suq leading towards the main west-east spine
C   Garden courtyard
D   Upper terrace overlooking the garden courtyard
E   Open-air theatre

1   Suq connections to southern section of Boukhrareb avenue
2   Passenger station
3   Railway servicing storage space
4   Shop units
5   Storage space to be subdivided
6   Service staircases
7   Main west-east spine of central suq connecting across the river
8   Garden terraces with small water channels
9   Water cascade and lower river basin
10 Existing water channel
11 Upper level shopping concourse
12 Pedestrian bridge above existing suq
13 Existing caravanserai to be rehabilitated
14 Traditional restaurant with private rooms
15 Specialty restaurant and cafeteria
16 Offices for rent
17 Library
18 Artisans' centre and exhibition rooms
19 Upper gallery of open-air theatre
20 Youth centre
21 Working lofts

0 2 4 6   10   20m

263 Ground-floor plan of the northern terminal complex.

264 Plan of upper concourse.

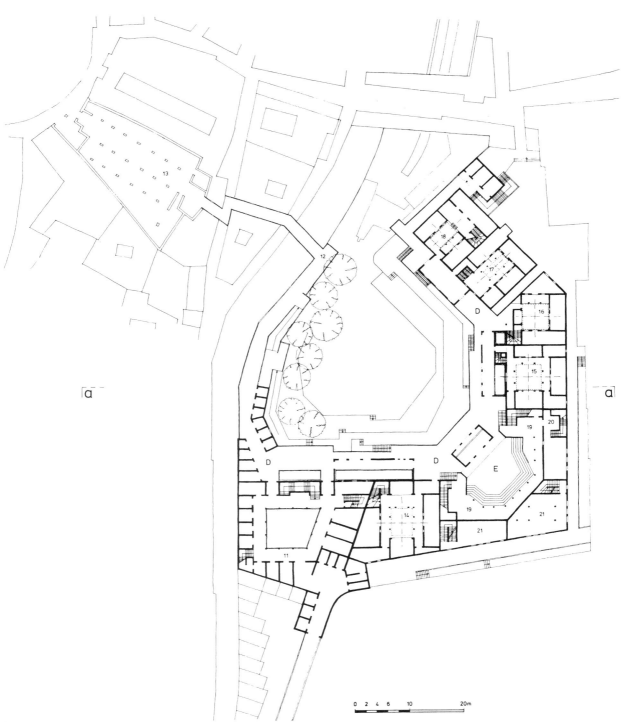

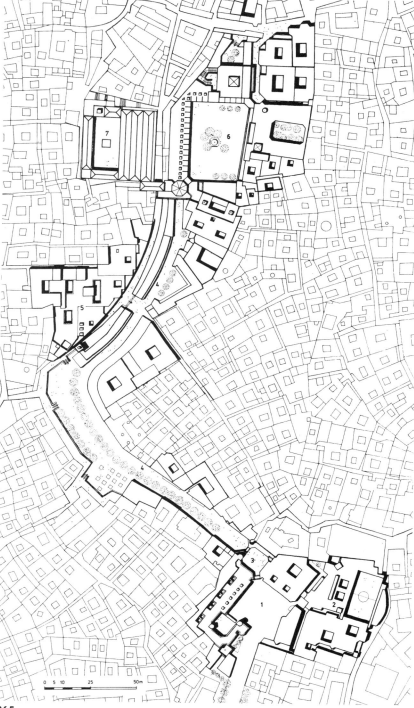

The infill project by Ruedi Bolli and Peter Gerber articulates the transition between the new and the old city in two stages. A vehicular service and public transport terminal in the Mokhfiya area acts as a filter for the subsequent pedestrian zone which leads to the compound of commercial and public facilities arranged around a large courtyard below the R'cif Mosque. From there, pedestrians have several possible ways to reach the existing central suq system. The "terminal" would only be accessible for taxis and minibuses. It is complemented by car parking and a bus station at the interchange between the southern end of the Boukhrareb and the ring road around the old city.

The lower Mokhfiya complex includes a small hotel/coffee shop, a first aid centre, transfer, dispatching and storage spaces for merchandise, as well as complementary facilities for the Mokhfiya residential community, such as a new primary school and sports and recreational facilities complementing the existing hammam. The northern compound contains a number of public buildings to sustain the nearby traditional city centre around the Qairawiyin Mosque, as well as commercial and service facilities. Along the new landscaped pedestrian spine further infill projects, including a small hospital, have been planned in order to repair the broken urban fabric and provide much-needed new facilities.

265 Site Plan.
1   Mokhfiya terminal complex
2   Neighbourhood facilities complementing adjacent hammam
3   Pedestrian entry gateway
4   Landscaped pedestrian area
5   Dispensary / hospital
6   New "R'cif Square" with public buildings and service facilities
7   Existing R'cif Mosque

266

266 Axonometric view of the Mokhfiya
terminal complex.
1 Unloading bays and storage on the
   ground floor, with offices above
2 First-aid centre and police station
3 Small hotel / cafeteria
4 Primary school
5 Sports and recreational facilities
6 Existing hammam

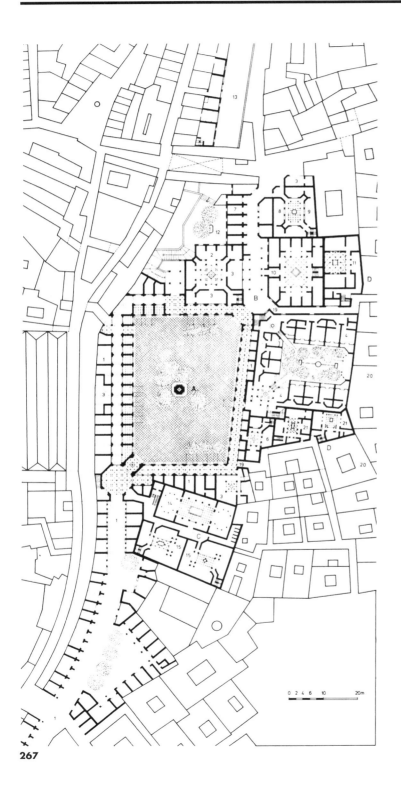

A New R'cif Square
B Service centre
C Old town municipality
D Residential units

1 Suq and shops
2 Restaurant
3 Coffee house
4 Hotel entry
5 Garden
6 Tourist office
7 Specialty shops
8 Bank
9 Post office
10 Artisans' centre and exhibition
11 Medical centre
12 Sunken open-air suq
13 Covered river channel
14 Court hall
15 Municipality offices
16 Multi-purpose hall
17 Bridge between court and mosque
   (on upper floor)
18 Mosque addition (upper floor)
19 Entry gates to residential district
20 Existing houses
21 New residential units

267 Ground-floor plan and section.

268 Eastern elevation.

269 Southern elevation.

270 Northern elevation.

271 Western elevation.

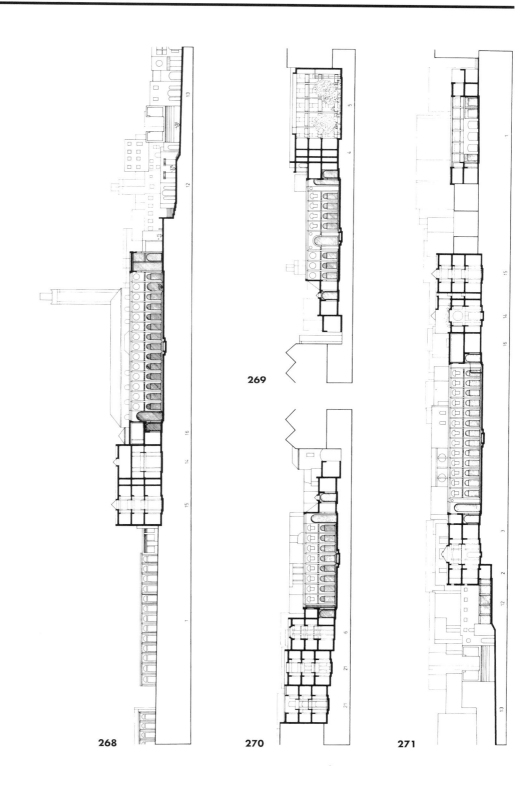

268

269

270

271

A Contemporary Version of Vernacular Housing for Low-Income Groups

During the master plan studies for Fez, it was recognized that upgrading the old city was not feasible without stopping the increase in densities and the trend towards multiple occupancy of historic houses by immigrant families in search of affordable housing. This, however, meant that viable housing alternatives had to be offered close to the medina, enabling immigrants to organize their own building activities with the support of the authorities, but without making them dependent on inappropriate and expensive governmental housing schemes. During the follow-up of the master plan organized with the Architectural School of the ETH in Zurich, it was therefore decided to explore the possibilities of an informal, process-oriented planning scheme for low-cost housing in a vacant area of the Aïn Qaddous district, parallel to the work on the Boukhrareb scheme.

The problem to be addressed was of more generic interest, since providing appropriate and affordable housing for low-income groups is currently one of the crucial problems of developing countries all over the world. The attractiveness of the new urban centres results in masses of rural immigrants trying to settle around the cities or in the declining historic quarters; yet the authorities are usually unable to deal with the problem – not only because of its sheer quantitative dimension, but also because of the institutional and technical prejudices which are part of Western-oriented administration systems. As in other vital areas, such as agriculture and nutrition, indiscriminate industrialization is not the answer to the problem, and in fact often aggravates the situation by imposing new cultural and economic dependencies, thus depriving people of their own traditional practices and resources.

While the housing problems in the developing world are certainly fuelled by rapid demographic growth, they are also an outcome of unbalanced development policies and inappropriate responses by governments and local authorities. Industrial production processes of housing components tend to rely on imported building machinery and raw materials, involve expensive transportation systems and introduce a distribution system which multiplies the basic costs by added intermediate profits for importers, wholesalers, retailers and construction firms. While this is part of the system in a Western-type industrial economy, it results in prohibitive costs for rural societies which are still rooted in pre-monetary economies. There, land is not a cost factor, building materials can be found locally and construction is done by the extended family group. Furthermore, modern formal-sector urbanization projects tend to become heavy administrative operations, involving land acquisition, legal procedures, construction permits, provision of infrastructure and services by the authorities, services of a contractor, etc.

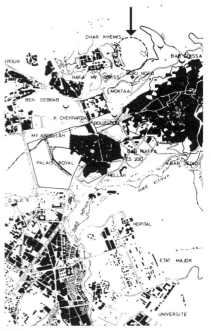

All this is alien to rural and pre-industrial societies, where construction is an integrated daily practice, managed by the community and its individual members. Societies which were accustomed to self-managed building processes for centuries have developed traditions which perfectly match both environmental conditions and social needs. Industrial housing schemes usually lack these qualities, as they are often climatically inappropriate in terms of material and layout, rarely fit the social patterns of the users and most of the time represent erratic foreign elements within a traditional townscape.

Although less pressing than in many Asian or African capitals, the various dimensions of this problem are clearly apparent in the case of Fez. Historically, there was always a close affinity between rural architecture and its more refined urban versions. Often the old city served to absorb and urbanize rural immigrants settling on the periphery or near the gates. However, the dimension of this process changed completely during the middle of this century, giving way to a mass exodus and favouring the constitution of a new "proletariat" seeking niches and new opportunities in the urban development process.

In the late fifties and sixties, during the transition from the colonial period to independence, there was a first attempt to cope with the emerging housing problems by founding the new district of Aïn Qaddous, on the hillside north of Fez, at a walking distance of 20 to 30 minutes from the medina and the colonial city centre. The satellite city of Aïn Qaddous, designed according to typical CIAM principles, was intended to take the pressure off the medina and to offer a new alternative to traditional housing. However, it was not fully successful in this respect. First of all, it was planned as a "dormitory town" with few or no work places and facilities included, and therefore largely dependent on the medina and the modern city centre. Its urban structure was dominated by a grid of vehicular roads with islands of isolated blocks in between, showing little concern for the socially and climatically attractive townscape qualities of traditional local architecture. Finally, its houses and apartments were too expensive to cater for the needs of rural immigrants and were therefore occupied by the emerging "middle class" of civil servants, government employees and merchants, while the rich "upper class" occupied the residential districts of the former colonial city.

The formally planned urbanization of Aïn Qaddous contrasts with the informal settlements of rural immigrants which emerged around the medina and in the former quarries above Aïn Qaddous. These squatter settlements sometimes grew overnight, as it were, by the collective efforts of family clans and groups of individuals who applied their traditional rural tech-

273

274

275

272 Map showing the selected project site northeast of Ain Qaddous.

273 Booming "illegal" markets in vacant areas of Ain Qaddous, along major pedestrian connections.

274 Ailing "planned" market in one of the residential complexes of Ain Qaddous, built in the mid-fifties.

275 "Illegal" settlement in one of the old quarries between the old city and Ain Qaddous.

niques, producing "spontaneous" villages of remarkable quality but devoid of any modern infrastructure and sometimes suffering from precarious physical and sanitary conditions. This illegal building activity put the authorities in an ambiguous situation: on the one hand, they found it difficult to accept the fact that people were occupying land and developing it independently of any government control; on the other hand, they knew that they were not

276

277

276 Map of the site selected for the new neighbourhood.

277 View of existing conditions before construction.

278 Project by Werner Rey / Martin Steinmann. Based on chosen planning constraints and on a limited range of typological models for individual housing units, a "spontaneous" urbanisation is proposed. Four stages in this process are depicted in this visual simulation of the project.

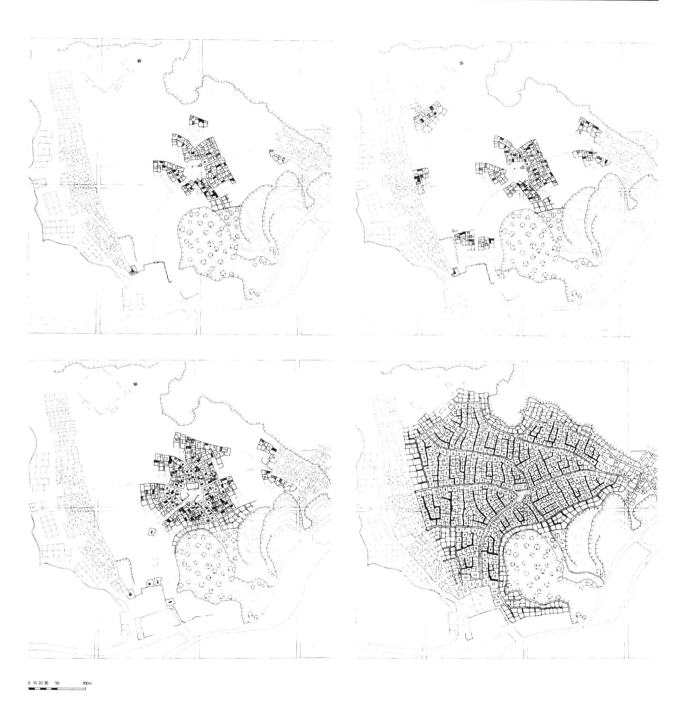

0 10 20 30 50   100m

278

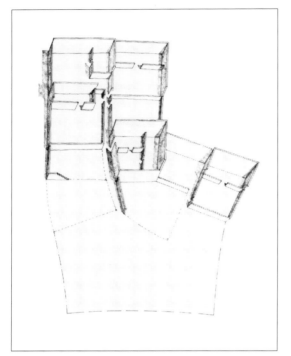
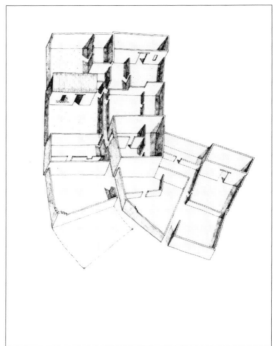
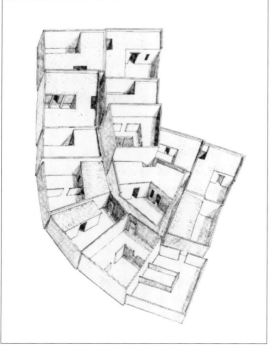
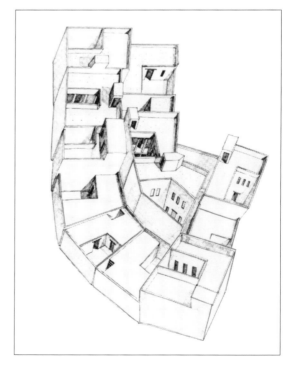

in a position to solve the problem by conventional administrative measures or to finance and subsidize large-scale development along Western lines. Therefore, most of the clandestine settlements ended up being accepted *de facto* and were eventually provided with water, electricity and sewerage. Some of them, however, were demolished by government decree and the inhabitants had to start from scratch elsewhere.

The starting point for the exercise was the fact that the self-built villages, besides showing obvious morphological affinities with the historic urban fabric of the medina, offered an interesting architectural model to be interpreted and re-used for a guided, informal building process. The students researched the layout of typical squatter houses in the "spontaneous" villages around Fez and often found typologies which were indeed simplified versions, if not archetypes, of the more sophisticated old town houses of Fez. This confirmed the hypothesis that a natural continuity exists between traditional and contemporary building patterns, provided the government does not interfere by introducing and imposing alien housing concepts. One of the objectives of the project was to support this continuity and to seek unconventional planning and implementation mechanisms which would encourage, rather than artificially suppress it.

The task, therefore, was to invent the right interaction between a general planning layout and the natural thrust of spontaneous individual initiatives. The "planners" had to define suitable ways of creating a flexible framework which the settlers themselves would fill with life and activities. The emphasis was not on the finished formal product, but rather on the rules of the game and the unfolding implementation process. Therefore the students had to think in terms of allocating areas and plots which would be developed by community groups and individuals, providing flexibility for step-by-step implementation of individual houses and clusters within the marked boundaries.

Here again, the students formed small teams of two or three participants and prepared alternative schemes, looking into both the general planning framework and individual house development. Special attention was given to the internal growth of the individual cluster as the relevant collective unit of ten to twenty families, who had to cooperate in organizing their shared territory. It was imagined that each group would have relative autonomy in the management of their land development within the allocated territory, but overall development scenarios and visualized models of individual house growth were prepared in order to simulate possible outcomes and provide basic design guidelines to the future users. The process was inspired by the age-old land occupation mechanisms used by the first Arab settlers in Mesopotamia ("Khittat"), which are still prevalent in urbanizing rural areas.

279 Visual simulation of the progressive growth of a cluster of houses around a common dead-end access ("darb"), as applicable to a sub-unit of the plan presented on the previous page.

280

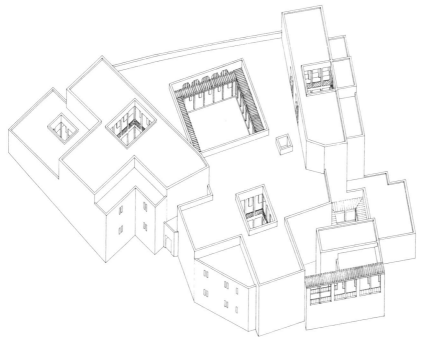

280 Final development plan established by the faculty and a group of former students in co-operation with the "Atelier du Schéma Directeur" in Fez.

281 Axonometric view of the primary-school building proposed as part of the neighbourhood centre.

281

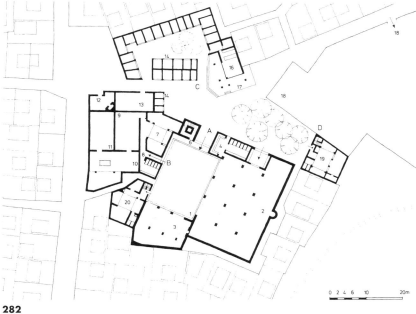

282

A   Mosque
B   Hammam and public bakery
C   Market
D   Public facilities

1   Mosque courtyard
2   Main prayer hall
3   Women's prayer hall
4   Ablution room and toilets
5   Auxiliary room
6   Minaret
7   Changing room
8   Toilets / showers
9   Cool room
10 Intermediate room
11 Steam room
12 Hammam heating
13 Public bakery
14 Shops
15 Niches for ambulant vendors
16 Coffee house
17 Terrace
18 Primary school
19 Medical centre
20 Women's centre

283

282/283 Two alternatives for the plan of the neighbourhood centre, as the core of the proposed site development.

284 Typological studies for individual housing units fitting into the overall neighbourhood plan (Christian Suesstrunk).

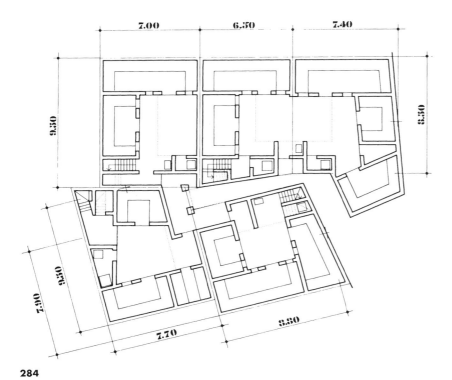

7.00   6.50   7.40

9.50

8.50

9.50

7.90

7.70   8.80

Postscript

While the projects presented in this chapter were initially conceived as an academic exercise, the results shown on pages 300/301 have informed the actual construction activities in Aïn Qaddous. The overall street layout, the neighbourhood centre and the school were implemented according to the designs presented here. When it came to individual plots and houses, the local representation of the Ministry of Urbanization engaged an architect to produce a range of new designs, which did not reflect the typology proposed by the study.

As regards the old city, the idea of peripheral service accesses, instead of the continuation of Ecochard's scheme for an Y-shaped vehicular road system cutting through the centre of the medina, has been pursued by a recent rehabilitation project for the historic city, sponsored by the World Bank.

The four student projects on the Boukhrareb area (of which only two are published here) were useful in demonstrating the range of existing opportunities, but no final infill project has been developed by the authorities so far. A decision is expected to be taken in the year 2000.

Case Study IV:
Aleppo – Urban Repair of a Destroyed Historic District

Historic Background and Project Context

Aleppo, one of the oldest continuously inhabited settlements in the world, is also one of the most outstanding urban monuments of the Islamic domain. Its site is dominated by a "tell", a steep hill dominating the city, which must have been settled since the third or fourth millenium BC and always served as an impregnable stronghold. In the Roman-Hellenistic and Byzantine period, the town came to be known as Beroe. Its structure was defined by a straight main avenue linking the western gate with the foot of the citadel hill. A large rectangular forum (or agora) was attached to this avenue. As in the case of its sister-city Damascus, Aleppo's special character is due to the fact that the Islamic city structure was built on a rectilinear Roman-Hellenistic framework which, since the Umayyad period, was gradually transformed and adapted to the needs of the new occupants, yet without completely losing the evidence of its previous pattern, particularly in the central districts of the walled city. By contrast, the suburbs developed from the 15th/16th centuries onwards show the usual non-planned urban structure, based on the direction of pedestrian traffic flows, location of markets and the irregular plot-shape of former orchards gradually being built over.

The heyday of Aleppo was during the early Middle Ages under Zengid and Ayyubid rule (12th/13th century), when the city came to play a decisive role in the confrontation between Islam and the Crusaders. It also started exploiting its geographic location, which made it a turntable of West-East trade. It was during this period that the citadel was built, an outstanding example of Islamic military architecture, with a remarkable structural and decorative use of stonemasonry. The north of Syria was always renowned for the art of its masons (many of Armenian origin), which influenced Islamic architecture in the Middle East and Egypt from the 10th to the 14th centuries and beyond, spreading the practice of stone architecture instead of brick. The domestic architecture of Aleppo perpetuated many features of Seljuk and Ayyubid architecture up to the 18th/19th centuries, and even today most buildings of the modern city are still faced with local limestone.

During the Ottoman period, Aleppo was still a flourishing trade centre, the third in importance after Istanbul and Cairo, and ahead of Damascus,

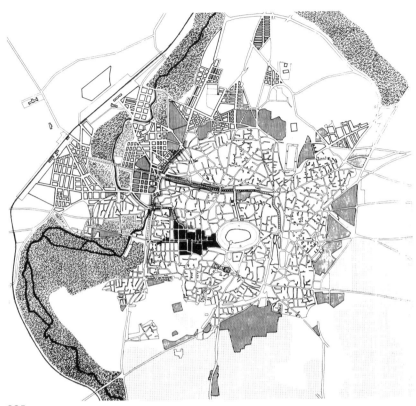

285

which had lost its leading status after the fall of the Umayyads. During this later period, in the 16th/17th centuries, the suq of Aleppo was a bustling centre of commerce, as reflected by the many khans added to the old linear suq structures. Many Western trade companies had their permanent representatives in the city which became a truly international community, with a high proportion of Christian residents.

By 1900, the old city of Aleppo included approximately 100 000 inhabitants, including the suburbs which had developed outside the main gates since the 16th century. The most important of these was the historic district of Jdeide, which today is still inhabited by Armenians and Christians. After the collapse of the Ottoman Empire and with the beginning of the French Mandate over Syria after World War I, Damascus resumed its former predominance and eventually became the economic and political capital of modern Syria. In terms of political and economic importance, Aleppo was again overshadowed by its old rival. However, it presently has about 1.7 million inhabitants and is the second city of Syria and the centre of the northern provinces. The urban growth of the past few decades has reduced

285 Plan of Aleppo around 1930. In black, the traditional city centre around the Umayyad Mosque and the covered suqs. In dark grey, the new service centre from the early 20th century in the Bustan Kullab area, opposite the gate of Bab al-Faraj on the northwestern corner of the old city, wich was to become a prime development area. Tramways (dashed lines) extended northwards and westwards into the new city, to serve the new extension areas constructed during French Mandate after World War I. Vertical hatching indicates location of cemeteries.

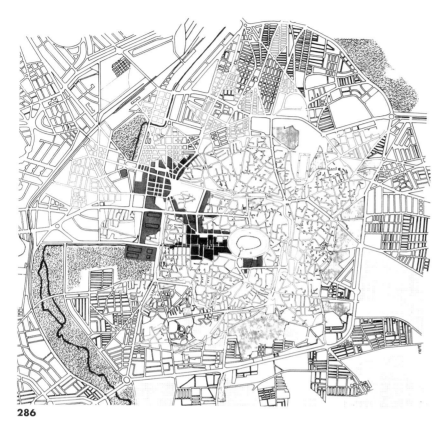

286

the relative importance of the old city, but its architectural and social fabric is astonishingly well preserved compared with the decline of other historic cities in the Middle East. Together with Fez and Sana'a, Aleppo thus constitutes one of the best surviving examples of a traditional Islamic city. At the same time, it provides a good example of modern urban development taking place immediately adjacent to the historic nucleus.

It is interesting to note that the beginnings of Aleppo's new town date back to 1868, when the Ottomans established a Western-style city administration in the newly constructed "Serail" building beneath the citadel. While the seat of power still remained in the old city for a few more decades, the Ottoman administration started developing a number of new residential districts *extra muros*, in particular Azizie, to the northwest of the old city, which clearly reflected contemporary European town-planning influences.

Another important urban intervention was the filling of the old moats and the creation of vehicular carriageways to the north and west of the walled city around the year 1900. After the demolition of the city walls and

286 Plan of the central area of Aleppo around 1980, showing further urban extensions around the old city, as well as a new road framework.

the southern edge of Jdeide (the Armenian suburb), the northern moat road was framed by two lines of terraced houses in a hybrid Ottoman-European style. This new spine, called Khandaq Street, became a major west-east connection between the periphery of the old city and the rapidly growing new town. In addition, a north-south spine, tangential to the western walls, was developed from the new quarters of Azizie towards Bab Antakia.

The intersection of the two spines on the northwestern corner of the city, near Bab al-Faraj, became an important node in the urban system. It is no wonder that this area developed very quickly into a major service and inter-change centre with a large number of hotels, restaurants, shops, garages and bus stations attached to it. Its importance as a focal point of the city was further stressed by the introduction of two lines for horse-drawn trams along the two main spines and crossing at Bab al-Faraj. The tramways were later electrified and operated until 1959.

Aleppo had thus become two cities in one. Although the old and the new parts coexisted peacefully during the first decades of our century, it would be hard to overlook the fundamental differences in their structural order. The old city grew as an aggregation of thousands of enclosed and introverted cellular units, taking the shape of private houses, mosques and markets, all enmeshed within a coherent urban fabric. The alleyways, totally absorbed by the built form, were meant for pedestrian circulation only and made a clear distinction between areas of public and private control. Mean-while, the new city was *a priori* defined by the geometrical grid of vehicu-lar traffic which dictated the size and shape of land subdivisions and, there-fore, the character of urban form: buildings were isolated from each other and dependent on the street rather than focused on their interior courtyards.

With the rapid growth of the new city during the French protectorate (1919–1945), and even more so after independence, the confrontation between two urban systems became inevitable. In the early fifties, when traf-fic flows were still modest, a somewhat utopian master plan was proposed by the French planner André Gutton. Together with the destruction of the western suburbs of the old city and their replacement by a modern city cen-tre, it envisaged two highways cutting through the historic fabric, north and south of the citadel, with a view to creating a direct road link "from the sea to the desert" and to "properly enhancing the citadel" (see scheme on page 180). There is no rational explanation as to why this axis, hundreds of kilo-metres long, should have cut its way through the heart of the old city instead of simply bypassing it. However, the concepts of celebrating highways as symbols of freedom and progress and exposing key monuments by strip-ping them of their urban context were consistent with European planning ideologies of the fifties and were to pop up again in later proposals.

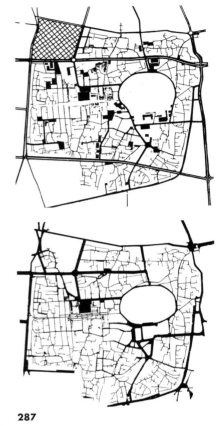

287

287 Above, the road scheme of the master plan by G. Banshoya (1974), and below, existing conditions in 1983, with only the northern road cut being partly executed. On the northwestern corner of the old city the Bab al-Faraj area, com-pletely surrounded by new vehicular roads.

288 Maps of the area north of the Umayyad Mosque, comparing conditions of the historic fabric around 1945 and in 1980 (after J.C. David).

Eventually, only minor elements of Gutton's proposal were implemented during the subsequent decades. Most of the western suburb, the glacis of the walled city, as it were, was gradually demolished and partly replaced by large markets and bus terminals (see page 209), without the planned new city centre being built. The idea of the two highways cutting through the walled city was reiterated in 1974 with the new master plan by the Japanese planner G. Banshoya. Many of its general concepts followed the model of a previous master plan established for Damascus in 1968 by M. Ecochard (including the idea of reviving the old Roman street grid by introducing corresponding new vehicular roads). Yet lack of funds and administrative problems prevented full implementation of the new highways. The northern axis was built only up to the citadel, from where traffic was brought back into Khandaq Street. In addition, a perpendicular road was constructed, leading to the entrance of the Umayyad Mosque (see below). The southern axis stopped in front of Bab Qinasreen, thus not really entering the old city and causing no physical damage.

By 1969, as a result of this new road construction, an area of two hundred by two hundred metres in the northwestern corner of the old city was surrounded by large avenues. The pressure for demolition and total redevelopment increased accordingly and was sustained by the fact that the Bab al-Faraj district, in the eyes of the authorities, had acquired a dubious reputation as the most popular amusement centre in Aleppo.

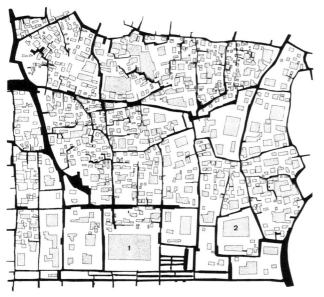
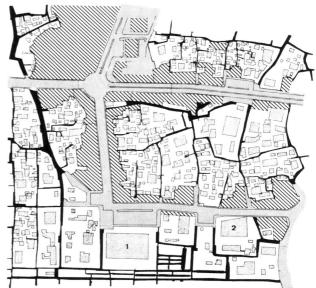

288

The Struggle with the Old Bab al-Faraj Project (1979–1983)

In 1978/79, an ambitious project for the redevelopment of this northwestern corner of the old city was worked out by a group of university professors on behalf of the then-Governor of Aleppo. It envisaged a number of 16-storey office buildings and an opera house on a two-storey commercial concourse replacing the historic fabric. The intent may have been to establish Aleppo as a modern metropolis which could rival or even outdo the capital city. However, quite apart from the fact that its design was totally alien to the surrounding urban fabric, the project's functional program was far from realistic in economic terms.

In 1979, the whole area was expropriated by the municipality. Most of the buildings were demolished, with the exception of two commercial streets, two mosques, a fragmentary courtyard frontage of the historic Rajab Pasha house and a group of buildings in the southwestern corner of the site, which were scheduled for later clearance. The project had a strong political backing, but there was also a certain resistance among the population. In 1980, a concerned group of conservationists under the leadership of Adli Qudsi, himself an architect, managed to persuade the Syrian Antiquities Department to ask Unesco for advice. As a result, the author was requested by Unesco in Spring 1980 to lead a mission on conservation problems in Aleppo, carried out with the help of J. C. David, a geographer who specialized in the history of Aleppo, and the architects B. Chauffert-Yvart, Y. Beton and G. Rizzardi.

Given the prevailing political circumstances, it was not possible for the group to directly criticize the project and its architecture as such. Yet, we argued that its implementation would induce further redevelopment pressures, with the corresponding effects of heavy traffic generation in a critical area of the old city. Eventually, this would result in a fatal tendency to further expand the modern Central Business District into the old city at the expense of the historic fabric. The report also stressed that the main problem was to find the right balance between two separate but interrelated central areas, one being an integral part of the traditional urban fabric and the other being structured as a modern Western city. The new city centre should neither destroy the old one, nor should the old city centre be dried out by cutting it off from the life-stream of the overall urban system. The problem was to define the right interface, to control the expansion and shape of the modern city centre, and to establish the right transportation modes in the intermediary zones, in order to achieve better traffic compatibility.

Consequently, the report pointed out alternative growth opportunities for the modern city centre in the area to the south – the already destroyed and badly used former western suburb. This site offered a better development

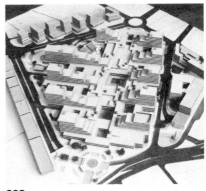

289

290

289 Model of the old Bab al-Faraj project, after reduction of the height of the towers.

290 Site plan of the old Bab al-Faraj project (1979).

potential than Bab al-Faraj, without jeopardizing the survival of the historic fabric. The proposed southern expansion would place the new centre in sequence with the old *via recta* and the suqs, as already proposed by A. Gutton, but in the context of an urban design concept emphasizing gradual transition instead of sharp confrontation. Basic principles were defined for achieving a progressive meshing of the two urban systems, in terms of both built form and traffic modes. By differentiating the new central strip into various types of land use and accessibility, the impact of vehicular traffic could be reduced step by step to meet the pedestrian system of the old city. Submitted in June 1981, the report received a positive response. Due to political pressures, however, the old Bab al-Faraj project was not abandoned; the buildings were merely reduced in height, without changing the basic layout or giving more consideration to the surroundings.

Finally, in 1983, excavation for the first phase of the project was started, and during the early works on the underground car park the foundations of the old city wall were exposed. Most of the stones had already been dis-

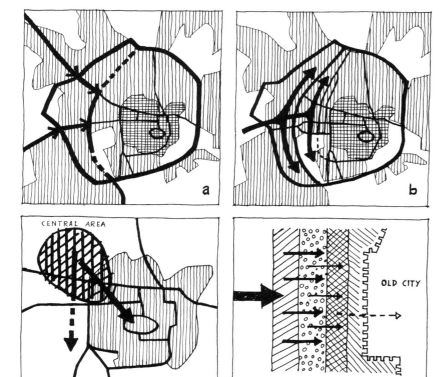

291 Diagrams illustrating development policies recommended in order to reduce pressures on the Bab al-Faraj area:
a) completing intermediate ring road
b) diverting through-traffic
c) reorienting growth of modern city centre southwards
d) Differentiating accessibility according to impact of traffic mode

291

293

mantled and taken away before the Department of Antiquities could intervene. The existence of the wall was certainly no secret but its upper parts, hidden by abutting houses and khans, had already disappeared in 1979 with the wholesale demolition of the district. However, the loss now became more evident, and the Antiquities Service managed to stop the project by imposing a large non-buildable zone east of the uncovered foundations. This caused yet another problem, for such a large unbuilt area, although preferable to the 16-storey towers, would have produced a strange "gap" in a strategic node of the central area.

At that time the author was requested, again via Unesco, to assess the range of possible alternatives in the light of the new situation. Three alternatives were investigated and discussed with the authorities as a basis for future projects:

a) To implement part of the old project, while maintaining the zone of *non-aedificandi* east of the wall remains. This was the simplest solution but hardly satisfactory, because the old project, rigid as it was, could not really be adapted to match this requirement. Furthermore, the problems of scale and urban form would remain the same in the eastern half of the large plot.

292 Existing conditions around the Bab al-Faraj site in 1983, after the demolition of around 90% of the old urban fabric in 1979 and partial excavation for the basement of the old project. In the front, the traces of the foundations of the old city walls. In the back, the Umayyad Mosque, the suqs and the citadel.

293 View of the site from the east, showing the excavation and first basement elements of the old Bab al-Faraj project, after its suspension (1984).

b) To leave the demolished district as a large landscaped open space and to create a park around the old city walls. This solution, although supported by a number of officials, was found to be inappropriate for the core of a central area, where a built environment with urban qualities was required. Landscaped elements should certainly be considered, but they needed to be integrated into an overall concept of urban form which would enhance civic life in the central area.

c) To start a completely new project that would take into account the special character of the adjacent areas and integrate all remaining historic structures, as well as the already built parts of former schemes, namely the underground car park. Compared with other historic districts in Aleppo, the surviving remains of the Bab al-Faraj district were by no means of exceptional quality, yet their conservation within the new project was a matter of principle, intended to mark a reversal of the previous way of thinking. Moreover, this alternative suggested looking at the new project as part of a more comprehensive central-area concept in order to resolve the interrelation between the two central areas, especially in terms of traffic flows.

As the municipality agreed to the recommended third alternative, the author started investigating the situation with the help of traffic planner Peter Davies (University of Nottingham). The surveys showed a considerable traffic congestion around Bab al-Faraj and in the adjacent areas of Bustan Kulab and Azizie, where radial roads penetrating the city from the west intersect with circular roads around the old city. Azizie and Bustan Kulab, both developed around the turn of the century, feature relatively narrow streets, bustling with commercial activities. The objective, therefore, was to relieve the node of Bab al-Faraj, to prevent or minimize west-east traffic through the old city and to divert north-south traffic further west, channelling it into more recent and less busy avenues which could become part of an old-city bypass. This circular system would engulf the walled city, as well as the historic districts of Jdeide, Azizie and Bustan Kulab, combining them into one large functional unit.

This protected low-traffic district would then be subdivided into a number of enclosed "pockets", each one having a separate loop (or cul-de-sac) traffic system accessible from the main outer roads. Public transport lines would be given the exclusive right of way to pass from one "pocket" to the other, in order to establish direct and uncongested routes, while private vehicular traffic would be confined to the loop system, with compulsory entries and exits into each pocket and no possible interconnections. The proposed new transportation concept did not imply any physical changes in the existing road network. It merely suggested operational changes, such as

294

295

296

297

closed circuits and one-way streets, to decongest the area and improve local access on the fringe of the old city (see diagrams on following page). The Bab al-Faraj area itself was conceived as a predominantly pedestrian environment in continuity with the old city, but offering better service access for public and commercial facilities.

Thus the stage was set for a new urban design approach to the Bab al-Faraj project by first providing better opportunities for organic linkages with the surrounding areas. A tentative new site plan for the future development was prepared, assuming building heights of 2–3 upper floors and defining the main components of urban form in terms of land use and overall volumes. The project planned to take advantage of the central location by providing a new civic core on the threshold between the old and the new city. To support this intention, it was suggested that Aleppo's new cultural

294-297 Existing conditions around the Bab al-Faraj site. The edge of the Bustan Kullab district to the west of Bab al-Faraj (294). The street-front development of 1900 along the covered moat, north of the site (295). The partly demolished southern edge of the site (296). The remaining structures of the 17th-century Rajab Pasha house on the eastern edge against the background of modern blocks from the sixties (297).

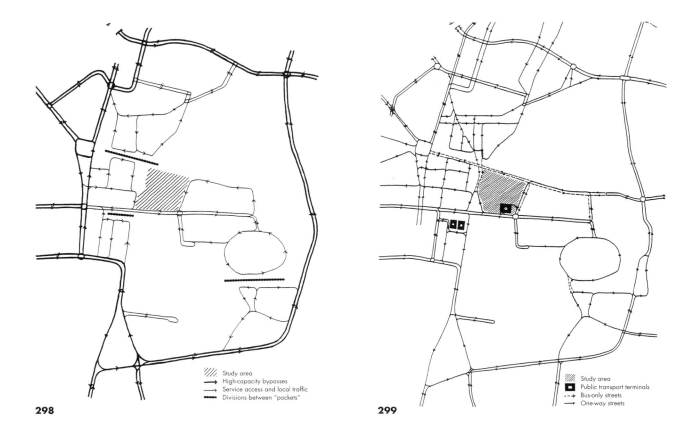

Study area
/// High-capacity bypasses
→ Service access and local traffic
▬▬ Divisions between "pockets"

298

Study area
■ Public transport terminals
--→ Bus-only streets
→ One-way streets

299

centre – previously planned on an isolated site in the new city – should find its place in the Bab al-Faraj complex and be combined with a pedestrian plaza, hotels, restaurants, cafés and commercial facilities.

The suggestions of this second Unesco report were fully supported by the municipality, and in September 1983 an international symposium was convened by the "Old City Committee" to discuss the redevelopment of Bab al-Faraj in the context of general conservation and town planning policies for historic Islamic cities. In the meantime, the main political players in Aleppo had changed, which made it possible to review former urban-planning policies in an open and professional manner. In this more relaxed political climate, consciousness of the values of the old city could be raised and the need for its protection and rehabilitation be explained in the light of recent international experience. As a result of this conference, the municipality announced its decision to abandon the old Bab al-Faraj project and start a new study along the lines of the above recommendations.

298 New vehicular traffic control scheme for the old city, proposed to eliminate through-traffic and enable efficient local service traffic within well-defined "pockets".

299 Correlated public transportation system, maximising accessibility within the given constraints of the old city.

The New Infill Project for Bab al-Faraj (1984-86)

In Spring 1984, the author was invited by the Syrian company Iskan al-Askari (Military Housing Establishment) to prepare a design concept at a scale of 1:500 for the reconstruction of the destroyed Bab al-Faraj area. The project was to be developed in greater detail (1:200) by the company's recently established conservation unit in Aleppo (Director Nabil Kassabshi, collaborator Thierry Grandin) under the author's supervision. The client of the project, the Aleppo municipality, followed the recommendations of the Unesco report, allowing for a maximum building height of two upper floors and requested a usable floor space ratio of 1.0 (such a low density being perhaps an over-reaction to the excessive land-use factor of the previous project and a concession to the idea of the park in the city centre). The new project, detailed in 1985/86, was drawn up according to the following agreed objectives:

300

–   To fill the large townscape gap of Bab al-Faraj by integrating all existing "fragments", old and new, into a coherent overall structure which should be flexible enough to cope with a variety of site constraints and historic references, and strong enough to produce an urban core with an identity of its own.

–   To take up the threads of the disrupted urban fabric, complete and inter-weave them with new structures which would show an affinity to the historic city in terms of volumes, scale and typology, without attempting to produce an archeological reconstruction of the *status ante quo*.

–   To redefine the edges of the old city along the major roads of the late-19th century and to establish a dialogue with the surviving remains of the old streetscape.

–   To provide an attractive focal point of urban and civic life which would connect the historic and the modern centres of Aleppo, while enhancing the status and prestige of the old city.

–   To establish a contemporary architectural style and vocabulary, which would make reference to typical Aleppine elements which have evolved throughout the centuries, having been continously adapted and re-used up to the recent past.

The dominating component of the new urban form was to be an enclosed public open space of irregular shape, defined by a theatre-cum-cultural centre, as well as commercial buildings linked with an adjacent hotel complex. These volumes were to occupy most of the destroyed northern part of the site, establishing a contiguous urban form with clear edges which evoke the boundaries of the old city walls. To the west, the streetscape of Bab al-Faraj

300 View of the last remaining old alleyway from Bab al-Faraj to the Omari Mosque, spared from demolition in 1983.

301

was completed and re-defined by a low and partly "transparent" suq build-ing, giving access to the sunken archeological area which will be described below in more detail. On the southern sector of the site the architectural treatment was somewhat different in scale and grain, since the main task here was to rehabilitate and complete the surviving urban fabric on either side of Bahsita Street, the old spine which leads to the restored Omari Mosque. Small-scale infill was used to repair the disrupted urban structure and re-establish the old pedestrian street network, while screening the street edge with new commercial buidings. Under the open plaza and the adja-cent public and commercial buildings it was possible to accommodate an underground car park, making use of the already constructed basement of the old project.

The following, more detailed presentation of individual buildings and spaces starts with the description of the central plaza. Its introduction re-flects a twofold rationale. Firstly, it was thought that a significant and undis-turbed central open space, with a strong urban character, was lacking in modern Aleppo, while in the old city, such a meeting place was only offered

301 Site plan of the new Bab al-Faraj project (1984).
1 Theatre/multi-purpose hall
2 Cultural centre with integrated remains of Rajab Pasha house
3 Urban plaza building with shopping arcades and passages covered on the ground floor and offices/apartments on the upper floor
4 Hotels
5 New covered Bab al-Faraj market
6 Omari Mosque
7 Commercial facilities

302

by the courtyard of the Umayyad Mosque. The Bab al-Faraj area, as a pivot between the new and the old city, was seen as an ideal place to provide
this new public open space. Secondly, it was felt that the rather low floor
ratio of 1.0 that was requested called for a large opening in the overall composition, in order to allow for sufficient density in the built-up areas around
it and to match the tightly woven texture of the traditional urban fabric. Thus,
the contrast between the rather narrow pedestrian streets and the central
open space was a deliberate choice, and was expected to greatly enhance
the spatial experience of the new complex. The buildings around the plaza,

302 Ground-floor plan of the new Bab
al-Faraj project combined with the remaining (undemolished) urban structures, showing the resulting pedestrian spaces.
Between the covered Bab al-Faraj market
to the east and the hotel complex, a
sunken archaeological park featuring the
remains of the city wall has been included.

while visually defining the open space and setting it off from the alleyways, provide several covered passages and arcades at ground-floor level to interconnect both elements. As explained below, the irregular geometry of the plaza itself absorbs and harmonizes the various directional systems of the buildings around it, reflecting a number of partly chosen, partly imposed constraints, which were turned into active design factors.

The southern edge of Khandaq Street was designed in response to the long line of late-Ottoman terraced houses on the northern side of the old moat. A new linear building compensates for the absent southern counterpart and completes the linear street space with arcades of similar scale, without attempting to replicate the features of the destroyed terraced houses. Two covered passages give access from Khandaq Street into the northern corner of the plaza, opening new "gates" into the pedestrian area.

The northeastern corner of the new development, including the hotel complex, follows a diagonal orientation as established by the structural grid of the old Bab al-Faraj project and its re-used basement structures. The hotels adhere to the imposed height limit of two upper floors and therefore extend horizontally across three courtyards, with a number of interconnected wings bridging the pedestrian alleyways. The surviving structure of the 18th century Antaki house, with its beautiful courtyard and iwan, has been attached to one of the hotel wings as a special guesthouse.

The orthogonal grid of the cultural centre, the theatre and the eastern section of the plaza is adjusted to match the surviving courtyard elevation of the 17th-century Rajab Pasha house, which was integrated into the cultural centre as a representative historic element.

The western and southern edges of the plaza are defined by a bent commercial building which provides an organic continuation, the "tail", so to speak, of the cultural compound. It contains arcades with shops, cafés, restaurants and public passages on the ground floor, office rooms on the two upper floors, and recessed penthouses and studios on the top floor.

The public square enclosed by these buildings and arcades is articulated into a sequence of interconnected open spaces: a small northern forecourt or precinct accessible through the main gates from Moat Street, the slightly raised central open space in front of the theatre and a more rectangular pocket in front of the cultural centre, where the plaza reaches its most formal and crystalline shape, emphasized by a central fountain and traditional geometric pavement patterns. The design of the plaza buildings is intended to strike a balance between individual buildings and overall urban form: the cultural centre, the theatre and the commercial multi-purpose building all use the same basic type of arch with a number of variations and different infills, corresponding to the specific character of each building. By

303 Model view of the new project from southwest.

304 Model view of the new project from northeast.

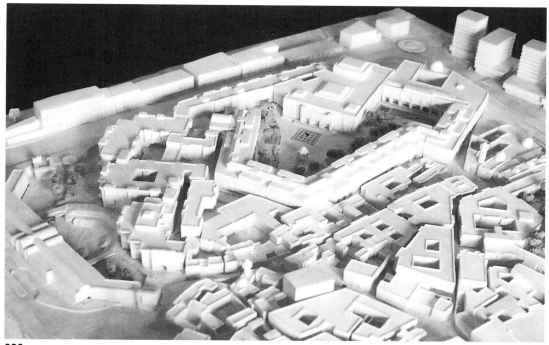

303

304

providing a common denominator in the elevations, the urban plaza is given a homogeneous character of its own.

Perhaps the most sensitive part of the new project is its western edge, since an appropriate setting for the remains of the old city walls had to be found – the raison d'être, after all, of the emergence of the new Bab al-Faraj project. A full reconstruction of the walls was not possible due to lack of historic evidence. It would only have resulted in a dubious "pastiche" – an undesirable approach when many original sections of the walls are still standing and awaiting proper restoration. Thus the excavated part with the old wall foundations was left at its present level (five metres below ground) and treated as a sunken archaeological park. In effect, this would create the visual impression of a new "moat" between Bab al-Faraj Street and the hotel complex. To make the best possible use of this topographic feature, a small open-air theatre, descending from the hotel terrace to the sunken archaeological garden, was suggested for cultural events or as an informal meeting place. The western front of the hotel complex was conceived as a visual substitute for the previous city walls. The elevations were given a strong mural character with relatively small window openings.

To the west of the hotels and on the other side of the sunken garden, a low commercial building along the street was introduced, to re-establish the clear spatial sequence of the Bab al-Faraj streetscape with its two typical nodes, north and south of the street channel. One of these nodes contains the clocktower of Bab al-Faraj, still a landmark of the inner city and a popular meeting point. The pedestrian north-south flows along Bab al-Faraj

305

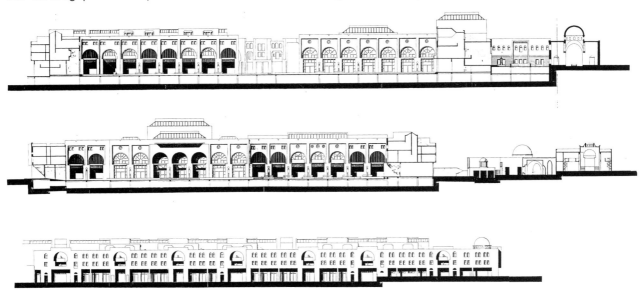

Street are intended to pass through the covered suq of the new commercial building, rather than being exposed to the vehicular traffic. The central part of this covered suq opens onto the sunken archaeological garden. A large balcony and wide steps in front of the open-air theatre complete the small "arena" which is further defined by two lateral pedestrian bridges. Covered by light trellises, these bridges would provide a pleasant at-grade connection from Bab al-Faraj Street to the hotel terraces.

The southern part of the new project is composed of a series of infills which are intended to repair and revitalize the district's old pedestrian spines, leading from Bab al-Faraj to the Omari Mosque, and from there southwards to the Umayyad Mosque and the central suqs. The new components are intended to re-establish the basic circulation patterns and activities without any attempt at archaeologically minded "reconstruction". Historic typologies are revived, such as the linear rows of suqs along the main alleys and the specialized markets and warehouses (khans) behind the suqs, with direct access from the street into their courtyards. Occasionally, workshops on the ground floor have been combined with offices and/or housing on the upper floors, introducing elevated courtyard houses.

Postscript

The project described in the foregoing paragraphs is now being executed after some minor changes and revisions requested by the municipality. Unfortunately, the budgetary provisions for developing and refining the initial 1984 concept – an extensive urban design study – were extremely limited and so was the time allowed for further detailing of the project. In total, little more than one year was conceded for necessary design revisions, detailing and working drawings – too short a time-span for a project of this size, importance and complexity.

A major concern was the phasing of the construction process. To allow for a smooth step-by-step implementation, the project was subdivided into six lots. The municipality decided to start with the southeastern corner, south of Bahsita Street and the Omari Mosque. This part, now almost completed, contains mainly shops on the ground floors, offices and administration on the upper floors, and a newly programmed supermarket in the freestanding khan-type structure. Phase two will concern the infill structures on Bahsita Street and the southeastern fringe of the surviving urban fabric; phase three the Bab al-Faraj suq on the western edge of the site; phase four the sunken archaeological park and the hotel complex; phase five the commercial structures around the plaza; and phase six the theatre and cultural centre.

305 Model view of the new project from southeast.

306 Sections / elevations cutting through the central square.

307

308

307 View of the nearly completed commercial complex in the southeastern corner of the new Bab al-Faraj development, as seen from the internal pedestrian street at lower level (1998).

308 View of the upper level pedestrian arcade of the above complex, with arcades connected to the walkways of the surrounding streets.

309 New pedestrian suq leading from the south into the Bab al-Faraj project area, through the southern commercial compound, before completion (1998).

310 Courtyard and passageway within the above commercial compound.

Fundraising for the further implementation of the project proved to be a major hurdle in a governmental setting which, for decades, has followed Communist models, with little or no involvement of the private sector. Yet selling or renting newly constructed shops and offices would have been easy, given the present demand and the rising interest of private investors in participating in this significant new development. The municipality could

309

310

have established a revolving fund for financing the subsequent phases of the project by the outright sale of land, development rights or facilities, but it preferred to maintain the governmental investment mode. The hotel is to be constructed on behalf of the Ministry of Tourism and may be leased to a particular operator or international chain. Being the only modern high-standard hotel in the central area, and given the present demand, its economic viability would seem assured. As to the theatre and the cultural centre, they are long overdue facilities which had been programmed by the Ministry of Culture for years, and so it is to be supposed that high priority will be given to their construction.

The history of the Bab al-Faraj project from 1978 to 1987 reflects a significant change of attitude with regard to conservation during a critical phase of the city's development. It marks the end of crude redevelopment policies, which used to imply the total demolition of complete historic districts, only to replace them by poor replicas of "Modern Movement" architecture. Local architectural circles, concerned citizens and politicians alike were involved in this process, which reflects the growth of a city-wide and even national consensus. In fact, similar trends could be observed in Damascus, where the old 1968 master plan was cancelled, as far as the old city and the historic suburbs are concerned.

Conclusion:
Towards the Rehabilitation of Historic Muslim Cities

"The state should not claim what it cannot exact; for the gifts that love and genius are able to provide, cannot be forced. These the state should not touch, or else its laws should be taken and put in the pillory! By God, those who want to turn the state into a school of morals do not know the sin they commit. Indeed it was man's urge to turn the state into his heaven which transformed it into hell. Nothing more than a coarse shell around the kernel of life – that is what the state can provide. It is the enclosure around the garden of the fruits and flowers of human life. Yet what good is the wall around the garden, if the soil is arid? Relief can only come from the rains of heaven." (Friedrich Hoelderlin, "Hyperion", 1797)

The foregoing case studies illustrate the practical and physical consequences of the current conflict between conventional forms of modern development and the differently structured urban fabrics of historic Islamic cities. What emerges here are not merely technical problems which could easily be resolved at a professional level, but much deeper contradictions, rooted in diverging philosophies, ideologies and cultural attitudes. As described in chapters 8 and 9, any attempt at reconciling or resolving these opposed positions needs to get to grips with the prejudices implied by the dominant Western ideologies. An outgrowth of 19th-century positivism and supported by increasing economic and political power differentials, these prejudices have first introduced a somewhat artificial polarization between "tradition" and "modernity" and then cemented the hegemony of a singularly isolated and fragmented world view. By ascribing superiority and prestige to certain Western models, other cultural traditions were stigmatized as being backwards and fossilized. As a result, the creative potential of traditional urbanization processes was blocked, while the deficiencies of the dominant Western model with regard to a whole range of excluded cultural values, human resources and social opportunities were deliberately overlooked.

In the current transformation processes imposed by an unilateral concept of "progress", the issue at stake, therefore, is the continuity of local cultural identities, as materialized in the built environment. The correlation between man's identity and his environment implies that the question to be addressed is how to foster significant architectural forms which both solicit and express identification with deep-rooted human values. At their best, architectural forms represent the crystallization of a creative process and have a life and a "soul" of their own. They are not just accidental and superficial shapes, as is often assumed, but are potential carriers and conveyors of meaning, capable of evoking strong resonances in man's spirit, soul and body. Through his visual and intellectual senses, the beholder is able to intuitively perceive essential qualities inherent in formal structures, such as wholeness, unity and truth. The sense of beauty that such experiences can evoke is nothing but a reminder of a higher and timeless order in which human life is rooted. By this very fact it constitutes a prime source of and impetus for profound existential identification processes.

With this context in mind, we shall first attempt to analyze the conditions under which cultural identity (or creative diversity) is produced and how it can be maintained or revived. Secondly, we shall describe the vital role of historic cities in this struggle for cultural identity, which is by no means limited to the Islamic world. We shall then debate the limits of conservation as a procedure for keeping historic cities alive and conclude by identifying a number of enabling factors for an active regeneration and rehabilitation of historic cities in the Islamic world.

The Sources of Cultural Identity

Creative diversity in culture and in the built environment can be seen as a result of the development of a range of strong and specific local identities, grown over centuries of continuous interaction between man's inner vision and his evolving natural and cultural environment. Due to their spiritual orientation, traditional cultures had access to the sources of the sacred as a primordial and suprasensible reality which inspires and shapes material expression. They knew that the various layers of reality, from the material to the spiritual, coincide with and thus mirror each other through the chain of references and analogies implied in the relation between macrocosm and microcosm. An almost ritual observance of social and cultural practices related to overarching values allowed a coherent physical environment to gradually materialize, which in turn expressed the underlying non-physical values. Thus the growth of cultural identities was no gratuitous process. It depended on man's existential experience of human values and on his ability to actively practice and realize his beliefs. Such convictions may ultimately be rooted in shared universal values, but their physical embodiment will always differ according to individual interpretations and the conditions of the "medium" employed. This natural variety of expressions, each of them one approximation of a much deeper reality, has resulted in parallel but varying cultural identities.

For thousands of years, man's natural and cultural environment relied on a delicate balance, based on the variety and diversity of their components – a differentiation also implying the interchange and interdependence between individual creative manifestations, whether in nature or in the cultural domain. Within this system, natural growth, decline and transformation of single units could take place without affecting the survival of the whole. Curtailing this diversity means reducing the prospects for richness and liveliness, as well as the chances of creative renewal, as we are beginning to experience in the rapid degradation of today's human environment.

As a result of its excessive destruction of natural and cultural wealth, the single-minded development concept initiated by modern Western civilization in the late 19th century (and adopted by most other regions of the world since the mid-20th century), has amply demonstrated its lack of long-term viability. Meanwhile, international awareness of the risks of an overshooting technology has steadily increased over the past thirty years. From the warnings by the Club of Rome in 1972 ("The Limits to Growth") to the Rio Conference on environmental sustainability in 1992 and its recent follow-up, the 1995 Report of the World Commission on Culture and Development ("Our Creative Diversity"), conventional modes of development began to be questioned at a global level. Accordingly, the inclusion of environmental and cultural considerations is now being advocated with increasing strength and insistence, even by more conventional agents of development such as the World Bank. Concerns are being voiced that the rampant uniformity caused by modern development trends, such as technical standardization, bureaucratic concentrations of power, world-wide industrial trusts and centralized processing of information, all driven by powerful economic forces, are undermining the richness and stability of the inherited natural and cultural micro-systems. The common denominator of all these trends, it would appear, is the substitution of organic and social processes by abstract and artificial mechanisms which no longer appeal to the human senses and man's need for direct involvement and interaction.

Cultural identity cannot be produced by rational thinking alone; it must involve all human resources, including the bodily perception of space and place, the emotional attachment to fellow-beings and also the sense of the more subtle and invisible dimensions of spiritual reality. Without an open window to the metaphysical world, no lively and meaningful manifestations of reality can be born. Forms degenerate to dead shells, and aesthetic principles become arbitrary and interchangeable, since they provide no handle for a deeper understanding of reality and the integral nature of created forms. (Incidentally, the Greek word "aisthesis" that underlies the term "aesthetics" means human perception of reality in its fullest sense.)

Here, modernity is trapped by the limitations of its fundamentally agnostic perceptions, attitudes and sciences, which by definition cannot accept any recourse to transcendent powers as the prime sources of creativity, let alone the appeal to any kind of revelation. Obviously, a view which denies *a priori* the existence of non-material or non-quantifiable forces must find it hard to accept the existence of spiritual facts (let alone experience them), and can therefore only produce mutilated forms. At best, it may relegate spiritual facts to the domain of vague and non-committal intellectual constructs while, at the same time, tending to raise its own fragmentary interpretations of material phenomena to the level of scientific "facts". This results in a distorted sense of reality and, concomitantly, a restricted view of human nature and its capacity to generate sensible and significant forms.

What, then, are the processes leading to the formation of genuine cultural identity? Our contention is that the process relies on the existence of an integral vision and understanding of reality, shared by the community as a whole. Based on this resource, the patterns of cultural identity are woven through numerous cycles of interplay between, on the one hand, deep and largely spontaneous human impulses and, on the other hand, "productive" resistances encountered in a given environment, such as the bonds of a given social order and the principles of a shared ethical code. It is this creative interaction which integrates the human mind and grounds it in meaningful cultural patterns, thus producing shared emotions and values, and turning information into experience, knowledge and wisdom.

The same principles apply to the formation of a significant built environment, as a result of interacting material and non-material forces that eventually create a correlation of human values and attitudes with architectural qualities. Within this creative crystallization process, social and physical bonds and constraints represent a necessary counterpart to the vital energies of a community, since they are needed to enable life to coagulate, as it were, into successive formal structures which can embody the evolving specific identity of a given society and its place. This also means that the qualitative level of both impulses and resistances will condition the very structure of the built environment that materialises through the rhythmical interaction between opposite but complementary forces.

For both impulses and resistances, a hierarchy based on the implied values can be identified. There are what could be called spiritually rooted *primary* impulses, such as worship, creative imagination, joy of life, human solidarity; and there are more trivial *secondary* impulses, such as the striving for economic gains, social prestige or power. Likewise, there are primary, more "creative" resistance factors, such as the resilient constraints of the natural environment and the given building materials, or shared social conventions, rituals and practices legitimated by spiritual references; and there are secondary, less inspiring resistance factors, such as industrialised production processes, rigid economic development systems or administrative procedures and regulations lacking in emotional appeal and incentives.

Modern civilization has drawn much of its dynamics from the abolition of all sorts of traditional bonds and constraints, pretending to "liberate" man, but in effect tying him in much more restrictive fetters. From a modern point of view, it may thus seem puzzling to speak of "inspiring" or "creative" constraints. Yet there is a clear correlation between bonds and options; for while bonds without options may be oppressive, options without bonds result in rootless and meaningless creativity, if not in outright destruction. The architecture of traditional cultures demonstrates that it was the social constraints that conditioned the traditional urban form, backed by shared values and correlated social conventions. These ensured the right balance between individual and collective expression, instilling meaning into man's creations and constituting the basis for both the unity and the variety of architectural manifestations that we cherish in historic settlements.

It can therefore be argued that the distinct character, beauty and meaning of traditional settlements, such as historic Muslim cities, stem from the fact that primary impulses and resistances prevailed in the urban shaping process and the cities' growth over time. Through their rhythm, their symbolic reference and their pragmatic sense of interaction, they embody something which transcends their formal and material structures and yet pulses through them and makes them "alive". This is the reason why the surviving urban structures, rich in such imprints, still exude a sense of identification, even to later users. By analogy, the notorious lack of empathy prevalent in most modern urban systems can be attributed to the fact that secondary impulses have become dominant there and, particularly, that secondary resistances are stifling potential creative energies within society.

Our analysis of the genesis of cultural identity suggests two conclusions. One of them implies that modern ideologies and their related technologies have sapped the shaping forces of cultural identity, both by devaluing impulses and constraints and by undermining the direct interaction between man and his environment through the use of alienating intermediate tools, be it in the fields of actual construction or in the domain of human interaction. The other conclusion implies that cultural identity, as an evolutionary chain of creative tradition, can only be sustained and revived from *within*, starting with a strengthening of these very internal processes, and not by imposing external forms. This assessment is corroborated by the observation that cultural identities, once they cease to be sustained from within, can easily be corrupted. They then become mere fashions or are misused for ideological purposes, as we can observe in many of today's nationalist and fundamentalist movements.

Over the past decade, cultural identity and creative diversity have become highly publicized issues on the international development agenda, which in itself is certainly a positive sign. Yet the nurturing of such qualities has to be pursued at levels, in domains and under conditions which elude theoretical concepts and the prevailing means of information and communication. It can only succeed by re-anchoring the life of individuals and communities in the deeper layers of a timeless reality, as it were – a reality which is all-encompassing in the sense that it links past, present and future, and yet limited in the sense that it can only be grasped and materialized through individual realizations at a "grass roots" level in a given time and place.

The fact that spiritual values essentially transcend forms and yet have to be experienced through specific forms is a condition imposed upon human existence. Without the interplay between a transcendent vision and a tangible human embodiment, "culture" will remain either meaningless or unproductive, and so will the creation of the built environment, particularly if it is reduced to an abstract, mechanical and purely quantitative production process.

The Significance of Historic Cities

In the fragmented reality of our modern civilization, historic cities constitute a major physical repository of wholeness and identity, since they are an integral reflection of man's innate aspirations and of his faculties for shaping the different layers of reality that he was given to build upon. The fact that historic cities represent formidable assets for today's needs becomes immediately clear when we consider that they still provide the points of reference of wider urban agglomerations that have grown to become ten, twenty or fifty times the size of the original nucleus. In a desert of predominantly anonymous and sterile urban extensions, they have often remained the sole dispensers of the spiritual, emotional and sensory values that are key to cultural identity.

The value of historic cities resides in the complexity of their structures, which are impregnated with the record of life and of human thoughts and activities: the whole is much greater than the sum of the parts. Indeed, the meaning of an urban entity draws on the interaction between individual buildings and open spaces, i.e., on the interplay between monuments, houses, meeting places and places of work, patterns of movement, social habits and ritual commemorations. Through subtle transformations over time, the urban matrix incorporates and perpetuates the memory of past generations of users. It thus reflects the *genius loci*, as conditioned by the given site factors and by the imprint of respective communities who collectively shaped their living space and were, in turn, moulded by their environment. The continuity – one could say the tradition – of this rhythmical "give and take" accounts for the essential quality of historic cities, which must be carefully managed in order for it to remain alive in succeeding generations.

The issue, then, is how to use the architectural and urban heritage of the past. Should it be frozen, as it were, to be handed over as a museal legacy to future generations? Should it be commercially exploited by turning it into attractive meeting places or playgrounds providing relief to visitors frustrated by their "normal" urban environment? Should it cater for the residences of a happy few who can afford to adorn themselves with a prestigious identity? Or can historic cities become a source of inspiration which enables a society to innovate by re-interpreting the past, overcoming the dichotomies resulting from a single-minded pursuit of a narrow vision of "progress"? Can a creative exploration and a careful evolution of historic structures give birth to cultural processes which re-establish an organic link with the past – not for the sake of nostalgia, but for the sake of re-integrating a human wholeness, drawing on other motivations than merely the rational?

The latter questions imply that historic cities can teach us lessons that go well beyond formal aesthetics or an antiquarian historic interest. A critical review of the achievements and failures of modern city planning in the 20th century reveals that modern societies can hardly afford to dismiss the values of pre-industrial urban structures as obsolete. A creative interpretation of the principles embodied in historic cities offer, at least potentially, the opportunity to overcome the effects of the relatively recent mental and physical dis-integration processes introduced by the Modern Movement. This holds especially true for the societies of the so-called developing world, which in many respects are much closer to their pre-industrial cultural roots and to corresponding spiritual and social resources, but which are now at risk of discrediting their heritage for the sake of an alien, dogmatic and often deceptive notion of "progress".

Emphasizing the values embodied in historic cities does not automatically imply rejecting evolutionary forms of change, nor does it mean that all historic structures should be conserved at any cost. But it does suggest that certain essential structuring principles can be revived, adapted, and perpetuated to the advantage of contemporary societies. As examples, it may suffice to mention some of the outstanding features of historic cities: their richness in implicit or explicit symbols and spiritual content, their sense of human scale, their successful use of open spaces for face-to-face interaction, their ability to let residents live in the centre rather than marginalizing them and their capacity to sustain small-scale community networks which can trigger affective bonds, thus enabling the growth of specific cultural expressions and grounding people in their physical and social environment. Such qualities could indeed become an essential antidote to certain negative aspects of "globalization" which are threatening to erode local cultural values and identities.

In this sense, historic cities, beyond being mere repositories of cultural memory, should be able to act as effective nurseries of cultural continuity. Clearly, ways of life are conditioned by the circumstances of their origin, and yet they can express principles of universal validity that remain relevant under changed external conditions. Such values and principles can then help shape new formal expressions responding to a different set of challenges. Accordingly, continuity cannot be achieved by simply reproducing frozen architectural forms, but must be fostered by reviving internal shaping processes. Only then can it lead to the construction of an inspiring built environment reflecting the qualities man needs for his physical, emotional and spiritual welfare. However, before addressing the social, institutional and technical aspects which enable cultural rehabilitation to be pursued from within, the scope and the limits of conservation need to be put into perspective. In our modern context it is conservation that provides the conventional approach for coping with historic cities. Yet its intrinsic shortcomings (which are directly related to those of an unilateral and single-minded development) are too often overlooked, giving rise to false hopes and expectations.

The Limits of Urban Conservation

Preservation, in the modern sense of the term, was never an issue in pre-industrial European and particularly non-European civilizations, as long as they were rooted in a living tradition based on a strong and authentic cultural identity. In many cases, evolving cultural traditions provoked significant urban change over the centuries. Sometimes, an old tradition was overlaid by a younger one which did not hesitate to re-use the pre-existing architectural heritage according to its own needs. Age-old cities such as Rome, Aleppo or Istanbul show different, partly transparent historic layers, which account for their special charm. While their urban evolution may show a coherency in terms of a consistent *genius loci*, there was not necessarily a strict uniformity of style. Countless incremental interventions, carried out over many generations, produced the complexity and the very depth of historic patterns which fascinate the modern mind at a time when it is increasingly deprived of visual and sensory stimulation. Yet even the more dramatic changes, resulting from the succession of different cultures and civilizations, rarely disrupted the historic urban fabric in the way that more recent modern interventions have done. In response to certain accepted social and environmental constraints, their scale remained within a compatible range of variation and thus the individual elements blended into a well-orchestrated symphony of distinct, but correlated architectural forms. Today, conservationists would easily agree on the need to preserve the vestiges of the various layers of past interventions to the fullest possible extent, and yet we have to admit that the very genesis of this accumulated heritage was fundamentally "anti-historic" and "non-scientific" when judged according to our modern conceptions of preservation.

As Friedrich Nietzsche put it in his penetrating "Unzeitgemaesse Betrachtungen" (Untimely Observations), his period, i.e., the late 19th century, "suffered from an overdose of history, which undermined the plastic forces of life". The solution he envisioned was to reclaim the right to the "un-historic" (i.e., to let the past sink into oblivion) and the "para-historic" (i.e., to regain access to the eternal and primordial forces of being). In the late 20th century, history as part of a detached scientific system analyzing the life of previous generations from a merely archaeological point of view is as dominant as ever. But it also has become much clearer that it was released and conditioned by its counterpart, an extreme type of rootless modern development which engendered the very emphasis on the historicizing approach. Both constitute two sides of the same phenomenon, and as the French say, "les extrêmes se touchent".

Here we come across the dilemma of modern Western architecture, which goes back to the 19th century and its increasing alienation from authentic cultural values. As described in chapter 9, the Modern Movement deliberately rejected the depleted architectural symbols of the 19th century, but in doing so it also rejected historic continuity and failed to recognize the need for spiritual and emotional content as an implicit or explicit motive of architectural expression. This rejection meant that the common cultural ground which existed between earlier periods was replaced by a serious divide which has never been overcome. The result was a disruption of the natural flow between the past and the future, severing the creative communication between man and his cultural matrix. This, in turn, produced the fatal and sterile dichotomies which we are struggling with today: "modern" versus "traditional", "rational" versus "emotional", "cultural" versus "technical" and so on. The deepening chasm between past and future (or between romantic nostalgia and futurist utopia) not only emptied the present of much of its substance and significance, it also affected the qualities of the past and the future. For history now runs the risk of being mummified and relegated to the category of the sciences, while coherent and creative innovation is in danger of being aborted or replaced by the stillborn phantoms of a unilateral "progress".

In either case, the sense of a living culture is at risk, since it can only flourish through a sustained identification of people with a continuous and interactive process of creation, as reflected in a meaningful built environment. The gradual replacement of knowledge and practised values by abstract and often dogmatic sciences (or by the impact of an omnipresent information system) has not only produced a certain spiritual deficit in man's daily reality, it has also weakened the natural cultural bonds that the present has with both the past and the future. Under such circumstances, historic buildings and artefacts are reduced to the status of "dead", at best aesthetic objects of scientific interest, while modern architects are left with the choice of either interpreting a reduced range of merely material needs, or relying on the expression of their individual originality, however limited in scope. Modern preservation efforts are thus intrinsically linked to the disruption of the very basis of traditional ("organic") cultural growth processes and the corresponding need for protective measures in order to safeguard the inherited patrimony and transmit it to future generations.

While the unprecedented rapid and massive change brought about by modern development since the late 19th century in many ways justifies and enhances the role of preservation, there are also certain conceptual pitfalls to be pointed out. One of them is that cultural heritage can now be perceived as a "frozen" or museal object, no longer subject to a natural evolution; another one is the fact that the sudden break in traditions, defined as the continuous flow of values and practices, has created an artificial split between "ancient" and "modern", or between "conservation" and "development". Conservation is indeed at risk of becoming a science of its own, detached from the daily concerns of society. One way to prevent this is to see conservation as part of a much wider development process. This means bringing in social and economical forces to support the survival of the heritage, while at the same time introducing a cultural dimension into the current development concept, which is far too limited if it excludes such social and cultural values.

At any rate, when it comes to historic cities as a whole, preservation in the strict sense of the word is simply not viable. Considering the complex task of urban conservation and the many aspects involved in it, one immediately realizes that only small parts of the heritage can be treated in archaeological or museal terms, that is, by physically isolating a monument from its original context and creating an artificially protected environment around it. While it may be relatively easy to deal with key buildings, such as a cathedral or a mosque, the situation becomes much more complex once it comes to the physical and socio-economic context, made of roads, busy public open spaces, historic houses, traditional commercial or industrial facilities, and all the activities and support structures needed to operate and maintain them as part of a living environment. Furthermore, problems of private land ownership and building use arise, which require softer types of rehabilitation and cannot be fully resolved by direct government intervention. All these complications have to be tackled, since the overriding objective is to maintain the viability of the historic city, which implies allowing for a natural evolution of the historic fabric. Restoration of individual monuments without conserving or rehabilitating their historical environment and without supporting the vital social and economic forces that sustain them would make little sense and would eventually deprive the historic city of its "nutrients", as it were.

In short, conservation cannot be conceived in an ivory tower if it is to be successful. It must take into account (and integrate as far as possible) the society's current aspirations and living patterns. It must look out for appropriate uses in restored or converted structures in order to keep them alive – except, of course, in the case of archaeological monuments or museal conservation. On the one hand conservation needs to consider proper maintenance and be financially affordable; on the other hand it must harness potential sources of economic income inherent in the cultural heritage as a development asset. Often, appropriate new buildings will have to be introduced to fill irretrievably ruined plots or to cater for complementary functions that will keep the city alive.

This suggests that conservation cannot be pursued as a separate discipline, but needs to be seen as an integral part of a more comprehensive environmental planning and economic development process – although a very special part, since it deals with highly sensitive, non-replicable resources and is therefore dependent on a special set of rules and regulations. Experience shows that conservation objectives, unless included in an overall development framework, will be difficult to implement, or will lose their raison d'être. For without such a pro-active approach, the heritage to be preserved may already be partly gone once conservation measures are ready to be applied. Integrated procedures are therefore mandatory, acknowledging that compromises will have to be made and certain trade-offs will have to be accepted as part of the overall negotiating process between divergent objectives and constraints.

Regeneration from Within

While analyzing the genesis of cultural identities and the significance of historic cities, we found that their revitalization needs to be tackled from within, i.e., by reverting to the inner forces that are able to nurture a living culture and re-establish a sense of presence, integrity and continuity. Problems such as cultural disruption, fragmentation of human purposes and the pretentious inflation of isolated aspects of life can only be transcended by making appeal to the vital sources of creativity – or, as Hoelderlin put it, to the "gifts of love and genius" which sustain the "fruits and flowers" of man's garden on earth.

Re-anchoring the main philosophies, attitudes and actions in the deeper layers of life has nothing to do with "regressing" in the sense implied by an obstinate philosophy of linear progress. It means, however, piercing or peeling off the dead crusts which have accumulated over time around the kernel of life. They distort human vision and judgement, since they obscure the supreme reality or, even worse, substitute it with their ideological or scientific makeshifts. This can happen to such an extent that individuals and societies, being fixated on lifeless surrogates of reality, forget their natural inner potential. As a result, the powers of supreme being that are active in human nature may suddenly appear as something very remote or beyond human reach. Yet the contrary is true: the sources of life and truth are inherent in man and nature. It is only the abstract constructs of an artificial secondary reality which establish and perpetuate the alienation which most modern societies are suffering from today. As the Prophet Muhammad once said during a journey to his companions who were crying out loud for Allah: "O men! Be easy on yourselves and do not distress yourselves by raising your voices; verily you do not call to one deaf or absent, but to one who heareth and seeth; and He to whom you pray is nearer to you than the neck of your camel!"

Reactivating the hidden inner resources means discovering that the timeless and the contemporary do not need to contradict each other but can work hand in hand. It is this type of empowerment which enables societies to absorb inevitable changes, by remaining in control of outer development forces and using them in a productive and synthetic manner. Instead of futile controversies between opposing forces, a real transformation from within can then take place, drawing on the forces of man's creative imagination and its ability to shape an envisioned new reality.

Transformation from within implies, above all, a new awareness. In order to become culturally relevant, the fundamental definitions of reality and meaning must be shared by a majority of people and must be transformed into accepted rules of action and decision-making. Hence "vertical" perception needs to be laterally extended and solidified by spreading the seeds of a new vision, harnessing community support and nurturing the social and material application of cultural principles. For unless humans are moved in their heart to actively implement acknowledged concepts, no cultural or architectural expressions will ever become whole and alive. Spiritual and emotional motivation are needed to build up the social capital which in turn will sustain internal renewal, producing effects which are not attainable through mere rational insight or administrative coercion.

In the following, we shall pursue the idea of mobilizing hidden resources through various levels of action pertaining to the rehabilitation of historic cities in the Islamic world. As intimated above, mental awareness of the cultural values of Islam and its cultural expressions is of paramount importance, since it is only through this awareness that the prejudices and blockages imposed by an alien philosophy can be removed or overcome. Thus it will be necessary to do away with the stigma of backwardness (and the cultural inferiority complex) that haunts the elite of many Islamic societies with regard to their own heritage. The collateral prerequisite is the recognition of the shortcomings, fallacies and illusory compensations of a misguided, largely utopian modern development process. By removing these mental blinkers, individuals and communities may again become open to influences capable of "widening their breasts " – an image often used by the Qur'an. The role of a reinterpreted Islam as a source of inspiration for a specific cultural identity and specific social practices should not be underestimated. Approached in an undogmatic sense, it may continue to serve as a timeless point of reference, informing the human search for the right way of life and assisting the various cultural metamorphoses taking place in the transient dimension of reality.

Enlightened leadership is perhaps the most concise definition of the quality needed to support creative and productive social transformations at various levels of society. It must inspire, solicit and direct the internal rehabilitation processes in the various domains of human activity. In an institutional sense, good governance would tend to develop and rely on innate human resources, at both individual and collective levels, and to reinforce natural social bonds. Empowering local communities to achieve as much as they can on their own and enabling self-sustained processes to happen in the domains of private enterprise, provision of shelter and grass-roots urban management is a precondition for regeneration from within. The right incentives must be given – incentives that are capable of releasing and developing the large potential of internal energies rather than stifling private initiative by external constraints and bureaucratic procedures or having the state provide all social services and benefits (which is in itself an utopian task). In this sense, development would mean setting a consistent framework, enabling direct action by the various groups concerned and coordinating individual efforts in order to produce desirable synergies. Applying the principle of subsidiarity involves delegating power to local authorities and specific non-governmental bodies and interest groups. Corresponding legal and administrative provisions would need to be taken and new practices to be developed in the context of a more humanized grass-roots governance, for which models from traditional Muslim communities can be adapted to contemporary needs.

Internalized control and decision-making mechanisms obviously call for planning procedures that are quite different from conventional modern planning methods. Instead of imposing, from outside, abstract schemes preconceived in the minds of estranged "professionals" (or simply copied from other projects), development plans and strategies have to be nurtured from within, involving the active response and participation of the communities concerned, or at least of their legitimate representatives. Apart from the obvious procedural implications, such an approach entails changes in the function of architects, planners and designers with regard to conventional modern role models. In order to overcome the division between "subject" and "object" in planning, architects must learn to act as agents and facilitators of the involved social groups, which means listening to, creatively absorbing and interpreting people's needs. At the same time, community representatives and local institutions will have to gain more insight into the consequences of technical decisions, to be able to exert leadership and assume responsibility.

Such fundamentally different approaches would have to be reflected in the training of both professionals and laymen. Academic barriers and privileges need to be overcome by providing students with real exposure to the social context they have to work in and by creating an intermediate layer of "barefoot architects" growing out of local communities and capable of assisting people at grass-roots level. By means of such a system it would be much easier to revive and sustain appropriate and inexpensive local building traditions which are at the heart of cultural continuity but all too often discredited by academically trained architects, engineers and decision-makers. Wherever possible, people have to be reinstated as the builders (or at least conditioners) of their own environment, particularly in rural and suburban settings. Technical advice and design support can be provided to upgrade such construction from marginal to mainstream activities.

The architect as a "prima donna" dictating short-lived fashions would become redundant in such a context, since building would change from an object-oriented activity to a process-oriented one, involving the real stakeholders of architecture. There would, however, be a need for creative "cultural agents", i.e., professionals with a combination of sharp intellectual insight, artistic creativity and sense of practical realization, capable of translating spiritual values and principles into material expressions. Their task must be to activate and interpret what we called "primary impulses" and to make proper use of "primary resistances". Architects of the future may qualify for this function in the way Islamic craftsmen did in times when the cultural context was so self-evident that no explicit analysis of creative processes was required.

"Regeneration from within" is a concept which must first grow its roots in people's heart and imagination. Once the need for it is felt profoundly enough, there are perfectly rational rules which can be devised to develop it in terms of social, institutional and educational procedures. Yet its full implementation will be dependent on its economic viability. The most powerful arguments against the rehabilitation of historic cities and softer, culturally rooted forms of development always rely on economic justifications, claiming that the sheer costs of such an "additional" burden make cultural priorities impractical, particularly in a Third-World context. The fatal error of this wide-spread misconception is that it deliberately segregates "culture" from "development" and thereby establishes a self-fulfilling prophecy. For if culture is artificially separated to become an optional add-on instead of being conceived as an essential inbuilt component or, even better, the lively spring of human development, then it is indeed difficult to finance cultural activities. From a different and more comprehensive perspective, cultural activities constitute in themselves a basic and powerful resource. They can unleash processes which may not be of a predominantly economic nature, but can generate financial benefits and side effects. Internal rehabilitation processes must therefore rely on this integral vision of human development, exploring and exploiting to the greatest extent possible the interrelations between cultural and economic factors.

The production, maintenance and adaptation of the built environment – an eminently cultural task – traditionally involved economic activities that gave emotional gratification and at the same time were of high material value for those sharing in them directly or indirectly. The collateral arrangements, conventions and exchanges related to such activities built up much of the social capital on which traditional communities drew. Industrialized modern construction techniques tend to weaken or undermine such processes; yet in many Islamic countries it is not only possible, but indeed imperative to maintain the participation of local communities in the construction, upgrading and maintenance of historic cities, popular districts and rural settlements that are under threat by alien modes of development. In these countries, labour-intensive and participatory construction processes will boost income generation and the development of small enterprises, together with a growing sense of cultural identity. This will be the only solution in the many cases where two parallel problems have to be tackled simultaneously: the problem of preserving the architectural heritage and culturally relevant urban patterns and the problem of providing or maintaining decent housing for a large segment of the low-income population which is socially and emotionally attached to the traditional fabric.

The social cohesion, the skills and the initiative of vernacular communities in the Islamic world constitute a tremendous and underestimated economic and cultural resource for renewal from within. Providing the right encouragement, guidance and incentives will set in motion an almost automatic rehabilitation process. Most important of all is perhaps the general attitude of the state and the decision-making institutions towards the patrimony of historic cities. Lack of belief in its values and its continuing viability, indifference to its decline or the even vague intention to demolish and redevelop in "modern" ways will all create a climate of disinvestment and will eventually place an enormous economic burden on the state – one which the community would have been ready to assume if allowed to do so. Inversely, declared support for the case of rehabilitation, even small investments in improving the public space of the historic fabric, technical support and guidance for appropriate investment and financial incentives (such as reduced costs of procedures, tax relief and development rights) will spark vigorous private sector initiatives and thus multiply the limited cultural and economic revitalization effects which governmental structures can achieve on their own.

Another hidden potential for revitalization from within lies in the often neglected or under-used traditional public facilities owned by the government or the waqf institutions. Introducing new uses in vacant caravanserais, madrasas or maristans, adding adapted new social functions to under-used mosques and redeveloping vacant or ruined sites in a morphologically appropriate manner will favour a functional re-adjustment of the old town equivalent to modern standards; at the same time it will generate investment opportunities, employment and direct or indirect income.

Many of these investments in infrastructure and public buildings will exert catalytic effects and eventually increase property value in the old city. While this is desirable in many ways, it is important to ensure that the benefits of economic improvement can be captured by the stake-holders of the old city and will not be hijacked by speculative investors who have no commitment to cultural heritage. The state will therefore have to invent mechanisms and procedures which enable the profits to remain or be reinvested within a closed circuit dedicated to the original purpose – the revitalization of cultural assets – in order to sustain the recycling of generated funds. An organised institutional form for achieving this is the model of the "urban development corporation". It can have access to land ownership, can pool individual holdings and assets and re-allocate them in the interest of the community as a whole. Due to its special privileges with regard to public property, as well as opportunities to establish productive coalitions between private and public sector, such a body can pursue focused rehabilitation tasks, thus developing and managing existing assets to the best advantage of the historic city.

The issue of increasing real-estate values is particularly critical in relation to improvements in vehicular accessibility, a rare luxury in Islamic historic cities, which have to be carefully managed in order to maintain the coherence of the historic fabric and the specific values of its social and spatial organisation. Any redevelopment schemes entailing new service roads or better accessibility must be carefully organised in order to ensure that the sacrifice in terms of built heritage is compensated for by taxes imposed on the commercial facilities benefiting from new road access. These revenues can be invested in the upgrading of less accessible and economically disadvantaged sections of the urban fabric. Skimming off some of the economic benefits of public infrastructure investment and converting them into cross-subsidies for the upgrading of less privileged historic districts is an important urban management principle which should be introduced before the rehabilitation exercise gains its own momentum.

Tourism is another source of economic revenue to be considered, as it can generate income via local craft industries, commerce, small hotels, restaurants and guest houses which are, in principle, compatible with the historic city structure and may bring opportunities for re-use and revitalization of existing structures. While tourists are always in search of genuine and authentic sites to visit, excessive tourism tends to erode or destroy these very assets by its own abuses. It is therefore essential that the economy of historic cities does not become totally dependent on the tourism industry but finds ways to integrate visitors and customers into a solid and self-reliant socio-economic framework of its own. Again, special care must be taken to ensure that financial benefits derived from tourism will reach the constituencies directly involved in the upkeeping of the historic fabric.

In any event, we must acknowledge that the rehabilitation of historic cities is an attempt to keep alive values which are not measurable with the instruments of a quantitatively oriented modern civilization but which are essential for people's spiritual, emotional and physical welfare. Special efforts must therefore be undertaken to recognize, protect and promote such values, and to support cultural rehabilitation as an integral but highly complex and sensitive part of overall human development.

The higher purpose of such rehabilitation efforts is not just to conserve earlier structures created under different material conditions, but to revive the internal forces of the society in order to enable it to reconnect with the past in authentic and innovative ways, instead of adopting inferior copies of alien cultural models which have never worked out satisfactorily in their own places of origin. This will require an acute sense of the essence of traditional values, creativity in the interpretation of traditional archetypes which may still be valid but need to be adapted to different circumstances, and above all, a shared commitment by the main parties involved, i.e., government, civil society and private sector enterprises. All three have been evolving in different directions and each one is often split into factions which find it hard to cooperate. Making all of them receptive to a common philosophy and shared objectives, balancing them and gradually increasing the area of overlapping concerns is a prerequisite for effective implementation of a new type of development that integrates the social and cultural dimensions and relies on mobilizing its internal resources.

When working in Chandigarh and reminded by the Indian architect Mulkarj Anand of the importance of local traditions, Le Corbusier replied in his proud and presumptuous manner: "Que signifient les coutumes indiennes aujourd'hui, si vous dites oui à la machine, aux pantalons et à la démocratie?" ("What sense do local customs and habits make, once you say yes to the machine, to trousers and to democracy?")

Forty years later, this statement seems oddly out of place. Today, we realize that we must look more deeply and more sympathetically at the perennial values of cultural traditions, their potential for metamorphosis and their eventual survival under new auspices. We have learned that we can no longer afford to romanticize about the benefits of a modern development epitomized by "the machine, trousers and democracy", that we must scrutinize the actual effects and side-effects of "progress" and that we must make sure to respond to the most essential human needs, as opposed to "needs" insinuated by seductive and overpowering market forces. We have experienced that even "democracy" is not immune from all sort of abuses and hidden totalitarian tendencies and that it is rarely able to instill the sense of legitimacy needed to mobilize, from within, societies and communities as a whole.

Thus we have become aware that progress is not a blessing in itself and should not be pursued for its own sake, but that it must integrate pre-existing values which can fill it with life and meaning. We acknowledge that human life is much more complex than the conventional tools and mechanisms used by simplistic planning techniques. We accept that in times of rapidly accelerating outer change, inner continuity has become of vital importance. Abandoning ourselves totally to each subsequent wave of progress would only mean falling from one abyss into another and thereby losing the freedom of individual choice and orientation which is perhaps the major privilege bestowed on mankind.

Appendix

Sources of Illustrations

With the exceptions referenced in the captions, the great majority of the drawings and photographs used in this book come from the author, or belong to projects directed or advised by him. While it is impossible here to mention everybody individually, the author would like to express his sincere thanks to all those who have contributed, in one way or the other, to the rich documentation of this book.

Bibliographical Notes

The following list is not intended to provide a comprehensive bibliography on the many subjects the chapters of this book have touched upon. Instead, it is to acknowledge a number of works from which the author has benefited during his own research, and to suggest a few basic titles where interested readers might find more detailed information than could be given within the concise framework of the present book. Whenever possible, English editions of books first published in other languages are quoted.

Translated Islamic Sources

Al Bokhari, "L'authentique tradition musulmane" (ed. G. Bouquet), Paris 1964.

Attar F., "Das Meer der Seele" (ed. H. Ritter), Leiden 1955.

Ibn Abdun, "Traité sur la vie urbaine et les corps de métiers – Séville musulmane au XIIe siècle", (ed. E. Lévy - Provençal), Paris 1947.

Ibn Battuta, "Travels in Asia and Africa" (ed. H. A. R. Gibb), London 1929 (reprint 1953).

Ibn Jubayr, "The Travels" (ed. R. J. C. Broadhurst), London 1952.

Ibn Khaldun, "The Muqaddimah – An Introduction to History" (ed. F. Rosenthal), Princeton 1958.

Ibn Luyun, "Tratado de Agricultura" (ed. J. Eguarez-Ibanez), Granada 1975.

Kai Qabus, "The Qabus Nama – A Mirror for Princes" (ed. R. Levy), London 1951.

Muhammad Ali M. (editor), "A Manual of Hadith", London 1978.

Nizam al-Mulk, "Siyasatnama – Gedanken und Geschichten" (ed. K. E. Schabinger von Schowingen), Freiburg 1960.

Rumi Jalaluddin, "The Mathnawi" (ed. R. A. Nicholson), Cambridge 1926 (reprint 1982).

Sohravardi, "Le Livre de la sagesse orientale" (ed. H. Corbin), Lagrasse 1986.

On the Spiritual Dimension of Islam and Islamic Art

Ardalan N./Bakhtiar L., "The Sense of Unity – The Sufi Tradition in Persian Architecture", Chicago 1973.

Burckhardt T., "Art of Islam – Language and Meaning", London 1976.

Burckhardt T., "Mirror of the Intellect" (Essays on Traditional Science and Sacred Art), Cambridge 1987.

Burckhardt T., "Sacred Art in East and West", Bedford Middlesex 1967.

Corbin H., "Temple and Contemplation", London 1986.

Nasr S.H., "Islamic Art and Spirituality", Ipswich 1987.

Schuon F., "Understanding Islam", London 1963.

On Islamic Societies – Past and Present

Abu Lughod J., "Disappearing Dichotomies: First World - Third World; Traditional - Modern", Traditional Dwellings and Settlements Review, Vol. III, No. 2, 1992.

Aga Khan Award for Architecture, "Toward an Architecture in the Spirit of Islam" Seminar No. 1, Gouvieux 1978.

Akbar J., "Crisis in the Built Environment", Singapore 1989.

Arkoun M., "La Pensée arabe", Paris 1979.

Chelhod J., "Les Structures du sacré chez les Arabes", Paris 1965.

Gardet L., "La Cité musulmane – vie sociale et politique", Paris 1965.

Gardet L., "L'Islam, religion et communauté", Paris 1967.

Haarmann U. (editor), "Geschichte der Arabischen Welt", München 1987.

Lapidus I. M., "A History of Islamic Societies", Cambridge 1988.

Levy R., "The Social Structure of Islam", Cambridge 1957.

Planhol X., "The World of Islam", Ithaca 1979

Sardar Z. U. (editor), "The Touch of Midas – Sciences, Values and Environment in Islam and the West", Manchester 1984.

Schacht J., "An Introduction to Islamic Law", Oxford 1966.

Shayegan D., "Cultural Schizophrenia – Islamic Societies Confronting the West", London 1992.

Watt W. M., "Muhammad, Prophet and Statesman", Oxford 1961.

Watt W. M., "Islam and the Integration of Society", London 1969.

On Islamic Architecture

Barrucand M./Bednorz A., "Moorish Architecture in Andalusia", Köln 1992.

Creswell K. A. C. "A Short Account of Early Muslim Architecture", Aldershot 1989.

Creswell K. A. C., "The Muslim Architecture of Egypt", Oxford 1959.

Grabar O., "The Formation of Islamic Art", New Haven 1973.

Frishman M./Khan H. U., "The Mosque – History, Architectural Development and Regional Diversity", London 1994.

Goodwin G., "A History of Ottoman Architecture", London 1971.

Hillenbrand R., "Islamic Architecture", Edinburgh 1994.

Hoag J., "Islamic Architecture", London 1979.

Kuban D., "Muslim Religious Architecture", Leiden 1974.

Marçais G., "L'Architecture musulmane d'occident", Paris 1954.

Mitchell G. (editor), "Architecture of the Islamic World", London 1978.

Monneret de Villard U., "Introduzione allo studio della archeologia islamica", Venezia 1966.

Pope A. U. / Ackermann Ph., "A Survey of Persian Art", reprint Tokyo 1977.

Sauvaget J., "La Mosquée Omeyyade de Médine", Paris 1947.

Vogt – Göknil U., "Mosquées", Paris 1975.

On Islamic Gardens

Brookes J., "Gardens of paradise", London 1987.

Galotti J., "Le Jardin et la maison arabe au Maroc", Paris 1925.

Icomos, "Les Jardins de l'islam" (Granada Symposium 1973), Paris 1975.

Khansari M., Moghtader M. R., Yavani M., "The Persian Garden", Washington D.C. 1998.

Lehrmann J., "Earthly Paradise – Garden and Courtyard in Islam", London 1980.

Macdougall E., Ettinghausen R. (editor), "The Islamic Garden" (Dumbarton Oaks Colloquium), Washington 1976.

Moore Ch. et al., "The Poetics of Gardens", Cambridge Mass. 1988.

Moynihan E.B., "Paradise as a Garden in Persia and Mughal India", London 1980.

Petruccioli A. (editor), "Il Giardino Islamico", Milano 1994.

Prieto-Moreno F., "Los jardines de Granada", Madrid 1973.

On Historic Cities

Abdelkafi J., "La Médina de Tunis – espace historique", Paris 1989.

Abu Lughod J. L., "Cairo – 1001 Years of the City Victorious", Princeton 1971.

Berardi R., "Lecture d'une ville – la médina de Tunis", L'Architecture d'Aujourd'hui, No. 153, 1970.

Bianca S., "Hofhaus und Paradiesgarten – Architektur und Lebensformen in der islamischen Welt", München 1991.

Chevallier D. (editor), "L'Espace social de la ville arabe", Paris 1979.

Cuneo P., "Storia dell' urbanistica – il mondo islamico", Roma 1986.

Gaube H./Wirth E., "Aleppo", Wiesbaden 1984.

Fusaro F., "La città islamica", Rome 1984.

Germen Aydin (editor), "Islamic Architecture and Urbanism", Dammam 1983.

Hakim S.B., "Arab-Islamic Cities – Building and Planning Principles", London 1986.

Hourani A.H./Stern S.M. (editors), "The Islamic City", Oxford 1970.

Lapidus I.M. (editor), "Middle Eastern Cities", Berkeley 1969.

Le Tourneau R., "Fez avant le protectorat", Casablanca 1949.

Micara L., "Architetture e spazi dell' Islam", Roma 1985.

Olsen D.J., "The City as a Work of Art", New Haven 1986.

Petruccioli A., "Dar al-Islam", Roma 1985.

Raymond A., "Grandes villes arabes à l'époque ottomane", Paris 1985.

Sauvaget J., "Alep – Essai sur le développement d'une grande ville syrienne", Paris 1941.

Serageldin I./El Sadek S. (editors), "The Arab City, its Character and Islamic Cultural Heritage", Riyadh 1982.

Serjeant R.B./Lewcock R., "Sana'a, an Arabian Islamic City", London 1983.

Torres-Balbas L., "Ciudades hispano-musulmanes", Madrid (n.d.)

On Traditional Housing

Bonnenfant P., "Les maisons tours de Sana'a", Paris 1989.

Boughali M., "La représentation de l'espace chez le Marocain illettré", Paris 1974.

Bourdieu P., "Trois etudes d'ethnologie kabyle", Genève 1972.

Cahiers de la recherche architecturale 20/21, Marseille 1987.

Depaule J.-Ch., "A travers le mur", Paris 1985.

Eckert H., "Struktur und Funktionen der Familie in Tunesien", Dissertation, Köln 1975.

Eldem S.H., "Turkish Houses – Ottoman Period" (I–III), Istanbul 1984–1987.

Galotti J., "Le Jardin et la maison arabe au Maroc", Paris 1925.

Greenlaw J.-P., "The Coral Buildings of Soakin", London 1976.

Kasba 64 Study Group, "Living on the Edge of the Sahara", Den Haag 1973.

Kuban D., "The Turkish Hayat House", Istanbul 1995.

Maury B./RaymondA./Revault J./Zakaria M., "Palais et maisons du Caire", (I/II), Paris 1982/83.

Musselmani M., "Damascene Homes", Damascus 1988.

Orihuela Uzal A., "Casas y Palacios Nazaries", Barcelona 1995.

Reuther O., "Das Wohnhaus in Bagdad und anderen Städten des Irak", Berlin 1910.

Revault J., "Palais et demeures de Tunis" (I/II), Paris 1967/71.

Revault J., "Palais et demeures de Fès" (I/II), Paris 1985/89.

Tillion G., "Le Harem et les cousins", Paris 1966.

Warren J./Fethy I, "Traditional Houses in Baghdad", Horsham 1982.

On Urban Conservation and Rehabilitation

Aga Khan Award for Architecture, "Conservation as Cultural Survival" (Seminar No. 2), Istanbul 1978.

Aga Khan Trust for Culture (Symposium), "Architectural and Urban Conservation in the Islamic World", Geneva 1990.

Antoniou J., "Environmental Management – Planning for Traffic", Maidenhead 1971.

Appleyard D., "The Conservation of European Cities", Cambridge Mass. 1979.

Cervellati P.L. (editor), "Bologna – centro storico", Bologna 1970.

Feilden B.M./Jokilehto J., "Management Guidelines for World Cultural Heritage Sites", Rome 1993.

Mimar, Archtiecture in Development, issue no. 12, Singapore 1984.

Mimar, Architecture in Development, issue no. 24, Singapore 1987.

Purchla J. (editor), "The Historical Metropolis – A Hidden Potential", Krakow 1993.

Schuster I.M. (editor), "Preserving the Built Heritage – Tools for Implementation" (Salzburg Seminar), Hannover 1997.

Serageldin I., "Revitalising Historic Cities: Towards a Public-Private Partnership", in "Culture and Development in Africa", The World Bank, Washington 1994.

Zuziak Z. (editor), "Managing Historic Cities", Krakow 1993.

On Modern Architecture and Urban Design

Aga Khan Programme for Islamic Architecture, "Theories and Principles of Design in the Architecture of Islamic Societies" (Symposium), Cambridge Mass. 1988.

Alexander Chr., "The Timeless Way of Building" (I-III), Oxford 1975-79.

Alexander Chr., "A New Theory of Urban Design", Oxford 1987.

Blake P., "Form Follows Fiasco – Why Modern Architecture Hasn't Worked",

Boston/Toronto 1975.

Krier R., "Urban Space", New York 1979.

Krier R., "On Architecture", London 1982.

Rowe C./Koetter F., "Collage City", Cambridge Mass. 1978.

Trancik R., "Finding Lost Space", New York 1986.

An excellent overview of contemporary currents in architecture and urban design in the Islamic world, including related philosophical, social and environmental issues, is provided by the series of books of the Aga Khan Award for Architecture documenting winning projects of each of the subsequent three-year cycles of the Award, starting from 1980.

On Science, Technology and Philosophy

Burckhardt T., "Scienza moderna e sagezza tradizionale", Torino 1968.

Guénon R., "La Crise du monde moderne", Paris 1927.

Guénon R., "Le Règne de la quantité et les signes du temps", Paris 1945.

Jünger F. G., "Die Perfektion der Technik", Frankfurt 1946.

Steiner G., "Real Presences", London 1989.

Tenbruck H. F., "Zur Kritik der planenden Vernunft", München 1972.